Talkin' Texan

Copyright © 2004 by Joe Kent Roberts

ISBN 1-59113-593-1

All rights reserved. No part of this book may be reproduced in any form or by any electronic or mechanical means, including information storage and retrieval systems, without written permission from the publisher, except by a reviewer who may quote passages in a review.

Published by Booklocker.com, Inc.

Manufactured in the United States of America.

Talkin' Texan

Joe Kent Roberts

Illustrated by Stephen Thompson

Contents

Foreword xi
Acknowledgments xiii
Introduction xv
A 1
   Dictionary 1
   Ama-rilla— Amarillo 5
   Aromas 9
   Texan – English 11
   Aws-tun—Austin 11
B 14
   Dictionary 14
   Bow-munt—Beaumont 17
   Texan – English 18
   Be-ugh Bay-un—Big Bend 18
   Texan – English 20
   Braowns-vul—Brownsville 20
   Bugs of Texas 24
   Texan - English 27
   Boz-urds—Buzzards 27
C 30
   Dictionary 30
   Camp Town Ladies 32
   Big Sandy 32
   Honeybunch 34
   Texan – English 39
   Canna-loap—Cantaloupe 39
   The City Slicker and the Pistol 41
   Texan – English 43
   Kor-pis Kristy—Corpus Christi 43
   Texan – English 48
   Cor-sa-kana—Corsicana 48

D 51
   Dictionary 51
   Dale-us—Dallas 54
   Days of the Week 59
   Deer Hunting 62
   Texan – English 64
   Do-mus—Dumas 64
E -F 66
   Dictionary 66
   El Duh-ra-duh—El Dorado 69
   Texan – English 72
   Owl Passo—El Paso 72
   Eyes of Texas 76
   For Better or For Worse 78
   Texan - English 84
   Foe-urt Warth—Fort Worth 84
   Texan - English 86
   Frad-racks-barg—Fredericksburg 86
G 89
   Dictionary 89
   Gail-ves-tun—Galveston 92
   Texan – English 95
   Jards-tay-own—Georgetown 95
   Grandma 99
   Grandma's Christmas Tree 103
   Grandpa and the Coffee 107
   Grandpa and the Pellet Gun 109
   Grandpa and the Snakes 113
   Growing Up in Texas 115
H 117
   Dictionary 117
   Hail-e-yuts-vail—Hallettsville 119
   Holidays in Texas 121

Valentine's Day	121
Easter	121
The Fourth of July	122
Halloween	123
Thanksgiving	124
Horny Toads—Horned Toads	129
Texan – English	131
Hew-stun—Houston	131
Hunters and Hunting	137
I-J	**139**
Dictionary	139
Er-vun—Irving	140
Texan - English	142
Thigh-lun—The Island	142
Jaz-purr—Jasper	144
Texan – English	146
Jung-shun—Junction	146
K	**148**
Dictionary	148
Kur-vail—Kerrville	149
Texan - English	151
Kangs-vail—Kingsville	151
L	**153**
Dictionary	153
Luh-ray-duh—Laredo	155
The Lone Star State	157
Texan – English	160
Loang-vue—Longview	160
Texan - English	162
Lob-uck—Lubbock	162
Texan – English	165
Laf-ken—Lufkin	165

M **170**
   Dictionary 170
   Mamaw 173
   Texan - English 179
   Mar-shul—Marshall 179
   Texan – English 182
   Med-lun—Midland 182
   Jan-yary—January 186
   Feb-yary—February 186
   Marsh—March 186
   A-prul—April 186
   Mae—May 187
   Jew-une—June 187
   Jew-lie—July 188
   Aw-gus—August 188
   Sap-tam-bur—September 188
   Ok-toe-bur—October 188
   Noe-vam-bur—November 189
   Dae-sam-bur—December 189
N **191**
   Dictionary 191
   Naga-dough-jez—Nacogdoches 194
   Texan - English 197
   Nu Bra-fuls—New Braunfels 197
O **201**
   Dictionary 201
   Oh-des-uh—Odessa 203
   Texan – English 205
   R-unge—Orange 205
   The Outhouse 208
P **211**
   Dictionary 211
   Pay-nots—Peanuts 213

Texan - English	215
Pick-um-ups—Pickups	215
Texan - English	217
Plane-vue—Plainview	217
Texan – English	221
Play-no—Plano	221
Q	**223**
Dictionary	223
Texan – English	225
Quee-hee—Quihi	225
R	**227**
Dictionary	227
Romancing the Cow	229
Raown Rok—Round Rock	231
S	**235**
Dictionary	235
Sane Angie-lo—San Angelo	238
Texan – English	243
San Un-tone (or San Ann-tone, by very happy residents)—San Antonio	243
Texan - English	246
Say-un Mar-cuss—San Marcos	246
Texan – English	247
Shoo-lan-borg—Schulenburg	247
Texan – English	250
See-geen—Seguin	250
Texan – English	252
Shy-ner—Shiner	252
T	**254**
Dictionary	254
A Texan's Map of Texas	256
Texan - English	257
Tax-er-kan-uh—Texarkana	257

Taxes Beg Tay-ouns—Texas Big Towns 259
Texas Cactus 263
Texas Chili 266
Texas Insects 268
Texas Rabbits 271
Tourist Season 275
U-V **278**
Dictionary 278
Una-var-sal Siddy—Universal City 280
Texan – English 282
Yuh-val-dee—Uvalde 282
Texan - English 286
Vic-tor-ya—Victoria 286
W **288**
Dictionary 288
Way-koe—Waco 290
Texan - English 294
Wart-er-mel-uns—Watermelons 294
Wish-et-ah Faws—Wichita Falls 296
X-Y-Z **300**
Dictionary 300
Ax-et—X IT 303
Texan - English 305
Yale—Yell 305
Texan – English 306
Yoh-kum—Yoakum 306
Texan - English 311
Za-pot-uh—Zapata 311
Outdex **317**
Backword **319**
Epilogue **321**

Foreword

A few thoughts on *Talkin' Texan*. First, a small caveat: If you are a history major or a geography student who has bought this book with the intent of using it as reference material for your final exams, you might want to double-check one or two of the facts. Don't get me wrong, it's not that Joe doesn't have a vast and bottomless well of knowledge when it comes to his native state, it's just that—oh, how can I put this?—he just tends to see things in a slightly different light. For example, even though I know he's no spring chicken, I have trouble believing he and Sam Houston were on the same Friday night bowling team. Lucky for us, his take on things is usually far more entertaining than the usual dry histories one encounters in the more scholarly texts. Some people see the world through rose-colored glasses; frankly, I think Joe's are more of the kaleidoscopic variety.

    I don't think there's a square inch of dirt in this massive, sprawling state that Joe hasn't set his weathered lizard-skin boots on. Nor do I think you could find a more knowledgeable guide on the planet, unless you resurrected old Pancho Villa himself, and he'd probably rob you and bury you up to the neck in sand for the vultures to feast on—so, yeah, I'd have to say Joe was your better bet for a tour guide. His colorful observations on everyplace from Amarillo to Zapata will be sure to tickle ribs and raise eyebrows.

    Having knocked around our second-largest state myself a bit, I can attest to the fact that passing for a native will be of immeasurable value when associating with the locals. This book is full of essential pronunciation tips for those looking to seamlessly mesh with the natives. Conversely, native Texans will find Joe's translations mighty helpful in figuring out those damned Yankee blatherings. They might even find out a thing or two about home they never knew before too, although, once again, let me reiterate, it might not be anything you'd want to base your Ph.D. dissertation on. So, go on, put on your ten-gallon hat, clip on your spurs, and hang on for a winding, sometimes bumpy, but always exhilarating ride through the Lone Star State with one of its favorite sons.

—Robert Domonkos

Acknowledgments

I'm not really sure what this acknowledgment section is all about, but my editor insisted that I have one in this book because everyone else has one in theirs. So here goes.

I'd like to thank my parents for not tossing me out with the bath water—elsewise, if this hasn't happened before, why would they have the statement "Don't throw the baby out with the bath water"?

I'd also like to thank all of the friendly people who live in the great state of Texas for their most unique and unusual accents. Until I left Texas, I did not realize that I had an accent. I did, and don't now, but will again as soon as I spend a week or so in Texas. You know, when in Rome, do as the Romans.

Probably the most thanks should go to Professor Emeritus Bob Domonkos, BA, MA, Ph.D., for his enthusiastic support of this project and helping me with writing terminology that I knew absolutely nothing about, such as fleshing out, query, niche, and voice. I'd also like to thank him for allowing me to call him Bob, instead of Mister. Professor Bob has written several books under various pen names. Many of his former college students have graduated from his classes to become very successful writers and authors.

Initially, I felt that a book about the rapidly vanishing language and customs of Texans should be written with the utmost seriousness. Professor Bob suggested that I use just a little bit of humor to keep the book politically correct concerning such a serious topic. Professor Bob also told me never to use two ands in a sentence and I hope that I just didn't.

Since the computer program I've been using to "spell check" all the words in this book doesn't speak Texan, it was a most difficult task to spell check. Hopefully in the future, we will have computer programs available that will speak fluent Texan. It would also be a great help if school districts outside of Texas would teach Texan for language credits.

    I work for a very small local dairy, and each of us has the responsibility for milking our own dairy cow. Mine is a beautiful two-year-old Holstein with big blue eyes and she goes by the name of Veronica. I'd like to thank Bob Walker, my boss at the dairy, for taking over my milking chores while I was trying to meet the deadline for finishing this book. It's not easy working around dairy cattle, but Bob never lost his grip with all the added work.

    I'd also like to thank my youngest son, Daniel, for his help and support while I was trying to meet the deadline for this book. Not only did he help me with all sorts of computer jargon (like why they call that little pointy arrow thingy a cursor, because I did let out one or two), he also took out the trash, vacuumed, and was very quiet while his ol' dad took a nap or two. He also had a couple of great suggestions that are included in this book, things that I had forgotten about Texas. If this frequent forgetfulness keeps up, I'll soon be able to throw my own surprise birthday parties and hide my own Easter eggs.

    I'm kinda hoping that someday one of the numerous Texas colleges will bestow an Honorary Absent-Minded Professor degree upon me. Either that, or at the very least, quit sending me all this stuff for completing my college degree at this late age. Whenever I've filled out any job applications, I've always included my four hours of college after graduating high school. It's not four hours of college credit; it's literally four hours of college.

    Once when I conveyed this to my youngest son, he said: "Hey, Dad, you missed lunch! You can't even complain about college food at the cafeteria." Hopefully, in the near future, I'll be able to accompany him to the cafeteria at his preferred college. He tells me that they'll have bratwurst and pecan pie on Fridays.

Introduction

The purpose of this book is not just to help visitors to Texas understand Texans but to also be a very valuable public school textbook for preserving the native Texan language. Many actors and actresses may also find this *Talkin' Texan* manual very useful when portraying a Texan on television, in the movies, or on stage.

    This is just a brief guide for those who wish to tour Texas and do not wish to be treated as a tourist, or treated any differently than any native Texan. This, my friend, will take a bit of study on your part and a slight change of attitude, not to mention a whole new way of walking, talking, acting, and so on.

    You may believe that you just crossed a state border or two and that you are still in America. Perhaps this is your first visit to Texas and this is how naive you are. You, my friend, are a foreigner—and a foreigner you will be until you study and digest this simple little guide to talking Texan.

    Once you have crossed the border, you are in a completely different country: you are now in the Great State of Texas (formerly the Republic of Texas, before we joined the Union) and any similarity to the speech and mannerisms of the rest of the nation is totally coincidental.

    Perhaps you picked up this little book because you are just a tad overwhelmed by the speech and mannerisms of these Texans. Just because you didn't need a passport doesn't mean a thing. See, you thought that you were just going across the border and were still in the United States. You, my friend, have just entered a whole nuther country.

    Welcome to Texas!!! Hopefully, you haven't entered through one of the big "city slicker" megacities of Dallas, Houston, or San Antonio, where the vast majority of the population talks and acts just like you. However, if you have made your entry through

Joe Kent Roberts

any of the small border towns or if you have ventured outside of any of the big cities, then this little book will be most helpful.

I hope that you haven't taken your trip to Texas during "Tourist Season." I also hope you're not just standing here at the bookrack reading this little manual and picking up tips on how to understand Texans and not paying for it. With a wife, six kids, and twins on the way, I really need the money.

A

Dictionary

AAH—This is not an expression of satisfaction or relief.
   Aah means "I."
   As in: Aah hoap yew-ul go.
      "I hope you'll go."
AAH PUET—This is actually two words.
   Aah puet means "I put."
   As in: Aah puet yore aws inna glace.
      "I put your ice in a glass."
AAHMONA—Not to be confused with ammonia.
   Aahmona means "I'm going to."
   As in: Aahmona warsh muh paints.
      "I'm going to wash my pants."
ALE—They are not talking about some type of alcoholic beverage—they are referring to a flying animal.
   Ale means "owl."
   As in: Thay-ut ale shore es purdy.
      "That owl sure is pretty."
ALL—Pronounced just like "all."
   All means "oil."
   As in: Aahmona chines muh all.
      "I'm going to change my oil."
ALM—This is not a type of panhandling or begging as it first sounds.
   Alm means "I am."
   As in: Alm bout sax fit tew.
      "I'm about six foot two."
A-MARE-KUN—Nothing to do with a type of horse.
   A-mare-kun means "American."
   As in: Aahm A-mare-kun.

>>"I'm American."

ARE—Not we are or they are; this refers to the time of day.
Are means "hour."
As in: Thay-ers ownly sew manie ares inna die.
>>"There are only so many hours in a day."

AST—Naw, Texans are very friendly and courteous and they are not referring to any part of the anatomy. They are even more friendly when you attempt to learn their language.
Ast means "asked."
As in: Aah ast fur uh tom-ollie.
>>"I asked for a tamale."

ASTER—Well yes, in most parts of the states, this is a girl's name or a flower. This is actually a female form and extension of the word ast.
Aster means "I asked her."
As in: Aah aster ta daince.
>>"I asked her to dance."

ASTUM—Yep, now you are getting it—this is the masculine version.
Astum means "I asked him."
As in: Aah astum fur a bare.
>>"I asked him for a beer."

ATAT—At first, this sounds like some kind of a military machine gun.
Atat means "at that."
As in: Alm rally gud atat.
>>"I'm really good at that."

AWIS—No, this is not a derivative of a wuss.
Awis means "always."
As in: Aah awis hav aws emma T.
>>"I always have ice in my tea."

AWL—Nope, this is not a carpenter's tool.
Awl means "I will."

As in: Awl be thar.
> "I'll be there."

AWS—Sometimes this word is interchangeable and you must really hear it in a full sentence to get the correct meaning. Aws means "ice."
As in: Aah aster fur sum aws.
> "I asked her for some ice."

Joe Kent Roberts

Texan—English

Ama-rilla— Amarillo
Have you noticed that all the really great towns in Texas have a song about them? Someone will sit down and write a song about their hometown and then have some famous singer record it for them. There are a few exceptions to this great town rule, because some really great towns in Texas are really difficult to rhyme. So you'll probably never hear a song about Corpus Christi, Fredericksburg, Halletsville, Orange, Nacogdoches, or Schulenburg.

I suppose that arriving in Amarillo by morning is nice, but my family and I prefer to arrive in the evening. There is a cozy little motel on the east side of town where we like to stay. It has a few antique cars that the kids love to admire and an indoor swimming pool with a whirlpool. Just about a mile down the road is our most favorite restaurant in Amarillo.

This is Amarillo's famous steak house and its biggest steak is a whopping five-pound T-bone. This steak comes any way you want it cooked and the meal includes a giant baked potato, beans, iced tea, shrimp salad, and Texas toast. If you can eat this approximately seven-pound meal within an hour, then there is no charge. The very first time we visited the steak house, a fellow at the next table ordered this five-pound steak. I ordered a twelve-ounce top sirloin at about the same time.

Every so often, my family and I would glance over and see how this fellow was progressing in his attempt to consume so much food in such a short period of time. We were amazed that he had completed over half of his dinner within twenty minutes. During the last fifteen minutes or so, this fellow was a-huffin' and a-puffin'. He was using the same type of technique that my bride uses in the delivery room, although this gentleman was using the technique to obtain completely opposite results. After he had finished his dinner within the hour time limit, the whole restaurant gave him a big round of applause. During the next half hour, he just sorta sat at the table savoring his victory then rose up, tipped his hat to the crowd, and slowly walked to the front door. "Walked" is probably not the correct word here, as the gentleman's walk resembled my bride's gait a few hours before giving birth to one of our children.

    I was absolutely amazed that he could eat all that food, as I was probably a few inches taller than he and we probably weighed about the same. I had to request a "doggy bag" for the remaining six ounces of my twelve-ounce steak. Some guys are "macho men" and some guys are dessert kings. Well, they had a pecan pie à la mode that I didn't want to miss. Plus, the only way I could have gotten rid of a seven-pound meal within the one-hour time limit would be by stuffing it under my shirt. I don't suppose the whole meal would fit under my shirt. I'd probably be able to drink the iced tea, eat the Texas toast, slip the baked potato into my coat, and use the shrimp as a trail to find my way back to the restaurant.

    This restaurant also has a large gift shop complete with a live six-foot-long rattlesnake in a glass-enclosed case. I've often wondered how many of these rattlesnakes they sell in a year. I'll have to remember to ask someone the next time we're there. The gift shop also has rattlesnake billfolds, rattlesnake heads, rattlesnake hatbands, rattlesnake rattlers, and they even have rattlesnake on the menu. Rattlesnake tastes nothing like chicken, although it may remind you of a giant ultralong chicken neck, because it is rather bony. It must have been a very brave or extremely hungry person who ate the first rattlesnake. They also have chicken and chicken-fried steak on the menu, but unlike rattlesnake, they don't have any stuffed chickens, or chicken parts for sale in the gift shop.

    Since they make rattlesnake boots, it seems to me that chicken boots would be fun to wear also. Chicken feathers sorta tickle, so it seems that anyone wearing chicken boots would be giggling, laughing, and happy all day long.

My sons like to visit the action-packed shooting gallery. There are all sorts of things that light up, ring, bong, twang, whiz, or play music whenever they hit the bull's-eye. When they hit the bull's-eye on the piano player, he starts playing an old saloon song on an old-timey piano. They always want me to join them at the shooting gallery and I always do. We always have a great time together.

There are hundreds of animal heads on the walls all over this restaurant; I think this is called atmosphere. There are deer heads, elk heads, moose heads, javelina heads, mountain goat heads, rabbit heads, complete pheasants, and so on. I'm surprised that there is no elk, moose, mountain goat, deer, javelina, rabbit, or pheasant on the menu. Then again, cow and chicken are on the menu but there are no cow heads or chicken heads on the walls.

Joe Kent Roberts

Aromas

They say that aromas will affect the psyche, and some stores even pipe in pleasant aromas to get us in a good mood so that we will buy more products while we are in their stores. Aromas also bring back memories to us, in many various and different ways. I do believe this is so, for I, too, am affected by aromas from the past, bringing back pleasant memories of many happy times.

There is a certain perfume that reminds me of an old girlfriend, and fresh baking breads and cookies remind me of my grandma. The smell of fresh cedar reminds me of Grandma's Christmas tree. The smell of the ocean reminds me of my carefree days spent on Padre Island not far from Corpus Christi. Then there was the time I got some catfish bait, and the smell was so awful that—after ten showers and three days—my wife finally let me come to bed with her again.

However, the aroma that really gets me nostalgic and brings back my favorite memories of Grandpa and Grandma and many wonderful days spent on the ranch outside of Hondo is cow manure.

Yep, if you really want to get me nostalgic and happy, just let me pass a cattle truck on the highway. I'll even slow down and roll down the windows just to get a good whiff of that earthy heavenly aroma. It was never fun stepping in it 'cause you wouldn't be allowed in the house until you cleaned it off. And we do have a yearly "cow chip" tossing contest here in Texas. If you are out of kindling, dried cow chips help start the fire and will keep you nice and warm. However, I wouldn't recommend them if you are looking forward to a romantic evening in front of the fireplace.

Joe Kent Roberts

Texan – English
Aws-tun—Austin
Well, every state has a capital, and Texas is no exception to the rule. The state capital is called Austin and is conveniently located in central Texas. Austin was named after Steven F. Austin, one of the early settlers in Texas. If you happen to be visiting from Los Angeles or New York City, you may become a little homesick while driving here during rush hour.

There is really no rush, as you'll probably be doing about three miles per hour in your car or stuck in a major gridlock. The Texas legislature did this on purpose so that tourists visiting from out-of-state big cities would feel right at home.

When I was in high school, our civics class took a field trip to see the Texas legislature in action. They call them field trips because we would have to cross a field to get to the school bus. I didn't see much action in the legislature, except for one fellow kinda flirting with his secretary, while another fellow was standing at the podium talking about traffic, streets, highways, and stuff, and most of the other legislators would be reading books, walking around, sleeping, eating donuts, drinking coffee, and apparently doing their legislative-type stuff. Most government workers at least try to look busy while on the job, and I suppose that since a bunch of people elected them to their jobs, they just don't have to put up with this pretense.

The following are some actual Texas state laws; Folks, I ain't making these laws up, although at times I wish I were.

It's against the law for anyone to have a pair of pliers in his or her possession. Apparently, there is no law against anyone having blowguns, machetes, knives, or axes. I suppose that this law does work, because I've never heard of a "plier murderer."

When two trains meet each other at a railroad crossing, each shall come to a full stop, and neither shall proceed until the other has gone. Well, folks, now you know why train travel is not as popular as it once was in Texas. They should have added all railroad crossings shall have picnic areas. Then again, now I know why I was never elected to higher office.

A recently passed anti-crime law *requires criminals to give their victims twenty-four hours' notice, either orally or in writing, and to explain the nature of crime to be committed.* I really feel safer just knowing that this law is on the books, because it shows that our Texas legislators saying that they are tough on crime is not just a lot of talk—they have rolled up their shirtsleeves and made bold, brilliant decisions against crime. Ain't it nice to know that the next time you're gonna be a crime victim, the perpetrator is highly educated and has good communication skills? Plus, you'll have twenty-four-hours' notice to correct any flaws in their writing skills. My old English teacher must be absolutely thrilled.

It is illegal to have more than three sips of beer while standing. This law seems to be a safety issue. Although making it mandatory that all bar stools require seat belts could possibly be the next addition to this law. What's nice is that there is no law that forbids taking more than three sips of beer and dancing at the same time. If you happen to observe an individual lying in the gutter drinking a beer, please be aware that there appears to be no law against this activity. However, as soon as this individual stands up and takes more than three sips of beer, please report this activity to the nearest law enforcement officer. If there is no law enforcement officer in sight, please check the nearest doughnut shop to see if one or more officers are available.

There is also a very confusing law about drinking and driving in the state of Texas. Signs are posted everywhere that say it is against the law to drink and drive. As a good citizen, I do try to obey each and every law. However, there should be a law against someone tempting you to break the law. Just the other day when I pulled up to the local drive-up window at a fast-food restaurant and placed my order, they asked me, "Would you like something to drink with that?"

I replied, "No, thank you, I'm driving."

The entire Encyclopedia Britannica is banned in Texas because it contains a formula for making beer at home. The people at the Encyclopedia Britannica are now working on a revision on this making-beer-at-home part to see if they can get this ban lifted. They will be adding that you might also be able to make beer in limousines and at state capitols. Hopefully, if in the meantime your home is raided by the local SWAT team because you happen to have a banned copy of this encyclopedia in your home, you won't be standing around sipping a beer. It would probably be a good idea not to have any open containers of doughnuts in your home too. It is also against the law to tempt or bribe any officer of the law.

B

Dictionary

BADE—Perhaps someone bade you farewell before you crossed the border.
    Bade means "bed."
    As in: Aahmona bade.
        "I'm going to bed."

BAH—Not really a bah humbug.
    Bah means "buy."
    As in: Aah wunna bah thay-ut.
        "I want to buy that."

BAR-BRA—This is not a special garment that females wear in a bar.
    Bar-bra means "Barbara"—I suppose that three a's in a word just takes too long to pronounce.
    As in: Woncha meat muh gale Barbra.
        "I'd like you to meet my girlfriend Barbara."

BARE—Nope, not as empty, without clothes, or buck naked.
    Bare means "beer."
    As in: Awl hava bare; yont wun?
        "I'll have a beer; do you want one?"

BARNT—Just what do they mean by barnt?
    Barnt means "burnt."
    As in: Muh sopper wus rally barnt.
        "My supper was really burnt."

BARTH—At times, this word gets confusing, even when it is used in a sentence and you take the word in context.
    Barth means "birth."
    As in: Muh waf gayve barth tew uh gale.
        "My wife gave birth to a girl."

BARTH-DAE—Yep, that's just what it means.

Barth-dae means "birthday."
As in: Hay-pe Barth-dae tew yew.
"Happy Birthday to You."
BAT-TREE—A tree from which we make Louisville Sluggers? Nope.
Bat-tree means "battery."
As in: Aah nade uh nu bat-tree fur muh pik-um-up.
"I need a new battery for my pickup."
BAYS-BOL—Now you're getting the hang of it.
Bays-bol means "baseball."
As in: Texus Raingers Baysbol Tame
"Texas Rangers Baseball Team"
BAY-UST—No, it's not a bay named ust.
Bay-ust means "best."
As in: Duh bay-ust tames cum frum Taxes.
"The best teams come from Texas."
BLAY-UCK—Sounds like some sort of a contagious disease, doesn't it?
Blay-uck means "black."
As in: Ats muh blay-uck pik-um-up.
"That's my black truck."
BODACIOUS—Strictly a word first formulated and used in Texas. Similar to the Yankee word giganticous, bodacious means "really, really big" or "really, really nice" or "really, really fabulous." You know, bodacious!
As in: Whale, shay shore is bodacious.
"Well, she sure is bodacious."
Without being there and seeing what he is seeing, it's really difficult to determine what he is talking about.
BOWIE—Nothing to do with a Bowie knife, which is pronounced Boo-ey.
Bowie means "boy."
As in: Ain't he a han-sum bowie?

"Isn't he a handsome boy?"

BRE-FUSS—In many parts of the country, this is the first meal of the day.

    Bre-fuss means "breakfast."

    As in: Whale, awl hayve saw-sage un aigs fer bre-fuss.

        "Well, I'll have sausage and eggs for breakfast."

BROUGHT—Pronounced like "I brought her flowers."

    Brought means "bright."

    As in: Duh brought lots e-yun tay-oun.

        "The bright lights in town."

BUB-EYE—They are not making any reference to your facial features.

    Bub-eye means "bye-bye."

    As in: Bub-eye, y'all

        "Bye-bye, you all."

Texan—English

Bow-munt—Beaumont
Located way down in southeast Texas, Beaumont was named after Beauregard Beaumont, the French governor of Texas. France was one of the six countries that ruled Texas for a brief period of time. Since Beauregard had the seat of the government here and was governor of this part of the country, he got to name this town. I believe this is where we get the term "ruling by the seat of your pants," because when Beauregard was governor, he got to sit down a lot. When someone is governor, he can pretty much do whatever he wants, so he named the town.

Thereafter, he was known as Beaumont of Beaumont, or Beau for short. Beau is pronounced like "bow" and sometimes "bo." *Beau* is a French word that means "sweetheart" and *mont* means "mountain." Those of you who know French will not find a mountain here, although you may find a sweetheart. Anyway, Beau ruled the land with a "velvet fist"; he was a pretty fancy dresser. Beau wore these long velvet gloves, velvet suits, silk vests, and silk ties.

You may still be able to see this "velvet" tradition that Beau instilled in his children and grandchildren. Every so often, you can be just driving down the street and there on the corner are a few of Beau's grandkids. Usually, they have a minivan surrounded by lots and lots of "velvet paintings." Just go on ahead and stop the car, get out, and take a look at what they're selling. You won't have to speak French to them, because you can probably speak Texan. I purchased a painting of the Eiffel Tower a few years ago, and I couldn't believe the low price. Seems the French not only gave us the Statue of Liberty, they're practically giving these paintings away.

Texan – English
Be-ugh Bay-un—Big Bend

Way down in southwest Texas, where the Rio Grande river makes a huge bend, is where you're gonna find Big Bend National Park. There is no big clock anywhere around here; that's Big Ben, the famous clock in London, England, that helps them tell the time. Big Ben has chimes that ring on the hour and half hour, just to let everyone know when it's teatime, lunchtime, and stuff. If you want to know what time it is in Big Bend, you'll probably have to bring your own clock.

It may surprise you to learn that there are an awful lot of no parking zones, even though this is a national park. There are also quite a few very friendly park rangers, but they know absolutely nothing about parking, so it would probably be best for you not to even ask. Just like the Texas Rangers highway patrol, these park rangers can also give you a speeding ticket. Please buckle up, observe all speed laws, traffic laws, road signs, traffic lights, and especially parking areas. There is nothing worse than getting a parking ticket at a national park.

Big Bend is the largest and most famous park in America, although most folks have never heard of it. I think if more folks owned a map of Texas, then Big Bend would be better known, because this park covers over 1,250 square miles, is larger than some of the smaller states back east, and covers a huge area on the Texas map. Big Bend may even be the largest park in the world, although there might be a park in Africa with elephants, giraffes, monkeys, and stuff that perhaps is larger.

Probably the largest animal in Big Bend is the black bear, although a few brown bears have been spotted. The largest insect in the park is the giant mosquito; however, recently there have been sighting of the historic giant tarantulas. These giant tarantulas stand over five feet tall and sit over three feet tall, so it's quite difficult to understand why we refer to them as insects.

Talkin' Texan

    The park contains over half of the known 900 species of birds in America, coyotes, wolves, bear, elk, deer, armadillos, roadrunners, jackrabbits, jackalopes, giant rabbits, longhorn rabbits, horned toads, falcons, eagles, chameleons, lizards, Gila monsters, scorpions, coral snakes, copperhead snakes, diamondback rattlesnakes, water moccasins, giant mosquitoes, tarantulas, and giant tarantulas. It's best to stay on the designated hiking trails during your visit to the park, unless you'd like to make the obituaries as another of the park's fatalities.

Texan – English
Braowns-vul—Brownsville
In the mid-1800s, there were three gentlemen—Mister Les Brown, Mister Moe Green, and Mister Benny Lush—who discovered this beautiful valley on the Rio Grande. These gentlemen were determined to build a great city in this area and got into a very heated discussion about what the town should be named. Benny suggested Lushville or Bentown, Moe suggested Greenburg or Moetown, and Lester demanded Lesterville. They nearly got into a brawl and finally decided that there should be some kind of a contest to decide the name of the town.

The men quickly ruled out rock, paper, scissors or horseshoes or any type of card game, but Lester did have an ace up his sleeve when he suggested a tomato war. Wild tomatoes were growing all over this part of the valley, and the men had an ample supply of ammunition with which to conduct the battle. When the men squared off at high noon on the banks of the Rio Grande on a cloudy day in June, Les clearly had an extra edge on Benny and Moe.

Les possessed an awesome blazing tomato and a pretty nifty curve. Legend has it that Les had these other gents completely baffled that day, and Benny and Moe didn't have a chance against him. Les won the tomato war easily and then proclaimed, "To the victor belong the spoils, and the ketchup." Les also won the right to name the town and decided on Brownsville instead of Lesterville. Les must have also passed on his skills to a few of his descendants, because several of them have had very illustrious careers in major league baseball.

In the early 1900s, Brownsville built one of the first schoolhouses in the area and brought in a fellow by the name of Hyrum Skool to teach their children for the first time. Mister Skool was a very friendly, intelligent fellow, and his students affectionately called him Mister Hy. This first schoolhouse only taught up till the eighth grade, and Hy felt the students should be allowed to continue their schooling through higher education. Mister Skool suggested to the community that they add grades 9, 10, 11, and 12, which they did, and Mister Skool's students started calling it Hy Skool.

As the growing community kept adding students to this small schoolhouse, they decided they would need to build a separate school for grades 9 through 12. Once this new building was completed, everyone continued to call it Hy Skool. Mister Skool was a rather shy, humble individual and wasn't one to be tooting his own horn, so he suggested that they call the school something besides Hy Skool. The town folk all got together and formally named this building for higher education the Skool High School. The school has been completely restored to its original condition and is listed in the Texas Historic Register.

Should you happen to visit this historic site during your stay in Brownsville, please remember that although the high school is there, Hy Skool is no longer around and has since moved on to another big high school in the sky. Please be sure to sign both the Hy Skool register and the high school register while you are there and have some photos taken in front of the high school, because you can no longer have any photos taken in front of or beside Hy Skool.

Brownsville is a thriving community and is well known for its shipping port, sometimes referred to as the Port of Brownsville. This is a very sweet, robust wine with very little aftertaste made from red grapes from the many local vineyards. Fortunately, the vineyards enjoy very good weather conditions throughout the year, and they are famous for producing some of the finest Texas wines. Be sure to plan your trip during the annual "Stomping of the Grapes Festival" held each year after the harvesting of the grapes. You don't have to be a professional grape stomper to be able to join in on the stomping of the grapes. Just jump on in and enjoy the fun and the festivities.

The wineries are located right next to the ship channel, so you will be able to not only visit some of the wineries but you can see some of the ships coming in and out of the docks. A few of the wineries have big picture windows overlooking the ship channel in their wine-tasting areas, so you can sip wine and watch for your ship to come in.

Brownsville is a delightful town with a vast array of things to offer citizens and tourists alike. Just off the coast of Brownsville, you'll find South Padre Island, with its beautiful white-sand beaches and warm surf from the Gulf of Mexico. South Padre Island is similar to Padre Island, it's just farther south. There is also a North Padre Island that they named Matamoras Island, just so they wouldn't confuse anyone about the similarities between these islands.

During one of our family outings to South Padre Island, we had the pleasure of meeting Rip Tyde, one of the local lifeguards on the island. Rip is a young, tan, handsome lad and takes his lifeguard duties very seriously. Rip is a very busy fellow and is constantly fending off enamored females while watching for anyone in distress along the beach or surf.

Other than the more common dangers of jellyfish, man-of-wars, toe-biting crabs, sharks, manta rays, electric eels, and being swallowed by whales, there are also the ever-present dangers of undertows and rip tides. Despite all this, everyone seems to have lots of fun at the beach, and I'm sure you will too.

Beach parties and family cookouts are very popular diversions on South Padre Island. I especially enjoy fighting off the seagulls trying to steal our food from the grill during cooking, because it keeps my metabolism up while I'm wildly thrashing around chasing them off. Once the meal is prepared, I can invite my bride and children to join me and have some hamburgers, hot dogs, bratwurst, and cold drinks. The nice thing about cooking out by the sand- and wind-blown sea is that I don't have to add salt to anything, because it's already salted—and unfortunately, it's also sanded. My family seems to really look forward to these cookouts on the beach, although I'm not too thrilled by the taste of sea salt and sand in my mustard-and-onion bratwurst. I'm told that sea salt is very healthy, and I'm sure that there must be some sort of vitally needed body minerals and nutrients in beach sand.

Bugs of Texas
Gee, I don't suppose any book about Texas would be complete if I didn't say a few things about some of the more interesting bugs of Texas. Some of my favorite bugs, and perhaps one day they may be yours also, are the "doodlebug," "dung bug," "lightning bug," and "June bug."

    We were pretty poor as I was growing up, and I didn't have many toys. Nothing much has changed; I'm still poor and don't have many toys, so I have to entertain myself with the simple things in life. Doodlebugs are quite fun to watch, because they have a unique way of capturing their prey and eating other bugs. While spiders have their webs and hide to await their prey, doodlebugs wait for their prey at the bottom of a hole in the ground. The doodlebug will dig a cylindrical hole in the ground that resembles a dirt funnel. Somehow, the doodlebug has the ability to churn the dirt into a very fine powder. Once the trap is complete, the doodlebug will wait at the very bottom of the hole under the dirt. Then an unsuspecting insect will come merrily walking along, and when it steps on the edge of the hole, the powdered dirt reacts like quicksand. The victim will try frantically to get out of the hole, but the dirt is so fine that the insect can't get a grip. In just a few short seconds, the insect is at the bottom of the hole, and the doodlebug gobbles it up.

    Doodlebugs are also pretty picky about what they will eat. If you were to drop an M&M or red hot or a doughnut sprinkle into their hole, they won't eat it. I tried. They also won't eat any pieces of cookie crumbs, cake, candy, or chocolate. I suppose doodlebugs just don't have a sweet tooth. I suppose kids and doodlebugs are completely different, because I tried to eat one of their insects one time, and I didn't like it.

    Another interesting bug is the dung beetle. There is a more common name for them down in Texas, but I can't use it because this is a G-rated book. The dung beetle is found mostly around barns and corrals—anywhere there's lots of cow and sheep manure. I suppose that nowadays if you were to tell young children to "go play," they wouldn't be hanging around the corral watching dung beetles. These bugs are most fun to watch as they gather their most unusual prize of fresh manure. Once the bug has found a pile of manure with just the right texture and temperature, it forms the manure into a perfectly round gumball size and rolls it home.

Mama dung beetle and the kids get really excited when they see what daddy dung beetle has brought home for them. They all get together and roll this great bounty into their dung beetle home. It's actually just a hole in the ground and probably doesn't smell too nice. Coyotes and wolves bring home lamb chops, rabbit, veal, and bacon; dung beetles bring home manure. I suppose all kids are happy to see Dad, no matter what he brings home.

Lightning bugs appear on cool summer evenings as soon as the sun has disappeared beyond the horizon. It was always great fun chasing them around the yard, as they seemed to dance in the dark, lighting up their tails and filling the air with their soft yellow blinks. I'd still like to chase them, but my wife says I should act my age. Perhaps I should suggest that she visit the mall some summer evening, and then I could indulge in one of my childhood pastimes.

Anytime you're gonna catch something, you need a little advance preparation—well, unless you were to catch a cold or the flu, then you wouldn't need to prepare at all. A clean screw-top jar with holes punched in the top and filled with grass makes an excellent lightning bug container. The lightening bug jar is just for temporarily observing the bugs that you have captured. Just like "catch and release" in fishing, we do the same thing with lightning bugs. One night, I captured a whole bunch of lightning bugs in a jar, and even though they lit up quite brightly, I couldn't read a comic book by their light—so I went ahead and released them into the night sky and got me a flashlight.

June bugs are well named because millions of them appear every summer in Texas, mostly in June. Some also appear in mid-May and last until the end of July. Initially, they were called May, June, and July bugs, but by the time you said their name they were already on you or had flown off. They also don't call them summer bugs because there are so many bugs flying around in the summer that it would have been too confusing.

June bugs are about an inch long, big, brown, and fat. Like most bugs, they just love porch lights. Therefore, anytime there is a summer get-together in the backyard, there will be June bugs. Well, unless you just mill around back there in the dark. Any kind of a bright light attracts a June bug, so they're everywhere on summer nights. They pretty much hide and sleep all day and then fly around looking for the bright lights in the evening. I think I know a few folks just like this.

Grandpa had installed a light in the backyard with a cord that ran from the house to the hackberry tree. Grandpa, Grandma, and some of my aunts and uncles would gather there on summer evenings to chat. The June bugs would also be there and be buzzing around and bothering everyone. To ease some of the problem, Grandpa would fill a washtub full of water and set it under the light bulb. When the June bugs flew into the hot light bulb, they would fall into the water. June bugs don't swim.

It always seemed to be such a waste, to have all these millions of June bugs and not be able to use them for anything. They would make really unique earrings and necklaces. Don't laugh; I've seen women wear all sorts of unusually weird things on their ears and around their necks. I'll bet you have too. Plus, tourists will buy just about anything as a souvenir to take back home. Seems to me if we can have stuff like fried grasshoppers and chocolate-covered ants to eat, we could at least try baked or deep-fried June bugs. They might even replace beer nuts as a snack.

Texan - English
Boz-urds—Buzzards

Buzzards are members of the condor family, and most of the buzzards you will see in Texas are actually black vultures rather than turkey buzzards. Observing them soaring high in the air, there is very little difference between the two because both birds are magnificent fliers. Black vultures seem to flap their wings a bit more than turkey buzzards. Buzzards rival eagles in their prowess in the skies; catching wind currents and updrafts, they will barely move their wings as they play among the clouds in search of their next prey.

They prey upon carrion—such a pretty-sounding word that so gently rolls off the tongue that I'm surprised someone has not named his or her daughter "Carrion."
Carrion actually means dead, putrefying flesh. Perhaps the nurse or doctor read the intended name on the birth certificate of the newborn girl and gently whispered the meaning into the proud parent's ear.

These turkey buzzards (*Cathartes aura*) have black bodies with red patches on their throats and bald heads—and unfortunately taste nothing like turkey. Black vultures (*Cora gyps atratus*) a.k.a. buzzards have a black body, gray neck, bald head, a twenty-two-inch length, and a fifty-four-inch wingspan. I'm not sure how much they weigh, as I've been unable to induce one to get on the bathroom scale.

Occasionally, you see them circling lower and lower in the sky over a sick, wounded, or dying animal. If you happen to be fortunate enough to see them close to the highway while you are traveling, you'll be able to see a feeding frenzy. They will rip, tear, and gouge the flesh from their prey, all the while keeping the others at bay and fighting amongst themselves for the choicest morsel. Perhaps it may remind you of a dinner at the in-laws. Without buzzards, we would have dead animals and stuff littering all of our roads and highways. Without wives, we wouldn't have in-laws—so it's very important that we choose our wives carefully.

Most of us may not have considered a buzzard as a pet, but they do have a distinct advantage over the popularity of dogs and cats as household pets. For one thing, buzzard food is very cheap and easy to obtain—when your pet buzzard is hungry, just open a window and let your pet outside. This is just one reason you never see a "buzzard food" section in any of the pet shops or grocery stores. Plus, unlike dogs, you won't have to leave your comfortable home to walk your buzzard. Unlike cats that shed hair all over your furniture, your buzzard will only shed feathers. I collect these feathers and give them to one of my female friends who makes feather pillows out of them. She calls them "vulture pillows" and the kids seem to like them; I think the name makes them feel like superheroes.

It's a little-known fact that the frontier doctors back in the 1700s and 1800s used buzzards for determining the seriousness of a patient's illness. If you weren't feeling too well and went to see the doctor, he would have you go sit in a chair in the field. When the buzzards started circling high in the sky and then flew down to a tree to be close to you, then both you and the doctor knew that you were really sick. It's such a shame that nowadays doctors try to keep the seriousness of an illness from their patients; sometimes the old ways are the best.

A pet buzzard is especially helpful if you don't have room for a garbage disposal in your house because, just like teenagers, buzzards eat almost anything. Remember how thrifty you felt when you saved those leftovers? Well now, if you forget about them, you won't have to fret, because you have made your own "buzzard food" from spoiled leftovers. Cleaning out the refrigerator actually becomes a treat for both you and your pet.

Talkin' Texan

At present, home security and personal safety are a big concern in our society; like the Viper car alarms, "no one would dare to come close" to you and your buzzard. Comforting, isn't it? You can learn more about buzzards by visiting your local library and checking out a copy of *Raising Buzzards for Fun and Profit*. You might not be the first on your block to have a pet buzzard; you might be the second, for I might already live on your block.

C

Dictionary

CAPE—I suppose a woman in a cape looks mysterious.
>Cape means "keep."
>>As in: Cape yore paints own.
>>>"Keep your pants on."

CAW—Romance languages twirl the "r" but Texans drop the "l."
>Caw means "call."
>>As in: Awis caw fust
>>>"Always call first."
>
>It gets most confusing if they just say "caw may" (call me).

CAW-FAY—No, they don't want you to call Fay.
>Caw-fay means "coffee."
>>As in: Caw-fay, please
>>>"Coffee, please."

CAY-UP—Similar to giddy up.
>Cay-up means "cap."
>>As in: Ave y'all sane muh cay-up?
>>>"Have you seen my cap?"

COE—Similar to famous Coe Porter.
>Coe means "cold."
>>As in: E-yuts awful coe.
>>>"It's awful cold."

COLT—You may think it's some kinda horse.
>Colt means "cold," past tense.
>>As in: E-yuts awful colt
>>>"It's awful cold."

CONT-NILL—If a word has too many letters, they just don't use 'em.
>Cont-nill means "continental."
>>As in: Wanna seama Cont-nill?

"Want to see my Continental?"

CRAIM—Rhymes with rain.
    Craim means "cream."
    As in: Wonesome craim en yore caw-fay?
        "Want some cream in your coffee?"

CUMEAR—Just a strangulation of two words joined together.
    Cumear means "come here."
    As in: Hay looky, cumear.
        "Hey, look at this, come here."

Camp Town Ladies

In these modern times, many of us promise our wives or sweethearts the moon and the stars, the sun and the rain, eternal bliss, moonlit walks, and at times, we may even be wealthy enough to name a boat or something or the other after them. Many of our male ancestors were a bit more romantic than many of us would suppose. These men should be highly respected for their foresight in letting their wives' or sweethearts' names remain for all time.

These very wise ancestors were very appreciative of what their wives and sweethearts endured in the early West. I suppose that after bringing her across oceans, through Indian attacks, in bumpy covered wagons, while the kids kept asking "Are we there yet?" the very least he could do was name a town after her. Some men did so and some men didn't. The following towns were named by some of the men who did. Although I'm sure some of the kids asked, "Hey, Dad, how come you named it Christine instead of Mom?"

There are many famous camp town ladies throughout the state of Texas, and there are the very well known towns of Alice, Carrolton, Edna, Odessa, and Victoria. In this section of the book, I'm just gonna tell you about a few of the lesser-known camp town ladies.

Big Sandy

She stood a very statuesque 6'6" and weighed about 225 pounds, with long golden hair that looked like new-mown hay kissed by the morning sun. They called her Big Sandy and named the town and a nearby river after her. When Big Sandy was in her teens, she figured that chickens, ducks, geese, and peacocks outnumbered dogs and cats about a thousand to one and so she opened up a poultry dressing operation in town. It seems that the local folks didn't take too well to dressing their fowl up in all sorts of fancy duds, and Big Sandy soon had to close her poultry dressing operation. The local folks adored her wit and determination and later changed the town name from Fowl City to Big Sandy. There is a big bronze statue dedicated to her in the town square, complete with some of her most popular poultry outfits. It's a very popular site for having your picture taken.

Christine

This little town is less than a two-day ride by horse going south from San Antonio, and much faster by car or truck. Named after one of the prettiest girls in Texas, Christine had long blonde hair, sky-blue eyes, and a smile that could melt the polar ice caps. Some of y'all may think that the "greenhouse effect" is causing this, but Frank swears that his wife, Christine, has such a dazzling smile that is why these ice caps are rapidly melting. I tend to agree with Frank. I'm just glad that Christine doesn't have a sister or we'd all be swimming in this part of the state.

Clairmont

Clairmont is located just a bit south of Lubbock. Well, the fellow who named this town after his wife, Clair, was really smart because *mont* also means mountain. Mont is also an abbreviation for his home state of Montana—so I suppose you could say he killed three birds with one stone.

Devine

Just a few miles southeast of Hondo, you'll find this sleepy little town named after Dee Vine. Her husband, Beau, felt that he was married to one of the most brilliant ladies in all of Texas. Dee was the one who suggested that one of the first horse washes in the state be built in town. These horse washes were very successful, and many of the local teenagers were able to earn some extra money working there after school. Folks were mighty impressed when someone rode up to church on Sunday morning on a freshly washed and shampooed horse. Dee would even clean and wash the bridles and saddles if her customers requested her to do so. She'd always attach a little packet of potpourri to the horse's bridle to keep that fresh horse scent. Unfortunately, there is no Devine Car

Wash in Devine, because Dee's descendants thought the horseless carriage was just a passing fad and invested the family fortune into designer horseshoes. There are quite a few Beau Vines remaining in the area.

Elsa

She can be found northwest of Brownsville. Elsa was very concerned that many of the local dogs and cats would get pretty doggone cold in the winter season. She was a whiz on her ol' Singer sewing machine and started making all sorts of coats for the neighborhood cats and dogs. Later, the town folk asked that Elsa make coats for their pets, which she did. Harold Coats asked that the town be named after his wife, Elsa. Elsa later went off on a bit of a tangent when she started making coats for the local cattle, although the local dairy cows looked quite fashionable in their udder garments.

Honeybunch

Located among the rolling oak-tree-covered hills in south central Texas is Honeybunch, the town named after my sweetheart of a bride and my most favorite place in Texas. I suppose all married couples have some kinds of signs or signals that they relay to each other when they want to get the other's attention. My bride's signal is to kick me in the shins whenever I say anything that she doesn't completely agree with. Normally, I'm pretty safe if I'm sitting in a chair or on a couch. However, if I'm sitting at a table, I really have to be careful about what I say.

If we are having dinner at home or if we've been invited over for dinner at a friend's house, I'll usually say little or nothing at the table, because I just know she'll haul off and kick me under the table. During the first few years of our marriage, I'd just keep talking and she'd keep kicking me harder and harder in my shins each time.

My shins are always battered and bruised, and I am unable to wear shorts around the house or during those hot Texas summers. I'm probably one of the few guys wearing long pants out on Padre Island. Sometimes my kids will ask, "Hey, Pop, how come you never wear shorts or go swimming with us?" I normally tell them that my legs are so beautiful that it will drive the other women wild, and I don't want to upset their mom.

Several years ago while my bride and I were attending Sunday school, the entire class sat at tables as the preacher instructed us from behind a covered desk. I really do love to discuss the Bible with others, and my sweetheart was continually kicking me as we would discuss certain passages in the Bible. I was always badly bruised after class and at times would have great difficulty even being able to walk out of the room after the lesson. It always seemed that my wife's lesson and the preacher's were totally different.

One Sunday after church, the preacher asked me if I'd like to teach his Sunday school class the following Sunday. I tried to leap for joy but because I could barely walk, I just told him that I would be happy to fill in for him the next Sunday. It was a real treat for me to teach the preacher's class that next Sunday because I was well out of range from my bride and protected by the preacher's desk.

After class, I was surprised to see the preacher behind the podium during church services. I had assumed that he just wanted me to fill in for him while he was on vacation or something. After church, I asked him about the Sunday school class, and he informed me that he wanted me to take over his class permanently. I was flabbergasted that he wanted me to take over "HIS" class, but I told him I would do my best.

They say there are no longer any "healings" in church, but I can readily attest to the fact that in less than a year my shins were completely healed. I was well protected from my honeybunch by the preacher's desk, and I would also beg out of any dinner invitation that was not a lap dinner. Anytime I am forced into accepting any sort of a sit-down dinner invitation, I always wear some loose fitting pants and some shin guards underneath.

I'm probably the most perfectly faultless husband in the country, and I suppose every married man has a wife with just one or two teeny faults that can be overlooked. My bride is worth more than her weight in diamonds, although I'd rather bring her a big bouquet of flowers than a box of chocolates.

Honeybunch is difficult to find without the aid of a wonderful, loving wife. Most modern men never ask for directions. Rather than ask someone where the post office is located, while traveling in a strange town, a real man will just follow a mail truck around knowing that eventually it will return to the post office.

Verdina

Back in 1903, my great-grandfather and one of my great-uncles donated some of their property to provide a location for a new schoolhouse. They also wrote to several locations throughout the state in search of a schoolteacher for this little one-room schoolhouse. The schoolhouse was nearly complete when they received a reply from a Miss Verdina Marm in response to their inquiry.

Verdina was well educated, charming, friendly, witty, a great cook, quite a looker, and the school kids loved her dearly. She taught grades 1 through 12 in this schoolhouse, and many of her students went on to receive college degrees because of her superior teaching talents. Young and old alike affectionately called her the "School Marm."

My great-uncle built her a small house adjacent to his house, and Verdina would leave each and every morning, via horse and buggy, to teach the kids at the new schoolhouse. The schoolchildren would arrive for classes each morning from up to six miles away. Some families would have only one child attending class, and their dad would have to accompany them by horse to and from school. After the child reached the age of seven or eight years old, they could ride to and from school by themselves. Families that had several children attending school were fortunate enough to let the older child accompany younger siblings to and from school, so there was no need to form "horse pools" the way we are required to form the many carpools in use today.

    One of my great-uncles explained how he would have to ride his horse over to Verdina's house when he was courting her. Sometimes they would go on picnics by horse and buckboard down by Verde Creek. He said the creek got its name from all the wild green chili peppers growing alongside the banks of the river. He said one day they had to postpone their picnic when they arrived at the creek because a bear was trying to get some honey from a beehive inside a large tree. He said he especially enjoyed the times that they would be out riding at night, because the sky would be covered with stars and they could see thousands of fireflies. The only sounds in the night were the chirping of the crickets and an occasional howling wolf.

    The town of Verdina is located about fourteen miles northeast of Hondo and about a mile east of the old Bandera highway. The old schoolhouse is no longer there, but you can still visit the old town hall and see some of the old photos and things. The Hondo Museum has a nice little section of their museum devoted to several historic objects and photos of Verdina. It's too bad they don't have a copy of her recipe for German chocolate cake, because it was one of the best.

Joe Kent Roberts

Texan – English
Canna-loap—Cantaloupe
People wonder why Americans have difficulty spelling and cantaloupe is one of those fringe words that are pronounced just a bit differently from the way they are spelled. Similar to bologna (a French word that translates "stuff swept up off the floor"), which is pronounced baloney, cantaloupe looks like it should be pronounced caint-uh-lou-pe. However, no matter how you pronounce it, Texas cantaloupes are some of the most delicious in America.

The best cantaloupes are grown on farms around Pecos. Cantaloupes were actually discovered by a straw farmer named Troy Beam, who also was a judge in Pecos County. Judge Troy grew the finest straw west of the Pecos by using a local grass called Johnson grass. There was also a Texas politician by this same name who went on to become an American president.

Anyway, Judge Troy had made a ton of money by selling his straw to the Texas farmers and was really looking forward to having a spectacular wedding when his beautiful daughter Clementine would marry the handsome Rufus Basslunker. Judge Troy knew that Clementine really loved Rufus to be able to give up such a cool name like Beam and be called Mrs. Rufus Basslunker.

Clementine informed Judge Troy that she had decided to forgo the wedding and was going to elope with Rufus. Judge Troy would have none of it and became so furious that he picked up one of those roundy, softball-sized, orangey-greenish melons that grew wild among the Johnson grass and slung it at her as she was running away. He hollered at her as he threw the melon "Yew kaint elope!" (translation: You can't elope!) as the melon squashed up against the fence post. As Judge Troy sat on the ground next to the melon consoling himself, he decided to take a bite of this melon. Well it was juicy, ripe, and delicious, and he decided in his misery to call this melon a "kaint elope."

And Judge Troy made even more money by selling kaint elopes all over Texas. Just like the name catsup evolved to ketchup, the name kaint elope evolved into cantaloupe. Judge Troy became wealthy beyond his wildest dreams. I suppose it's true that money can't buy happiness because all his grandchildren were called Basslunkers.

The City Slicker and the Pistol
Grandpa and all my uncles were all country boys and also great deer hunters; they also all had Winchesters and 30-06 rifles and fully knew how to use them.

Then came Bob, my stepdad, the city slicker, to the ranch one Christmas Day. I dearly loved my stepdad because he always took up for me, played games with me, and gave me my love for fast and beautiful cars. Bob had movie-star looks with a slight build. He stood about 5'10" and weighed in around 170 pounds dripping wet.

Bob had bought a pistol and leather holster and been out just a few times, practicing plinking tin cans and bottles with his 22 caliber pistol. Bob owned an Arthur Murray dance studio so, with his unusual occupation, city-slicker looks and lack of knowledge about the great outdoors, he was not too well received by these "good ol' boys." Plus, he was wearing this pistol and holster this one particular day.

We had walked from the ranch house into the pasture and were near to the "Black Tank." My uncles asked Bob if he knew how to use the pistol he was wearing, and Bob said that he could do okay with it. A few moments later, one of my uncles spotted a sparrow about forty yards away sitting up in big old oak tree.

"Do you think that you could hit that bird?" he said as he pointed to the oak tree.

"Sure," Bob said.

I suppose they expected Bob to aim the gun at the bird with both hands the way they do in those cops and robbers movies.

Bob pulled out the gun from the holster and shot from the hip just like in the Western movies, and the bird instantly fell to the ground as dead as a doornail.

"Wow!" they said in unison. "Do that again!"

"Naw," Bob said, "I don't like to show off."

The respect that was shown on my grandpa's and uncles' faces was ample reward. They asked me later if Bob could make that shot again and I said that he was a pretty good shot.

Bob couldn't have made that shot again in a hundred years; someone was really looking out for him that day.

Talkin' Texan

Texan – English

Kor-pis Kristy—Corpus Christi

Situated on the balmy, breezy Gulf Coast, Corpus Christi is a year-round playground for those who love the sea, sand, and surf. With visions of beautiful bikini-clad young maidens dancing in their heads, eligible Texas bachelors come to Corpus Christi from all over the state. Sometimes ineligible men also make this same trip, and they mostly end up with an entirely different vision—usually the inside of the "doghouse" or on the Living Room couch.

The average wind velocity in Corpus is a breezy 36 MPH, so most of the locals don't wear hats, and hardly any of the men wear toupees. Most of the ladies who live here fret about what the wind and humidity does to their hair yet tend to forget that the high humidity is great for their complexion. The local women tend to look much younger than their years, so the sweet young thing that you think may be in her twenties might actually be in her late thirties.

It's an odd thing to me that young girls always state their age as being eight and a half or nine and three-quarters, then teenage girls always try to pass for several years older, yet when these same women reach their late twenties, they say they are a few years younger. It's probably a good thing I did not attempt to write a book on everything I know about women—I doubt I would have been able to fill up a page. Fortunately, I'm not alone, as most of my gender seems to be pretty much in the same situation.

One of the most popular drives in Corpus is Shoreline Drive. Some of you may be wondering why I'm just writing Corpus instead of Corpus Christi. Actually, it's just an ingrained habit, whereas Texans tend to expand and exaggerate a bit on some of their stories, we also like to save time when we are talking so we just lop off a word or two. Plus, there is only one Corpus in the state; it's not like we are taking about San Antonio and just calling it San.

Anyway, Shoreline Drive runs from downtown Corpus all the way out to the naval air station. They call it Shoreline Drive because it's right on the shore of the beach and it "shore" is a pretty drive. There are some really fancy homes on Shoreline Drive because most of the rich people in town live out there. It must be nice being rich because you can pretty much live wherever you want.

Since there were pirates that preyed upon unwary travelers around the coasts of the Gulf of Mexico in times past, Corpus celebrates these events by having an annual "Buccaneer Days" carnival from the last week in April until early May. Looting and pillaging is kept to a minimum nowadays, so families can have an enjoyable time at the carnival. If you happen to be over twenty-one, you may partake of the fare offered at the local beer garden. It's really not much of a garden, because the only "flower" on the menu is a foreign out-of-state beer. It's really a crying shame that they don't offer Shiner Bock or at the very least some state-brewed Lone Star or Pearl beer. It's a very sad state of affairs indeed, and I have tears in my eyes just thinking about it.

Perhaps these are just crocodile tears, because there are quite a few of these beasts in the local rivers and streams around the Corpus area. I was happily fishing for perch and brim on the Nueces River one warm summer day when I happened to be surprised by one of these lurking monsters. It was just a small crocodile—about four or five feet long—and seemed to be having much better luck at catching fish than I was. It also seems to me that I remember my favorite English teacher saying something about there being a rule about ending a sentence with a possessive adjective. Fortunately, I don't know what a possessive adjective is so I guess I'm okay because of this.

Talkin' Texan

There are also supposed to be rules about telling the difference between a crocodile and an alligator, but again I can't remember. I think it has something to do with the number of rows of teeth in their mouths. I'm sure that alligator wrestlers have the time to count teeth, but I didn't really want to stay around to find out. Someone should develop a jingle about the difference between crocodiles and alligators, similar to the one I almost learned in the Boy Scouts about coral snakes. It went something like: black and yellow can help a fellow, while red and yellow can hurt a fellow—or maybe it was the other way around. Anyway, the scoutmaster thought that it would be very helpful if we all learned this little jingle.

I'm sure by now the Boy Scouts, forest rangers, or swamp rangers have some little jingle about telling the difference between all sorts of things. When it comes to crocodiles and alligators, I sorta like one of the verses from a popular Beach Boys song: "Run, run, run, till daddy takes your T-bird away." I've often wondered if crocodiles really do shed tears, or if it's just something else that I've never really understood, like the coral snake jingle.

You'll not only come across crocodiles and alligators when you're strolling through the rivers and woods around Corpus—there are also the occasional coral snakes, diamondback rattlesnakes, copperhead snakes, water moccasins, scorpions, black widow spiders, or Texas-sized mosquitoes to contend with. The mosquitoes are fairly easy to avoid, as there are some very high-quality mosquito repellents on the market. At the present time, there are no repellents offered for these other varmints. For some folks, running, hollering, and screaming seem to work the best.

You'll also find mosquitoes around the ocean and along the beaches, along with seagulls, sand crabs, jellyfish, man-of-wars, electric eels, manta rays, sharks, and biting crabs. The seagulls are the easiest to deal with, because you just have to toss them food. With these other varmints, YOU are the food. Many folks have a great time on the many beautiful beaches around Corpus, and there are hardly any major fatalities at all. That's because Corpus has the highest per capita of doctors of any city in Texas. So if you happen to be on a crowded beach and are bitten by something, just holler out "Is there a doctor on the beach?" Chances are, you will have several doctors respond to your plea for help. If you happen to be bitten on your bellybutton, then you're really in luck, because there are lots of navel doctors in Corpus Christi. They have doctors that specialize in just about anything nowadays.

    There is a big navy base at one end of Corpus, so you'll see lots of navy personnel while you are visiting in and around town. Docked near the Bay Bridge, you'll find a beautiful decommissioned aircraft carrier called the *Blue Ghost*. This is a great way to educate the kids and have a really enjoyable day. This ship is built like a lady's shoe, for it looks small from the outside but is really big on the inside. They have tours of the ship about every hour or so that are very informative and entertaining. There are also lots of restored vintage aircraft above and below the decks of the ship. The *Blue Ghost* is all lit up at night and is visible from all over Corpus Christi Bay.

    When you take the tour of the ship, you'll notice many retired navy men and women who have volunteered their time and energy to keep the *Blue Ghost* all polished and shipshape. Each one of these individuals is a vast encyclopedia of information about this ship. They will be delighted to answer any question that you might have about this ship, so don't be afraid to ask a dumb question, because they won't make you swab the decks or send you to the brig even if you don't know the meaning of swab or brig, port or starboard.

    Every New Years Day, Corpus has a big to-do about how nice and hospitable the weather is in this part of the nation. They show films of bikini-clad young maidens happily frolicking in the surf and on the local beaches. As for me, I'm happy when my beautiful bride brings me food and drink (bratwurst, Shiner Bock, or pecan pie) no matter what the weather is like.

Texan – English

Cor-sa-kana—Corsicana

Not too far south of Dallas, on Interstate 45, you'll find the town of Corsicana. The town was settled by a group of German immigrants and one lone Italian around the mid-1850s. The town was named after Corsica, Italy, just because the Germans were used to being ruled by a czar, and the minority ruled. Well that, and the Italian fellow was really homesick. In the early years, the settlement was known for agriculture, bratwurst, rich pastries, cattle, and hats. The city fathers and mothers decided that the town was growing so large that it was time to have a stable water supply.

In the early 1900s, they started drilling for water and discovered black gold (oil), lots and lots of oil. They continued to drill for water and continually found more oil. They found oil on every farm, ranch, front yard, backyard, school, park, and empty lot in town. They all became wealthy and just decided to bring in railroad water tankers from out of town.

In the 1920s, Corsicana was a boomtown, with roughnecks, oil folks, bars, gambling, and dance halls. There were over twenty-one millionaires in town. In the 1920s, a million dollars was quite a bit of money, although nowadays Enron executives are able to make that much in just a few hours, plus they don't get their hands nearly as dirty. Well, not literally anyway. Seems that nowadays, while visiting banks, white-collar executives can make more money in a year than Bonnie and Clyde ever thought possible by barging in with blazing handguns. This just goes to show you the value of getting a good college education from an accredited university.

Other than black gold, Corsicana is world famous for the Collin Street Bakery. The bakery is located right on the main east-west highway going through town. My family and I love to stop in and make several purchases at the bakery whenever we are in town. The bakery is famous for making the best fruitcakes in the known world. These aren't the ordinary artificially flavored brick-hard fruitcakes that are sold in major department stores during the holidays. Those fruitcakes, sold in their colorful tins for a few bucks, make excellent decorative doorstops during the holidays and can be reused year after year.

If you would like to support the local economy while you're in town, drop by the bakery, buy a hat, and get some gas. There are a coupla different ways that you can get gas in town. Visit one of the local service stations in town. I realize in this age of self-serve that this may be shocking news to you, but there are several service stations in town. They'll fill your tank, check your oil, and wash your windows. To be completely gassed up, you may want to have a few bowls of chili before leaving town.

In the early 1950s, Corsicana continued to increase in population and again needed a local supply of water. They started drilling for water on the eastern side of town and again, discovered oil. They drilled some more and discovered still more oil. All told, they ended up with an additional 500 oil wells. Even the sheiks in Saudi Arabia envy the enormous number of rich folks in Corsicana. Nearly every home in town has an oil well in either the front or the backyard. If you're looking to buy an old home in town, it will most likely come with its own oil well, so the asking price may be a little bit high.

Hardly anyone in town has a water well on their property, and nearly every homeowner with an oil well just uses bottled water. There are no car washes in town, so if you have any road grime on your car from traveling, be sure to have it washed before journeying into Corsicana. Most of the locals will just use that fancy French bottled water to wash their cars. Normally, when you happen to see one of these cars being washed, it's being washed by the butler, or the driver, and not the actual owner of the car. Every so often, you may see one of the poorer folks in town washing their own car with some of that cheap bottled water, purchased at one of the local discount stores.

    If you don't want to appear like a tourist while driving through town, you may want to rent a Lexus, Mercedes, BMW, or a cowboy Cadillac before you arrive. Brush up on your petroleum knowledge, add a pair of Western boots and a Stetson hat to your wardrobe, and please avoid any fruitcake jokes.

D

Dictionary

DADE—Yes, it's also a county in Georgia.
 Dade means "dead."
 As in: Muh bat-trees dade.
  "My battery is dead."
 No bats in the trees, they just need a jump.

DAINCE—Rhymes with ain'ts.
 Daince means "dance."
 As in: Aah jus lock tew daince un hava gud tom.
  "I just like to dance and have a good time."

DARE—Not a challenge, but a term of endearment.
 Dare means "dear."
 As in: Moe caw-fay, muh dare?
  "More coffee, my dear?"

DAWN—Same word, but it has nothing to do with the sun.
 Dawn means "dying."
 As in: Muh doe-guhs dawn.
  "My dog is dying."
 Or: Alm dawn muh shart
  "I'm dying my shirt."

DAY-OWN—This has nothing to do with possessions.
 Day-own means "down."
 As in: Snot upits day-own
  "It's not up, it's down."

DAY-YUM—Sometimes Texans like to add a few more letters to a word for emphasis.
 Day-yum means "damn."
 As in: Day-yum, thay-ut chele as bodacious.
  "Damn, that chili is bodacious."

See "B" for reference to bodacious; Texans really like their chili.

DOE-GUH—Really important words require more letters for Texans.

Doe-guh means "dog."

As in: Ats muh doe-guh inna Cont-nill.

"That's my dog in the Continental."

DROGS—Not to be confused with dregs, rhymes with dogs.

Drogs means "drugs."

As in: Eyuff drogs ar alegil, hay-ow cum thay hayve drog stars?

"If drugs are illegal, how come they have drug stores?"

Talkin' Texan

Texan—English

Dale-us—Dallas
As I was doing some research before writing this short story about Dallas, I came upon a glaring bit of historical misinformation pertaining to the initial founding of Dallas. The history records state that a certain gentleman came upon a natural Ford on the banks of the Trinity River in 1841. Hey folks, I was born in the morning but not yesterday morning. We all know that Henry Ford didn't begin making Fords until the turn of the twentieth century.

This particular bit of history must have been written by one of those blasted Yankees from around Michigan way trying to fool us into believing that Fords were around in the mid-1800s. There has always been quite a rivalry between Ford and Chevy down in these parts, but this has to be the most unbelievable statement that any Yankee has ever tried to make about Texas and Fords.

This same history book stated that the origin of the name Dallas was unknown, but they thought that Dallas could have been named after a vice president of the Union. Yeah, un-huh, sure, I can't believe that those wonderful Yankees who came down here and gave us so many helpful innovations like Boston baked beans, maple syrup, and baseball would have Texans believe that we would name one of our towns after a vice president of the Union. Texas seceded from the Union during the Civil War. Most Texas towns and counties are named after the heroes of the Revolution—Austin, Houston, Travis, Crockett, Bowie, and so on and so forth. I surely hope they're not teaching this type of Yankee logic to any of my children or grandchildren in school.

Rather than rely on a history book apparently written by Yankees, I decided to interview a few of the descendants of Dallas and find the true origins of this world-famous town. I wasn't able to go straight to the horse's mouth, because the original settlers of Dallas are no longer around to answer any questions, so I decided to interview a few of their grandchildren. I took a bunch of notes while I recorded and interviewed several grandchildren.

Grandchildren are always fun to talk to because they always have the most factual information. The following will be the actual story of the early development of the Dallas that we all know and love.

In late 1839 or the early 1840s, several families with the surname of Dallas arrived on horseback and covered wagons on the banks of the Trinity River. There were Wally and Wilma Dallas and their boys Wiley, Waylon, and Willy, who opened up the first dry goods store on the banks of the Trinity River. This family was pretty smart because they figured that anyone who had just crossed this big ol' river would be needing some dry clothes. They also sold towels and flip-flops.

Ernest and Elsa Dallas along with their sons Erly and Edward Zachary, also known as EZ, were a family of buffalo hunters. Ernest, Erly, and EZ made a fine living hunting buffalo in these parts. After a successful hunt, they would haul their buffalo over to Waldo's Wild Game Processing Plant, and Waldo would butcher the buffalo into sirloins, filets, roasts, hamburger, and jerky. Ernest and the boys would provide most of the local saloons, cafes, and restaurants with fresh buffalo meat on a regular basis.

Then there were Larry, Burly, and Moe Dallas who owned the local tannery and an adjacent retail outlet called Buffalo R Fust—meaning that buffalo leather made the best in coats, jackets, and pants. They sold most of these leathers to folks back east, because it was way too hot in these parts to even consider wearing leather. The boys also designed some very fine buffalo fur coats accented with roadrunner feathers for the ladies back east. Dallas became very famous for its buffalo-hide trade. Back in the 1800s, it was pretty easy to hide buffalo in gullies, valleys, and forests. The buffalo-hide trade must still be pretty good, because whenever you're traveling throughout the Dallas metropolitan area, you won't see any buffalo at all. I kinda wonder where they're hiding them nowadays.

Another Dallas clan was Dizzy and Donna Dallas and their children Don, Doug, Dewey, Daphne, and Della. They named their youngest son Harold because they didn't want to name him Delbert, Dick, Desoto, or Donut. This family was well known for honesty and a straightforward way of writing, and with all of the other family members having their names start with the letter "D," of course, Harold became the one and only Harold Dallas. A few of the grandchildren I interviewed mentioned something about Harold being a newspaper writer.

Some of the other families that settled in this part of the state were Rich and Ginger Baker, who owned the local bakery; Hyrum (Hy) and Wanda Taylor, who operated the local tailor shop; Don and Carrie Cotton, operators of the local gin mill; and Doc Menteauh, the beloved town physician and his lovely wife, Dee. Seymour and Charlotta Byers owned the very first department store in town along with their partners, Les and Cindy Sellers. The store was originally called the BS Department Store, but they later decided to change the name to something more appropriate.

Probably one of the most famous individuals in Dallas is Russell (Rusty) Pocket, the inventor of the Texas army knife. This army knife contains a tent-stake carver, cactus straw, fishing line with hook, fish scaler, rattlesnake skinner, pecan sheller, magnifying glass, mosquito lasso, guitar pick, bird call, duck call, and wolf whistle. The wolf whistle is especially handy while deer hunting. When you see a deer, just blow the whistle and the deer will stop and turn around to see who thinks she's cute. While the deer is standing there primping, just squeeze off a shot and you'll be having venison for dinner.

In the 1600s, the Trinity River was called the River of Canoes. The Spaniards named this river the Trinity because of the three different forks of the river—the east fork, the west fork, and the elm fork. In addition to these forks, the modern-day Trinity also contains spoons, knives, old tires, car parts, truck parts, dead animals, raw sewage, and lots and lots of chemicals. In keeping with the biblical name Trinity, you can literally walk on water across this river, but you have to be sorta careful where you step.

The most picturesque entrance to Dallas is on the old causeway, just like the opening scene on the 1980s television program *Dallas*. There are over 3,000 millionaires within the Dallas city limits, and if we were to add in the suburbs there would be well over 5,000 millionaires in the Dallas metropolitan area. If we were to add in the poorer folks who only make $900,000, $800,000, or $700,000 per year, we are still talking about a bunch of rich people.

Try to "dress up" when you go out to dinner; wear a Rolex if you have one. About the only thing they didn't show you on the *Dallas* program was the Daytona 500 raceway traffic on the expressways. This may take a little getting used to if you and your family are not familiar with drag racing or the Indianapolis 500. Seems that the Dallas drivers are all competing to see who will get to be the pace car. There also seems to be some sort of a prize for the driver who gets home first. Either that or every Dallas driver has a million-dollar insurance policy and they want the rest of us to be able to become millionaires also.

Since they don't use turn signals at the Indy or Daytona 500 racecourses, they don't use them on Dallas expressways either. If you were to purchase a used car either in Dallas or from Dallas, the turn signals would be as good as brand new. This is because the turn signals were only used if the vehicle was a show car or if it was in a slow-moving parade. Never, ever buy a parade car because there is always some clown who will.

If you will not be taking a city bus or taxi while you are in Dallas and instead will be driving in your own car, please be sure to purchase a white flag to display on your car while you are in the

Dallas metropolitan area. This white flag will identify you as a tourist, and you and your family will be well protected as you travel the highways and byways around Dallas. Most of the department stores and drug stores in Dallas and the suburbs have these white flags in stock. If, by chance, you are unable to find a white flag, then the next best thing is to just take a clean old pair of white underwear and attach this to your car antenna. If your car does not have an antenna, then go on ahead and spend $8.00 or $10.00 and buy one.

     This will not only give you a place to attach your white flag, it will also give you better radio reception.

Days of the Week
Texan - English
Mun-de—Monday
    Some folks think this is the first day of the week; it ain't. This is the first day of the average person's workweek. The first day of the week is actually Sunday, which is a day off.
Twos-de—Tuesday
    For most people, this is when we really get into the flow of the workweek. This is the second workday and that's where the Two comes from. There are no Threesdays or Foursdays, and I suppose that's a good thing, because otherwise the days would be too numerical.
Whens-de—Wednesday
    Right smack dab in the middle of the workweek is normally when we ask "When is our new work schedule due?" "When is coffee break?" "When is lunch hour?" "When is payday?" "When is the next three-day holiday?" This is also the correct day of the week for mothers to ask their daughters "When are you gonna get married?" or "When can I expect to be a grandmother?"
Thurs-de—Thursday
    This is the second most exciting day in the week, because it's almost Friday. I think the eve of all holidays and weddings should be on Thursdays—that way we could have lots of three- and four-day holidays during the year and longer honeymoons.
Fry-de—Friday
    Friday is one of the most exciting days of the week for most working people. This day is well named, for this is when we can go home and enjoy a big chicken-fried steak with all the fixings. Texans eat an awful lot of fried foods—there are fried eggs, fried bacon, fried sausage, fried okra, and by golly, we even have fried ice cream! This is also the day that all the fast food restaurants really push the French fries by asking, "Would you like fries with that?"

Satter-de—Saturday
　　Come Monday morning, my friends will ask "So wa-ja dew Satter-de?" Normally, I just sat around the house playing with the kids or sat on a bench at the mall while my wife went shopping or sat on the riverbank with an ol' cane pole just a-thinking and waiting for a bite.

Son-de—Sunday
　　The first day of the week is a day off so we celebrate by getting all dressed up and going to church.

Talkin' Texan

Deer Hunting

One really cold day, Grandpa took me deer hunting on the ranch. Boy, was it cold! Grandma had me bundled up with about three shirts, two pairs of pants, two pairs of socks, plus a jacket and a hat. Grandpa told me to wait by this tree and he would go around and scare up some deer. We had gotten up so early that morning that I was still sleepy and decided to sit down and rest against the tree.

  I awoke to rustling leaves, and Bambi was grazing about four feet from my feet, and just a few feet farther was her mom. I could not shoot the doe and leave Bambi all alone so I did not squeeze the trigger. Even though we could shoot doe that season, Grandpa said it was okay that I didn't shoot.

  The next year when Grandpa took me hunting, I had a bad cold and I climbed up the big oak tree and settled into the deer blind. Grandpa trudged off to another part of the ranch and said he would be back later. Grandma had given me a whole box of Kleenex, and I kept blowing my nose and tossing the Kleenex outside the deer blind. I'm sure every deer within ten miles knew that I had a cold. When Grandpa returned at the end of the day, that whole oak tree was covered with white Kleenex and looked like some sort of an oddly flocked Christmas tree. Grandpa sorta chuckled as he asked me if I had seen any deer that day. I told him that I had not seen nary a one all day long. He always laughed and sometimes tears would come to his eyes as he told this story.

  A few years later, Grandpa and I went hunting again, and I took a deer blind in an oak tree with a small meadow at the base of the tree. After about an hour, a doe appeared—then two, then three, four, five, and six. Suddenly, the buck appeared and with his head held high, he was truly majestic as he overlooked his doe. I was just in awe as more and more deer entered the meadow. All told, there were eighteen doe, three Bambis, and three bucks. They were magnificent and I could not bring myself to shoot.

Grandpa returned and said he hadn't seen a thing all day. Unfortunately, I made the mistake of telling him what I had seen that day. Grandpa knew that I was an excellent shot for he had taught me. We never went again. I love to eat venison, but I just can't shoot them. Deer are just way too pretty, and I think that's why Americans eat so much chicken. I believe that's why we have Kentucky Fried Chicken and not Kentucky Fried Rabbit, because bunnies are just too cute and cuddly to eat.

Texan – English
Do-mus—Dumas

You will find Dumas just less than fifty miles north of Amarillo in the heart of the Texas panhandle. The town was named after the famous author Alexandre Dumas, who wrote *The Count of Monte Cristo*. The local folks are very intelligent and well read; their school system has the highest grade point average of any in the state. Just to show your good taste, it would probably be a good idea to have a copy of one of the classics under your arm during your visit in town. Just to let them know that you are also multilingual, carry a copy of this book around with you also.

    I've always enjoyed stopping there and staying overnight with my family. My wife and kids always look forward to visiting the local Braum's ice cream parlor. They have about fifty different kinds of ice cream, and they will make any one of them into a shake or malt for you. It's always lots of fun deciding on which flavor ice cream we would like. Since we are only here for one night a year, we'll usually have some ice cream at the store and get some more to take back and enjoy around the motel swimming pool.

    In the late 1940s, there was a very popular song called "I'm a Ding-Dong Daddy from Dumas." This song is still sung today at many of the family reunions and some of the local taverns. The song also inspired a very tasty snack cake by a large American bakery. You will receive a 30 percent discount when you sing "I'm a Ding-Dong Daddy from Dumas" when purchasing this item at any of the local establishments. Some folks are too embarrassed to sing and prefer to wait until their senior discount kicks in, or just pay full price. It seems to me that if some folks have to sing for their supper, it would be more fun to sing for our just desserts.

    "I'm a Ding-Dong Daddy from Dumas" also inspired the ever-popular electric doorbells that many of us use today. Before ding-dong, there was just a knock on the door, or a steady buzz, or ring. Seems that Mister Electric was singing along with this song one day and thought this would be a great idea for a doorbell. A doorbell that went ding-dong so revolutionized the doorbell industry that Mister Electric was promoted to a General.

E -F

Dictionary

EMMA—Perhaps you think it's a female name.
   Emma means "in my."
   As in: Atsma gal emma Cont-nill.
       "That's my gal in my Continental."
ENGINE—There is a motor and there is an engine.
   Engine means "Indian."
   As in: Muh kay-uds ur plane KO-boys un Engines.
       "My kids are playing Cowboys and Indians."
EVER-THIN—Wouldn't it be nice to be ever-thin?
   Ever-thin means "everything."
   As in: Mah waf wonts ever-thin.
       "My wife wants everything."
EYE-REEN—Sounds like a new kind of eye drops.
   Eye-reen means " Irene."
   As in: Aah draim uv Eye-reen.
       "I dream of Irene."
EYE-TALIAN—I was raised with this word until a friend said
   "Hey, there ain't no Eye- Taly."
   Eye-Talian means "Italian."
   As in: Whale, yew shore luck Eye-Talian.
       "Well, you sure look Italian."
E-YUN—Just say it phonetically "E-yun."
   E yun means "in."
   As in: Whale, cumon e-yun
       "Well, come on in."
       "I'm fixing to leave."
FANGER—Rhymes with anger.
   Fanger means "finger."
   As in: Thas muh fanger.

"That's my finger."
FAR—If it's not near, it must be far.
> Far means "fire"—that's why it's illegal to yell far!
> As in: Pul-ease, no porking inna far lane.
>> "Please, no parking in a fire lane"

FARED UP—Sometimes sounds like fart up.
> Fared up means "fired up."
> As in: Whut dew aah haf tew dew tew get yew fared up?
>> "What do I have to do to get you fired up?"

FAWNEY—Little fawns eat ivy.
> Fawney means "funny."
> As in: Ats purdy fawney.
>> "That's pretty funny."

FAXUN TUH—They're getting ready to do something.
> Faxun tuh means "fixing to."
> As in: Alm faxun tuh lave.
>> "I'm fixing to leave."

FAY-UT—If something is not slim, it's fay-ut.
> Fay-ut means "fat."
> As in: Whale, shay shores fay-ut.
>> "Well, she sure is fat."

FLAR—Nearly every town has a flar shop.
> Flar means "flower."
> As in: Them flars smale naws.
>> "Those flowers smell nice"

FORN—Since they used so many letters up above, they had to delete a few here.
> Forn means "foreign."
> As in: Yew frum a forn cuntree?
>> "Are you from a foreign country?"

FRAND—Pronounced fran with a duh—fray-und.
> Frand means "friend."
> As in: Ats muh frand.

"That's my friend."
FUR—Cuddly? Furry? Fuzzy-wuzzy?
　　　Fur means "far."
　　　　As in: Ats purdy fur.
　　　　　　"That's pretty far"

Texan—English

El Duh-ra-duh—El Dorado
The legend of El Dorado began over five hundred years ago during Columbus's exploration of the Americas. The Italians said they were looking for a shorter route to India so they could bring Indian spices back to Italy and avoid those long ocean voyages. Apparently, Italy didn't have stuff like salt, pepper, cinnamon, basil, parsley, garlic, oregano, and so on, so they had to travel across the seven seas to get them. It's pretty difficult to make a really good spaghetti sauce without these ingredients and Columbus pretty much convinced the queen that the world was round instead of flat and that the shortest route to India would be west instead of east.

    The queen really loved spaghetti with spicy meatballs so she gave Columbus a ship and a crew to obtain these much-needed spices. Columbus set sail in the spring of 1492 with great cheers and a few jeers. Some folks figured that since the Earth was flat, the ship would fall off the edge of the world, while others admired his bravery for living on the edge. A few weeks later, Columbus arrived in Spain and decided to give his crew liberty before departing to east India. They really didn't call it liberty back then, so Columbus just said, "Hey, y'all can go ashore if you want to, but please be back before noon tomorrow, because the queen is almost out of oregano."

    It may surprise you to learn that all of the crew returned to ship before noon the next day. The Italians really do love spaghetti and meatballs. While the crew was in port, they told some of the local folks about their journey into dangerous uncharted waters and that if they were fortunate enough to return, they would bring them back some spices for their rice. The Spaniards were thrilled, because spices were very expensive and very difficult to obtain in those days, and it's almost impossible to make a decent Spanish rice without them.

A few anxious months after leaving port in Spain, Columbus and his crew arrived on one of the islands in the Gulf of Mexico. Of course, back then it wasn't called the Gulf of Mexico—Columbus just figured that he was somewhere in east India. After anchoring the ship, Columbus and his crew rowed ashore in one of the longboats. They were greeted by some of the local folks, and Columbus said howdy to them in Indian. The locals were somewhat puzzled by this greeting, and one of the chiefs raised his hand and said, "How." Columbus then went into a long story about the queen, spices, oceans, stars, round versus flat, and so forth, and the locals were even more puzzled.

The legends of these island people stated that some day in the distant future a light-skinned man would come to them from the east and that upon his arrival everything would be hunky-dory. These island people would later learn that it's best not to listen to someone who just got off the boat and to study legends a bit more thoroughly, because these legends said nothing about this light-skinned man being accompanied by a bunch of guys who smelled like wet chickens with a slight hint of oregano.

Columbus informed these island people that they were East Indians, and they pretty much went along with whatever he said because they believed he was the actual light-skinned man spoken of in their legends. Columbus started asking them all sorts of questions about where their spices were located. The "Indians" replied that they really didn't need any spices, because their diet consisted of bananas, coconut, papaya, and seafood. Columbus replied that he couldn't return to the queen empty-handed or without a full load and asked them if they knew where any spices could be found. These newly named Indians replied that yeah, there were a bunch of spices, diamonds, emeralds, rubies, and lots of gold over in El Dorado.

Columbus was thrilled and asked the Indians to tell him more about El Dorado. Well, the Indians replied, El Dorado was over on the mainland. Each year during the Spice Festival, the folks in El Dorado would celebrate by covering the Spice King with gold dust, then they would put him on a boat and float him out into the middle of the lake and throw diamonds, emeralds, rubies, and other precious stones at him, and every so often some poor folks kids would toss bananas, broccoli, cauliflower, spinach and okra. Columbus really liked bananas and there was nothing like them in Italy, but he was very interested in finding El Dorado and all of the many riches that the Indians had described.

Early the next morning, Columbus and his crew set sail for the mainland in search of El Dorado. They were very excited and warmly greeted by the locals when they arrived on the mainland several days later. These Indians said that, yes, they did have spices and proceeded to show Columbus some chili powder, garlic, hot peppers, and oregano. Columbus was pleased because he reasoned that if the Indians were correct about the spices, they must know where he could locate El Dorado. Yes, they said, El Dorado was just over the mountains and only about ten moons and six sons away. Columbus thought hey, that ain't bad; we should be there in less than a few weeks.

The Italians couldn't find it, the Spanish couldn't find it, but y'all can find it just about forty-five miles southwest of San Angelo. See, the Indians were correct in their directions, because it would take a lot of romancing and about ten moonlit walks to be able to have six sons.

There are over 2,000 friendly folks in town and I do hope that you will enjoy your visit to Eldorado. Should you happen to take a moonlit walk out to the lake with someone you love, you may discover something more precious than gold.

Texan – English
Owl Passo—El Paso

The Spaniards named this area El Paso del Norte, which means "The Pass of the North." There are many types of allowable passes. There is the "long pass," the "short pass," the button hook," the "stop 'n' go," the "slant," and the "Hail Mary," just to name a few. These are all fun to watch when they are successful; however, it's just not allowable in Texas for a fellow to make a pass at another man's wife or sweetheart.

One of the Spanish officers in the group was unfamiliar with Apache protocol and customs. A Spanish second lieutenant, not realizing that he was flirting with Little White Dove, the wife of an Apache chief, inadvertently started yet another Indian war. Even today, in this age of enlightened political correctness, this behavior would probably not be accepted. We shouldn't spit into the wind, tug on Superman's cape, or mess with Texas married women.

Not only did this incident start a war with the Indians, it also resulted in the "Don't mess with Texas married women" signs that are seen on many of the Texas highways. This story is so well known throughout Texas that many of the signs just say, "Don't mess with Texas."

Little White Dove was banished from the tribe because of this pass, and she spent most of her remaining years walking up and down the road leading into El Paso. She never remarried because she loved her Apache chief and would not dishonor him by accepting any other man. Since she never had any children, she formally adopted this highway as her only child. Whenever you happen to see an "adopt a highway" sign during your travels throughout Texas, you may want to take a short pause in her memory. Legend tells us that whenever you happen to see two white doves flying together, it's Little White Dove and her Apache chief, reunited by the Great Spirit.

The road that Little White Dove traveled upon was originally called the Trail of Tears. She shed many tears upon the road, because of her broken heart over lost love for her Apache chief. Several archaeologists and historic researchers have attempted to find traces of her travels along this road but have had little success. With all of today's modern technology and the roads being paved over with asphalt by the lowest bidder, there are very few remaining remnants of her journeys. The locals still refer to this road as the Trail of Tears because of all the potholes and the high costs of balancing and realigning their tires.

For nearly two hundred years, El Paso was under Spanish rule, and they built many Spanish missions in the area. The Spanish monks had an abundant supply of wild Angora goats, cats, rabbits, armadillos and chickens. If you should happen to find any of these very rare and elusive Angora armadillos or chickens at any of the local pet shops be prepared to pay a pretty hefty price. Anyway, these monks were able to weave some of the mohair and angora into very beautiful yarns. From these yarns, the monks would weave all shapes and sizes of angora sweaters, coats, and jackets. They would also do the same things with the mohair. Unfortunately, it rarely got cold enough around El Paso for the local folks to wear any of these warm and beautiful items, so they shipped most of them back to Spain.

Every few months, the Spanish galleons would make the trip from the New World back to Spain. These ships would be loaded with treasures from the New World, including gold, silver, gemstones, jewelry, javelina jerky, angora, and mohair clothing. There were frequent and sudden storms in the gulf, and occasionally some of these ships would be lost at sea. Sometimes, one or two of these ships that were built by the lowest bidder would sink to the bottom of the ocean for no apparent reason. At times, these ships were attacked and looted by pirates. Even a pirate with a hook, an eye patch, and a wooden leg looked pretty good wearing lots of gold jewelry and a nice angora sweater.

Through the years, there have been several discoveries of these ancient treasures aboard these sunken Spanish ships. Searching for treasures of gold, silver, Spanish coins, and things is a very expensive project. Treasure hunters will spend several million dollars for the latest equipment to aid them in their searches. A few years ago, one of these sunken treasures was discovered completely by accident when a shark came swimming up from the bottom of the ocean wearing a really nice mohair jacket. I don't believe the part about the shark also munching on some javelina jerky, but sometimes truth is stranger than fiction.

El Paso is a very colorful town, literally. Influenced by the large amount of Spanish and Mexican cultures, most of the buildings in town are very brightly painted. These are festive and fun-loving folks and this is reflected in their arts, crafts, clothing, and the bright colorful buildings in town. Bright reds, greens, yellows, purples, and oranges dominate the area. Because of all the bright colors and festive music, walking down any of the streets or boulevards in town is a real treat; it will put a spring in your step and a song in your heart. I do hope that you will walk instead of drive, because most folks don't enjoy a spring in their seat.

The vast majority of the population in El Paso is Mexican, so you should brush up on your Spanish before your visit. More than 20 percent of the population are military personnel stationed at nearby Fort Bliss. Apparently, geography is not taught in schools as well as it once was, because many of the military personnel are greatly disappointed upon their arrival. Perhaps they thought that Fort Bliss would be in Hawaii or within the vicinity of the Garden of Eden. However, once they have gotten over their initial heat shock and learned a valuable geography lesson, they come to realize that El Paso is a great city. The local folks are very warm (no pun intended), friendly, hospitable, and gracious. They love it, I love it, and you'll love it.

Be sure to stop by one of the local Spanish missions and purchase some of their various selections of angora or mohair yarns and clothing. You might just want to thank a goat or a rabbit or a cat for your looking so much better than a pirate in your new clothing. It's quite simple: Just say "Thanks, goat," unless someone else made this purchase for you—then it's probably best to just thank that person.

Eyes of Texas

There is a song down in Texas that is called "The Eyes of Texas." The song goes something like "The eyes of Texas are upon you, all the livelong day." As an adult, I still don't understand what this song is about. Then again, perhaps I'm just old and haven't reached adulthood yet. When I was a young child and heard this song about "The eyes of Texas being upon me all the livelong day," it really scared the begeebers out of me. Geez, it's no fun being watched by a bunch of eyes all day long, especially when we're little kids. Perhaps really old people are comforted by the fact that they are being watched by a bunch of eyes all day long, but not me.

Childhood is pretty much a double-edged sword. On the one hand, they give us fun stuff like the Easter Bunny, Santa Claus, birthdays, trick or treat, the tooth fairy, firecrackers, and Valentine's Day candy. Then they scare us half to death with things like "switches" and the "boogey man." It kinda put a damper on staying out and playing after dark, because the boogey man would get us. Perhaps it was just my imagination, but I swear that I could hear the boogey man's footsteps at night as he was coming to get me.

It seemed to me, that these "eyes of Texas" were what was getting me in trouble all the time. Anytime I was having a really fun time, here came Grandma Denbo hollering "I'm gonna get a switch." She would be running towards me with her hand up in the air reaching towards the nearest tree for that dreaded switch. When I was a young lad, we all had to wear short pants that exposed our bare legs. I think it was just so they could use that switch. I couldn't wait to grow up and wear long pants. To this day, I still feel very uncomfortable wearing Bermuda shorts and stuff.

Sometimes, my children will ask me, "Hey Dad, how come you never wear shorts?" I just explain to them that as a young man, my legs were so pretty that it would drive the girls wild with desire, so I only wear short pants when I'm alone with their mom. Truth be told, my knees are so wrinkled at my age that I would probably be laughed off the planet if I wore short pants in public.

For Better or For Worse

Well, when my future bride and I met with the preacher to take our wedding vows, I suppose that I was so giddy about marrying my dream girl that I probably should have been listening more closely to what the preacher was really saying. I already knew the "for better" part because she was beautiful, talented, very smart, loved me dearly, and had exceptional taste. After all, she had chosen to marry me versus her many other suitors.

There must be a special "new wife" school that all new brides attend to help them train their husbands on how to toe the line. Johnny Cash's hit song "I Walk the Line" has been a big help to me understanding how I'm supposed to behave, because my training began shortly after my bride and I returned from our honeymoon. I thought that I was completely faultless and "pure as the driven snow" but apparently the love of my life felt entirely differently. Seems she sees me as a lump of coal and with just enough pressure exerted upon me, she will have a beautiful sparkling diamond to show off to her friends and family.

Miranda felt that I should be taught the fine art of shopping. When I need something, I go buy it at the store and immediately return home. Apparently, this is the completely incorrect way to shop. Seems that the correct way is to spend half the day looking for the particular item that you need in every store within a forty-mile radius of your home. Then you are supposed to take notes on this item at each and every store for future reference and return home with several alternate items that you purchased, because they were either "on sale," "cute," or "darling."

Another "for worse" part is when she insists that I accompany her into the lingerie department to look for something to tweak my interest in her. She will select some undergarment, hold it up to her, and ask, "Hey, honey, how do you like this?" Geez, apparently she thinks that I look much better when I'm beet red, stuttering, and stammering. She's built like a brick outhouse with the most beautiful, dancing, crinkly eyes, and would look quite sexy wearing a burlap bag. I would much prefer that she go shopping in the lingerie department by herself and surprise me when she got home. In the meantime, I could be doing something more enjoyable—like having a root canal or something.

    My honeybunch will never ask me to hold her purse for her when we are at home. She will always ask me to hold her purse for her when we are at Six Flags over Texas or somewhere very similar with thousands of folks walking past. I always feel extremely uncomfortable standing there with a ladies purse and I've tried several things to allay this particular feeling. Once a lady called the cops on me because she thought that I was a purse-snatcher when I acted like I was looking for something in the purse. Nowadays, whenever my wife asks me to hold her purse, I'll just stuff it up under my shirt and stand around nonchalantly and belch. I suppose that you would never want to be chalant while holding a purse, because someone might call the cops.

    Another "for worse" part is when she asks me, "Hi honey, do you notice anything different?" It took awhile, but I learned to never, ever, answer this question with an incorrect answer. There is no right answer; it's all part of our husband training process. The correct answer depends on the situation, and the circumstances seem to be either "Hey, the barn's on fire!" or "Hey, is that Tom Selleck?" I have to keep changing the name of the actor to whomever is currently popular to keep her somewhat off guard.

    There is also no correct answer to her question "Does this outfit make me look fat?" She knows that I am lying if I answer "Oh no, sugar, you look great!" and I am really in deep doo-doo whenever she thinks I'm fibbing to her. Over the years, I have learned to develop other answers to this question. If I can give her an answer that can give me at least a ten-minute head start, then she will have changed her outfit by then and will no longer pose this question to me. Two that have worked are: "Oh gee, I think I left the water running in the back yard!" as I dash out of the house, and "Oh gosh, I forgot to pay the electric bill!" as I grab my car keys and run out of the house à la Dagwood.

I can't get too cute with my answers, because one that didn't work was "My spidy senses are tingling—I think one of the children is in distress" as I dashed out the front door. Taking a nap on the couch is enjoyable; sleeping on it all night long isn't.

One statement that I always dread to hear from her is "We need to talk."

This always brings me way back to my early childhood, because I feel like I'm five years old again and I'm being severely scolded. The "we need to talk" sessions are pure torture and normally last at least an hour. I try to avoid them at all costs although I know they're part of my training. I try not to let my thoughts drift too much during one of these sessions because I usually have great difficulty answering the "What did I just say?" question.

Sometimes, for no apparent reason at all, she'll be fuming mad at me. Yep, there is something definitely different about her. I can tell, because I have this special sense that requires no superpowers whatsoever. I seem to be blessed with this great ability; I think it must be a guy thing. Whenever she is stomping around with a scowl on her face, I know that there is some type of storm brewing in paradise.

I'll ask, "Honey, are you upset with me?"

"Yes, I am," she'll reply.

"What have I done?"

"You know what you did!"

Actually, I never do know what I did wrong. I'm completely puzzled. "Gee, I really don't."

"Well, you just think about it," she'll respond.

It may not surprise some of you when I say that I spend an awful lot of time thinking. Well, time may heal all wounds, but

I've found that I'm a bit impatient so I'll go buy her a big bouquet of her favorite flowers. I read somewhere that "The power of flowers is only exceeded by the power of God."

Occasionally, I'll hear an affectionate, endearing question from my dream girl preceded by either "Honey?" "Darling?" "Sweetheart?" or something of a similar nature. Some guys might figure "Oh, no, I'm in the throes of another Honeydew." Nope, not me. I actually relish these requests from my bride because I consider these as pleas from a damsel in distress. The theme music from a popular Western movie explodes in my mind as I quickly leap into action wondering how I can possibly save her from some great distress. Visions of Dastardly Dan having tied my lover on the train tracks while some hissing, belching, fire-breathing train is rapidly approaching dance in my concerned mind. I jump on my trusty stallion and race to her rescue. Arriving just in the nick of time, with barely a moment to spare, I gaze into her desperate eyes and ask, "Yes, my love, how can I help?"

She'll usually reply with something like "Can you reach that platter on the top shelf?" or "Will you open this jar of pickles for me?"

My Stetson hat is slightly tilted on the back of my head revealing my golden locks and my Ritter shirt is partially open while I smile broadly and say, "Well, ma'am, I'm just happy to be of assistance."

Another mission accomplished, another foe defeated. Honeydews are actually quite fun. This is normally where the cowboy kisses the lady and sweeps her up on his mighty steed and rides off into the sunset. I'll kinda leave this part to your imagination.

My sweet darling cringes, though, whenever she has to ask me to get her something from the grocery store and she only asks me to do so in dire emergencies. "Sure, honey, I'll be glad to get you some sugar" (or whatever it is that she needs in these times of great distress). Our cats and dogs come running at the sound of a can opener. Our children come running whenever Dad has to go to the store. One reason is that they probably enjoy traveling short distances and the other reason is that Dad will let them get whatever toy each of them wants, plus any type of the newest cereals, cookies, candy bars, and stuff. Dad also buys all of the really great stuff to eat like: pizza, chili dogs, buffalo burgers, White Castles, genuine ice cream, fruit popsicles, Big Red soda pop, real root beer, black cherry soda, potato chips, corn chips, red chips, blue chips, and other assorted delights for the palate. You know, all the really neat stuff that Mom never seems to buy enough of while she is at the store. The children and I always make sure that we get Mom a bouquet of her favorite flowers while we are at the store.

My lover will anxiously await our return and will normally be found pacing around the front door. I know she really misses me and the children whenever we are not around. The first time she sent me to the grocery store all by myself and I returned to find her in this condition, my first thought was "Gee, I wonder how she can stand being away from me all day while I'm at work." To my great dismay, this unfortunately was not the case.

"Did you remember the sugar?"

"Yes!" I beam.

My sweetheart will give quick, furtive, distressful glances at our unhealthy junk food cargo as our precious children are rapidly unloading bag after bag of their newfound booty and will normally ask, "Why did you buy all this stuff?" and "Where am I going to put it all?"

"No problem, sugar, we'll probably eat most of it before dinner," I say as I hand her the flowers.

It is usually a great comfort to her when I ask "Honey, don't you remember our wedding vows? This is one of the 'or worse' parts." Then I'll give her a big hug, nuzzle her a bit, give her a gentle pat on the hip and a warm kiss and say, "I love you dearly and this is just another one of the 'for better' parts."

These "for better" parts of the wedding vows should always rapidly follow any of the "for worse" parts that occur in a marriage, because overnight stays in the doghouse or on the couch are very uncomfortable, although they do seem to be a necessary part of our training. I can fully understand why they call marriage an institution and not a sport. In baseball, we would go to "spring training" and learn the fundamentals in practice games, before the real games would begin. Unfortunately, marriage is not a recognized sport and I think that most married women would agree that most men belong in an institution.

"I keep a close watch on this heart of mine. . . . I keep my eyes wide open all the time."

But I sure seem to miss a lot.

Texan - English
Foe-urt Warth—Fort Worth
Travel about thirty miles directly west of Dallas to find the historical town of Fort Worth. There has always been a great rivalry—and much animosity—between these two sister cities. Dallas is pretty much the arrogant, high-falootin' rich sister, married to a successful doctor, and Fort Worth is referred to as the down-and-out poor sister who married a beer-swizzling, tee-shirt-clad couch potato.

The folks of Dallas call Fort Worth "cow town," and perhaps this supposedly derogatory statement stems from the fact that Fort Worth was the starting point for numerous cattle drives to Kansas City in the 1800s. There are no longer any cows roaming the streets of Fort Worth, so you needn't worry about avoiding them with your car or stepping in something as you walk along the streets of the city.

Once bustling with hundreds of cowboys and thousands of beef cattle, this proud city is now covered with hundreds of highways and thousands of shopping centers and malls. There is a handy little sign on one of the expressways that says "downtown" with a little directional arrow and everything pointing to downtown Fort Worth. You can still visit the old stockyards and train station where these cattle drives began. The city has preserved a few of the old red brick streets around the stockyards and train station.

After your tour of downtown, you can have a nice evening of entertainment at Billy Bob's country-western dance hall. Please be aware of the dress code: barefoot is acceptable only if you are wearing overalls, a straw hat, and chewing on a toothpick. All others are required to wear Levis, a Ritter shirt, boots, and a formal cowboy hat. You may either buy some Western outfits or rent one at the door—this is a pretty classy place. There's a sign on the front door that says "No Shirt, No Shoes, No Service." All of the really classy places in Texas have a sign like this posted on their front doors. I always kinda wondered why they didn't have a sign like this posted at the state capitol.

Texan - English
Frad-racks-barg—Fredericksburg
Originally of Hamburg, Germany, the brothers Rick and Frede Burg were traveling about four miles north of the Perdanales River when they discovered a strong flowing creek. Rick had dreams of one day becoming a cattle baron, and he wanted to name it Cattle Baron Creek. Frede suggested that they drop cattle from the name and just call it Baron Creek. Rick agreed and that's what it is called today. The brothers ventured a little farther into the forests and discovered yet another strong flowing creek.

    This was such a beautiful part of the country that they thought this would be a great place for a new town. They pondered over what to call this new creek and finally reached their conclusion after a game of rock, paper, scissors. They decided to name the town Fredericksburg, after themselves, and call the creek Town Creek. Frede sent a note back to New Braunfels via courier pigeon to some German immigrant friends of theirs. The note basically said, "Hey, if y'all think New Braunfels is great, then y'all ought to see this place." Well, the Germans in New Braunfels were overwhelmed with such a description of the new town because they thought that New Braunfels was one of the most beautiful places in the whole country.

    A group of about 120 of them decided to make the journey by uncovered wagon train up to this exquisite place. They traveled by uncovered wagons because this part of the country is very beautiful most anytime of the year, and they didn't want to miss any of the fabulous scenery by traveling in an old stuffy covered wagon. Most folks nowadays will retrace this historic journey in open convertibles; it's a bit faster—but please do observe all speed limits and road signs.

    The journey took several days, and the Germans complained of being constantly attacked by Indians. Actually, it was just curiosity on the Indians' part, or I suppose you might call it harassment. The Indians had never seen a dachshund before and were amazed that anyone could possibly use one of these dogs for any kind of help around the camp. The Indians called this animal Yipyaptowa, which translates to red-hot tamale with really short legs.

    The other thing that really piqued the Indians' curiosity was how the Germans made something called frankfurters and why were they all linked together. The Indians could understand why the Germans didn't use any hot dog buns, because they hadn't been invented yet. The Indians liked the idea of mustard on the frankfurters, but why did they call thick tomato sauce catsup, unless it somehow contained cat? The Indians also could not understand why anyone would want to add sauerkraut to a frankfurter. The Indians called this sauerkraut Ohyukpoo, which translates into Oh, yuk, poo.

    Each time the Indians would approach the German travelers, they would hear the same chant of "Vasislos, Vasislos" being called from the travelers. The Indians sorta liked the sound of this, so they started calling themselves the Vasislos Indians. Today, they have a place right on the main road into town and serve some of the best frankfurters around. If you happen to stop by, you'll find an ample supply of mustard, onions, and ketchup, but no catsup or dachshunds.

    When the German immigrants arrived in town, they were amazed by the great natural beauty of the area. However, once they unboarded their uncovered wagons, they began criticizing the brothers for using the term y'all. They were also quite shocked to learn that Rick did not have a German given name. They vowed that as long as the town existed, only German would be written or spoken. Fortunately for the brothers, the combination of their name was Frederick, which happened to be the name of a German prince. The people were happy that Frede had won the game of rock, paper, scissors and that they had not named the town Rickfredeburg.

For years and years, the folks of Fredericksburg spoke only German. During one town meeting, a fellow named Otto Maddick spoke up and suggested that since most tourists didn't speak fluent German, perhaps they should learn English. After much debate, they decided to vote on the measure. The majority ruled and forty folks were chosen to study and learn the English language.

Nowadays, most of the folks in Fredericksburg are quadralingual. They speak German, Mexican, Texan, and English. If you happen to rent a room at the famous Nimitz Hotel, don't be too surprised when your hosts start speaking Shakespearean English with a thick German accent. Sometimes, there are teeny little language glitches but I do hope you really enjoy your flat at the Nimitz Hotel. The staff at the hotel offers all sorts of entertainment for the enjoyment of their guests. They'll offer tours of the local sights, museums, theaters, hunting, fishing, and of course, foxhunting. *Othello* is normally performed during tourist season at the local theater. I do hope that you enjoy Shakespeare with a German accent.

Hey, tally ho the fox, y'all.

G

Dictionary

GALES—Nope, not strong winds preceding hurricanes. Hmm, then again?
    Gales means "girls," "females," or "ladies."
    As in: Them gales lock tew daince.
        "Those girls like to dance."

GARSH—Rhymes with marsh and just as mushy.
    Garsh means "gosh."
    As in: Garsh, aahmona mis yew.
        " Gosh, I'm going to miss you."

GAWD—Yes, you're getting the hang of it.
    Gawd means "God."
    As in: Iffin yore day-own, ast Gawd fer hep.
        "If you're down, ask God for help."

GAWDA—Not even close, are you?
    Gawda means "got to."
    As in: Aah gawda go.
        "I've got to go."

GEN-U-WINE—Yes, the real thing.
    Gen-u-wine means "genuine."
    As in: Aahma gen-u-wine K.O.bowie.
        "I'm a genuine cowboy."

GONE—It's neither here nor there.
    Gone means "go on."
    As in: Gone
        "Go on."
As a native Texan, this makes complete sense to me. You know, when someone is telling you a story and you want them to continue, you say "Gone."

GON-UH—Very similar to the above; variant of Aahmona.

Gon-uh means "I'm going to."
   As in: Alm gonuh go fashing.
      "I'm going to go fishing."
GREY-UTS—Most often ordered with breakfast.
   Grey-uts means "grits."
   As in: Bay-cone, aigs, ayun grey-uts.
      "Bacon, eggs, and grits"

Talkin' Texan

Texan—English

Gail-ves-tun—Galveston
Located just about fifty miles south of Houston, Galveston is a very popular destination for those who love the sand and sea. The short trip from Houston to this city on the Gulf Coast will take you less than an hour between the hours of 2 and 4 A.M. With over four million visitors per year, your daytime trip will take about four or five hours, one way. Nowadays, most folks avoid the hassle of the bumper-to-bumper traffic and make the journey on bicycles. Not only is riding a bicycle much more enjoyable, you also improve your cardiovascular system, lower your cholesterol, and have really shapely legs.

The causeway leading from the mainland to Galveston Island is jam-packed with fuming travelers and overheated cars, especially on weekends. These motorists don't feel any better when they glance over to see the smiling bicyclists whizzing down the road on the bicycle causeway. Tandem bicycles are very popular; dual bicycles with surrey-topped two-seaters are rapidly gaining in popularity.

For those of you wanting to avoid the causeway traffic, there are several catamaran rental locations on the southern shore of the bay. Traveling by catamaran to Galveston Island will help you avoid all the traffic on the causeway, plus you'll be able to build your upper body strength, lower your cholesterol, increase your metabolism, and possibly do some fishing. You'll also be able to get a great tan on your journey, with the proper planning, clothing, and suntan lotion.

Another way of avoiding the causeway traffic is to rent a paddleboat. Paddleboats are great fun, and you can peddle them just like a bicycle to operate the paddle. Nowadays, some folks are renting a paddleboat for a one-way trip to the island and renting a catamaran for a return trip, or vice versa. By traveling in this manner, they will be able to exercise both their upper and lower body during their travels, do some fishing, and get a great tan.

Galveston probably has some of the best-looking fishermen in the nation. Fish are well recognized as a "brain food," and these fishermen also have an opportunity to search for buried treasure during their travels. Galveston still lays claim to originally coining the slogan "healthy, wealthy, and wise."

Galveston Island was claimed by Spain in the early 1600s, and the Spaniards called the island Snake Island. The Indians who inhabited the island had a varied diet that consisted of fish, clams, shrimp, snake, maize, and squash. The Indians also made a delightful salsa that consisted of cactus, jellyfish, maize, jalapeno peppers, and tomatoes. You may be able to purchase some of this popular Indian salsa at any of the local grocery stores or gift shops during your stay on the island.

During the early 1800s, the island was headquarters for the notorious La Feet brothers, Pierre the older and Jean, also known as Stinky. The brothers were dirty, rotten, thieving pirates who terrorized the Texas coasts for over a decade. Jean was the most despised of the brothers, mainly because of his mean and nasty disposition. He earned his nickname as a young boy because his mom did not insist that he take baths, and he rarely took any baths when he grew older—although rumor has it that he always wore clean underwear, just in case he was ever in an accident.

Since there were no banks in Texas at this time, and the brothers didn't trust banks anyway, they would bury their loot in treasure chests around the area. Most of these treasure chests haven't been recovered, because the brothers would always kill off their crew after they had buried the treasure, to keep the whereabouts of the treasure a secret. There were always lots of ads in the classified section of the newspaper for "Pirate Crew Wanted" in the early 1800s. A crewman on a pirate ship could make a lot of money really fast but there wasn't much in the way of job security or retirement.

Texan – English
Jards-tay-own—Georgetown

Depending on the time of day, Georgetown is less than an hour's drive north from downtown Austin. The best time to make this trip is between the hours of 2 A.M. and 4 A.M. During the hot summer tourist months, this is the coolest time of the day with the least amount of traffic. If you really enjoy heavy bumper-to-bumper traffic, then you can make your journey during any of the other twenty-two hours of the day. Most travel agents will suggest that you make either a large east-west loop or a west-east loop from Austin and arrive in Georgetown from either Burnet or Sandow. This is actually the best way to travel, because you'll avoid the city-slicker drivers from Austin and enjoy the local folks at the same time.

I've traveled through thirty different states in America, and over two-thirds of them have a town by the name of Georgetown. I'd chat with these folks who lived in Georgetown and ask them questions. You can find out a lot of interesting stuff just by asking a few questions. One of my former teachers used to say, "Don't be afraid to ask a stupid question, just be wary of stupid answers." It turned out there was one common thread running through all these other Georgetowns: they had all been visited by a man named George Peaches.

Seems that wherever George traveled, he would have a wagonload of fabulous peach seeds and stop to plant them during his journeys. He was sort of the southern version of Johnny Appleseed. While Johnny was working the northern states planting apple seeds, George was traveling the southern parts of America planting and selling peach seeds. There was an unspoken rivalry between these two gentlemen to see who could have the most towns named after them. George was fortunate enough to have married a lady by the name of Georgia, and not only did George have over thirty towns named after him, but he had a state named after her, plus a town named Peaches.

Johnny didn't have nearly as many towns named after him; however, since apples needed a lot more fertilizer than peaches, a lot of folks affectionately called their outhouses "johns." Johnny was a sweetheart of a gentleman, so I won't get into what the ladies of the evening call their temporary clients. I think that George actually won the contest. There are several towns named Johnstown but very few named Johnnytown, Johnnyburg, or Johnnyville.

You may want to participate in the annual Peach Festival during your stay in Georgetown. The festival is held each year starting on the third Saturday after the harvest moon, unless the harvest falls on a month ending in the letter "y," and then the festival will be held starting on the second Saturday of the following month. The Peach Festival will last until the following weekend ending on a Sunday, after a Saturday beginning from the previous weekend. I don't know about you, but this confuses the heck out of me so . . . you might just want to check with the folks at the local Chamber of Commerce in Georgetown to find out when the festival begins. You may also want to ask them about when Easter and Thanksgiving are while you're finding out information about the festival.

The Peach Festival is lots of fun because not only are there bushels of peaches to try and buy, there are many peach products available to purchase. You'll be able to enjoy all your favorites such as peach pie, peach cobbler, peaches and cream, peach shortcake, peach jam, peach preserves, candied peaches, peaches on a stick, peach brandy, peach schnapps, peach vodka, and peach beer.

There is a huge rivalry between Texas and Georgia about who has the best peaches. Both states were given the same peach pits by George Peaches, and Texas uses pure artesian water for irrigating their peach groves, while Georgia doesn't. Georgia is actually winning the battle because they have a peach pictured on their state license plate while Texas just has a logo of the Lone Star State on theirs.

This is all about to change shortly, because the Texas State License Bureau just received approval from the state legislature to begin making all Texas rear license plates two feet tall and three feet wide. These new license plates will not only help us win the Peach War, but will also greatly increase state tourism. All the letters and numbers on these new license plates will promote all of the various things for which the state is famous.

As an example, if a Texan were to have a license plate with ALP 6390, the letters and numbers would be as following:

- A would have pictures of rodeos, cowboys, Indians, and longhorn cattle.
- L would have pictures of bicycling, hiking, hunting, and bass fishing.
- P would have pictures of islands, sun, sand, and surf.
- 6 would have pictures of citrus, peaches, pecans, and peanuts.
- 3 would have pictures of Big Bend, lakes, streams, and mountains.
- 9 would have pictures of beer, bratwurst, and chili
- 0 would have pictures of the Alamo, Spanish missions, and cityscapes.

These new two-by-three-foot license plates will bring a lot more tourists into the state because there are so many Texans who travel to other states during their vacations, and these new license plates will be promoting Texas. The Texas State Tourism Board is figuring that these new license plates will also show many native

Texans all the wonders of the state, and more folks will take their vacations within the state instead of traveling across state borders to foreign areas. The Texas Highway Patrol also loves these new license plates because while they may miss seeing all the letters and numbers on the front plate, they won't be able to miss seeing the rear license plates. Many of the donut shops in the state are already asking if they will be able to purchase advertising on any of these new license plates.

Grandma

At the end of each school year, I would travel from San Antonio to Hondo to spend my summer vacation with Grandpa and Grandma, and since I was their first grandchild, they always made me feel very special. Grandpa would pick me up at the Greyhound bus station in his old Chevy pickup truck and we would then travel through town and about a mile later arrive at the house. I loved the house; it had a huge front yard and some big trees to climb in, rain barrels with tadpoles, a big garden, storage shed, smokehouse, pigeon house, doodlebugs, June bugs, and a big two-story washhouse with steep wooden stairs to the bedroom where I slept all by myself when I was about ten years old. I used to love to listen to the rain falling on that old tin roof.

    Grandpa and I would pull up to the house around the back driveway. I can only remember using the front door to the house a few times. The screen door would creak as we entered the back door to the house, and I would be overwhelmed with the aroma of cookies baking in the oven. It always seemed to me that Grandma would have the oven door open, removing a big tray of cookies, each summer as I entered the kitchen that first time. I would look over on the kitchen counter and there would be two big two-gallon cookie jars. One would be full of cookies, and the other would be about half full, just awaiting the latest batch of cookies from the oven.

    Grandma would give me a big hug and offer me some cookies and milk. Then she would open a door from the kitchen to the living room, and behind this door was the measuring wall. All my aunts and uncles and me had our names and the date with our height measured in pen or pencil on the wall. It was always a treat to see how big I had grown since the previous summer.

    Most of the time, I got to go with Grandpa during the day, but every so often I'd spend all day with Grandma. Grandpa did a lot more fun stuff than Grandma. Grandma and I would wash all the dishes after Grandpa left for the morning. Then sometimes she would want me to help while she cleaned the house, but most of the time she didn't want me to help, and I would get to go outside and explore. Later, Grandma would start cooking lunch for Grandpa, and sometimes she would ask for my help and at other times she wouldn't.

Sometimes, Grandma would cook lots of good stuff, like fried steak, corn on the cob, and smashed potatoes with gravy. Her fried steak was the best and I especially loved corn on the cob. It was so much fun to eat because sometimes I would eat the corn in rows and at other times, I would spell my name by nibbling the corn in just the right spots. A pile of corn on my plate or creamed corn wasn't nearly as much fun to eat.

I especially enjoyed smashed potatoes with gravy, because Grandma would always make the most delicious gravy. I would watch intently as she prepared the fried steak and then she would add flour to the steak drippings to make gravy. After she made a big pan of gravy, she would pour the gravy from the pan into a gravy boat then place the gravy boat on the table.

Normally, Grandpa would always arrive home about five minutes before the gravy was being prepared. He would exchange greetings with Grandma and me, give Grandma a peck on the cheek, a soft hug, and a light touch on her hip. He would always ask how we had been doing and if I had been helping Grandma. I'd always say yes, and Grandma would agree with me, because I had the most wonderful Grandma around and I would do anything that she asked.

Grandpa would take his place at the table and Grandma and I would bring the food to the table once lunch was all prepared. Once we were all seated, either Grandpa or Grandma would say grace and then lunch would begin. Grandma would always take the base of the big spoon and make a hollow in the potatoes for a gravy lake. Gravy lakes were lots of fun because I could make all sorts of rivers, waterfalls, and stuff from the potatoes and gravy. Grandma and Grandpa didn't have nearly as much fun as I did with their gravy lakes. Occasionally, Grandma would pause from her lunch and ask if I was going to eat my potatoes.

We would always have bread and butter with every meal. Sometimes Grandma would have hot baked bread, and sometimes she would make biscuits. Whenever she baked bread, she would always cut me a slice of hot bread and put butter on it. She knew how good hot buttered bread tasted, and she would always give me the first slice. Grandma would do the same thing when she made biscuits. She'd take the hot biscuits out of the oven and she would put butter and sugar on them, but sometimes she would use butter and honey. She always made me feel very special and I miss her.

Grandma also fixed food for Grandpa and me that was not fun to eat and tasted awful. She would fix things like liver and onions, beets, turnips, broccoli, brussels sprouts, cauliflower, okra, and spinach. She told me that these things were good for me. I still don't understand why things that are good for us have to taste so bad. I always felt that perhaps I was being punished for doing something bad, but she assured me this wasn't the case. She would say, "Look at Grandpa, he likes it." I would study Grandpa as he ate the broccoli, turnips, and stuff. He wouldn't be making any faces, but I could tell that he really didn't like these things either.

No amount of sugar would make broccoli, brussels sprouts, cauliflower, okra, or spinach taste any better. The only reason I would even attempt to eat spinach was because of the Popeye cartoons. To this day, I still believe that the Popeye cartoons are some sorta diabolical plot by spinach farmers to get little kids to eat spinach. I've talked to farmers from over thirty different states, and whenever I ask them what they grow, I always get replies such as corn, wheat, oats, sorghum, milo, sunflower seeds, peanuts, cantaloupe, watermelons, and so on. No one has ever admitted to being a spinach farmer. Some folks say that they are truck farmers, but I think they're just saying this to throw us off the track, because most folks do like trucks.

It never was fun watching Grandma cook turnips, cauliflower, or spinach for lunch or supper. Probably the most nauseating was watching her cook okra, because okra had all those slimy spiderweb-looking things hanging off them. Someone really had to be superhungry to cook up and eat that very first batch of okra. It looks all slimy when it's rolling around on the plate and tastes awful. I guess they thought it would be good for them. Grandma would try to disguise okra by cutting it up, adding corn meal, and frying it. Nice try, Grandma, but it still tasted like okra. I'd peel of the corn meal, and eat that, but the remains of the okra would normally end up in a big pile at the edge of my plate.

Grandma would also make us eggs, grits, bacon, sausage, and biscuits with butter, jam, or jelly for breakfast. I loved the aroma of the breakfast being cooked and especially enjoyed watching the bacon curling up as it cooked. Sometimes Grandma would make us hotcakes for breakfast and I would get to help her mix up the batter. Grandma would always make me special "silver dollar" pancakes for breakfast with plenty of butter and sugar on them. And since I didn't want to eat tomatoes with lunch or supper, she would put sugar on these also.

She always made me feel so very special; I wish each of us could have a grandma like mine.

Grandma's Christmas Tree

For a young boy, Grandma's Christmas tree was a thing of beauty and it gave me much joy. She would have Grandpa and me cut a nicely shaped cedar tree from the pasture at the ranch, and we would gently put it in the back of the pickup, drive back to town, and bring it to the house. Grandma had already strung popcorn to trim the tree. Plus she had Christmas lights, all kinds of glittering ornaments, tinsel, and lots and lots of candy.

What was so neat was she would let me eat candy from the tree—a sweet, edible Christmas tree. The cedar Christmas tree always smelled so good and I could eat all the candy that I wanted off of it. She would put the Christmas tree in the front room where I used to sleep before I was old enough to sleep in the big room upstairs above the washhouse. It was always such a thrill to be able to sleep in the same room as the Christmas tree with all those glittering lights and ornaments—and especially all that candy!

Being a carpenter, Grandpa had welded a quarter to a nail and had nailed the quarter to the wooden floor of the living room. When an unsuspecting guest would be entertained in the living room, Grandpa would see what reaction the guest would have when he noticed the quarter. Some folks would point to it and say, "Joe, you have a quarter on the floor." Grandpa would say, "Thank you, I'll get it later."

It was the others that Grandpa had the most fun with: those who—when they thought Grandpa was not looking—would reach over and try to pick up the quarter. Grandpa would be delighted and would let out a great bellowing laugh.

My Grandma was a very special lady to allow Grandpa to nail a quarter to the living room floor.

Grandpa

It was always fun being with Grandpa during summer vacation. He was over six feet tall and had sky-blue eyes with a wide smile and a great bellowing laugh. He was a great carpenter and claimed that he had built over 50 percent of the homes in Hondo. He always wore his gray shirt, gray baggy pants, and an old beat-up, sweat-stained cowboy hat—except on Sundays, when he would wear his suit and tie and take his Stetson hat down from the closet and go to church with Grandma and me. Grandma taught Sunday school, and I always remember the little envelope filled with fifteen cents that she would give me for the offering plate.

Whenever Grandpa went to the lumberyard, I would get to play in the sawdust pile. The sawdust was four to five times taller than I was and great fun until I got some sawdust in my eye. Grandpa would always patiently remove it.

I always had my BB gun with me each summer and would look forward to going with Grandpa when he would go to work at Chapman Grain. There would be hundreds of birds there, and Grandpa told me I couldn't shoot any songbirds but I could shoot the sparrows. I would get on top of the roof of the granary across from a big oak tree and practice my marksmanship. After each shot, as the sparrow would fall to the ground, I would climb down from the roof and line up each sparrow. At the end of one day, I had 123 sparrows lined up when Grandpa came to take me back to the house. He had taught me how to shoot and was happy that I had done so well.

On the way home each day, Grandpa would drive up to the liquor store and I would wait in the pickup. In a few minutes, Grandpa would return with a pint bottle in a paper bag. He would immediately put it under the seat of the pickup. I can't remember but just a few times where Grandpa would take a swig or two from his pint bottle. It was always great fun being with him.

Talkin' Texan

We would go to Chapman Grain, the lumberyard, the hardware store, and the gun shop, and sometimes drop in to see Grandma at Fly Drug Store. The drug store was always great fun, because they had an old-fashioned soda fountain and I would get to spin around on the stools while I had a root beer float or a malted milk shake.

One time, during an election, Grandpa took me down to the courthouse while he voted and we stayed around as the election results came in. It would take Grandpa just a few seconds to vote, because he always voted straight Democrat. As the election results were being called, Grandpa would fuss just a bit anytime a Republican would be ahead in the count or win a particular election. Back then, we pretty much voted for those with the best qualifications. Voting now is much more difficult, because it seems to me that whenever I close the curtain behind me, I'm faced with a list of candidates that includes Attila the Hun, Ted Bundy, Jeffrey Dahlmer, Adolf Hitler, Jack the Ripper, and others of their ilk. They say that if we don't vote we may lose this right and many of our freedoms. I'd kinda like to have freedom from political commercials. Perhaps this is one of the reasons cable and satellite TV are so popular! Seems that we get what we pay for, both in television and politicians.

Grandpa helped me understand a lot of things while I was growing up—I just wish that he had taught me more about politics and voting. Then again, perhaps he did, because he once told me, "Sunny, when a politician's been born sneaky, he pretty much stays that way for the rest of his life." Whenever someone has a child who's born with a conniving mind, that kid'll probably end up as an Enron-type corporate CEO or as one of our elected officials. Seems that each Thanksgiving, our politicians have turkey instead of ham. It's called the "ballot box" tradition: it's easier to stuff a turkey than a ham.

I'm happy that I don't have to explain some of the more modern technology to Grandpa—like, "Hey, Grandpa, I lost my cell phone." He'd probably figure that I had ended up in jail like a few of our politicians and some of our unfortunate relatives.

Grandpa and the Coffee
Grandpa always had several steaming hot cups of coffee during breakfast and Grandma would always pour the coffee into his cup for him. She would notice that he needed a refill on coffee and would ask him, "Joe, would you like some more coffee?" Grandpa would always say, "Yes, please" and Grandma would bring the coffee pot over from the stove to the kitchen table and would pour the coffee into Grandpa's cup.

When the coffee was nearing the rim of the cup, Grandpa would say "Whoa." Grandma would respond, "Joe Brucks, I'm NOT a horse!" Grandpa would just smile, chuckle, and then take the coffee from the cup and pour it into the saucer. He would then proceed to drink his coffee from the saucer. As a young boy, I saw him drink coffee this way for many years and I always thought that this was the purpose for the saucer under the coffee cup. Each time that Grandpa would say "Whoa," Grandma would stop pouring the coffee.

One morning, Grandpa was having his breakfast and his coffee cup was getting low. Grandma asked him if he would like some more and he said, "Yes, please." Grandma started pouring the coffee and when it was close to the rim of the cup, Grandpa said "Whoa." Grandma just kept right on pouring and the coffee started to go over the rim of the cup. "Whoa," Grandpa said. "Whoa!" The coffee was running out of the coffee cup and into the saucer, then over the saucer and going onto the red-and-white checkered tablecloth. I lifted up my plate from the table and scooted out of the way. "Whoa," Grandpa said. "Whoa!" The hot coffee was running across the tablecloth and dropping onto the floor. Grandpa was flabbergasted and in a panic. Grandma kept pouring. "Whoa, whoa!" he said, which had always worked in the past. "Joe Brucks, I'm NOT a horse," Grandma said. Grandpa said, "That's enough, please," and Grandma finally stopped pouring the coffee. Grandpa never again said "Whoa" to Grandma.

Joe Kent Roberts

Grandpa and the Pellet Gun

There was a time when the ol' BB gun just plum wore out. As Grandpa and I were leaving the house one day and I took aim at a sparrow in the hackberry tree, I pulled the trigger and a bird ten feet below fell out of the tree. I received a brand new Benjamin pump pellet gun that same Christmas.

Grandpa had spent a bunch of money that year to drill a deep well and had hit an underground river about five thousand feet below the ranch. The water was cool and sweet. The previous summer, I had helped Grandpa dig postholes and we had put up a new barbed wire fence. I had much fun with the pellet gun that summer; with just a few pumps, it was much more accurate than my old BB gun.

Grandpa had seven other siblings, and this one fellow who had married one of his sisters was not one of Grandpa's favorites. Because Grandpa had this deep well, this uncle was using Grandpa's ranch to water his cattle.

There were over fifty of this uncle's cattle on the ranch that day, and after lunch Grandpa asked me if he could shoot my pellet gun. Grandpa put about three or four pumps on the pellet gun and took aim at the back of one cow's rump. He squeezed the trigger and POW! The cow jumped about three feet off the ground. Grandpa let out that big bellowing laugh of his, and for the next hour we took turns shooting cows until we had hit each cow at least twice. Grandpa was laughing so hard he had tears in his eyes. I was about twelve years old at this time and had no idea that this was harmful to the cattle.

A few days later, we were sitting on the fence rail at Great-Grandpa's ranch and there were a bunch of cattle there. Remembering how much fun Grandpa had shooting cattle a few days before, I asked him, "Hey, Grandpa, wanna shoot some cows?"

He said "Shhhhhh!"

Grandpa and the Ranch

Grandpa's ranch (which was separate from his house) was about fourteen miles from town, between Hondo and Bandera. We would get in the ol' Chevy pickup and start heading out of town towards the ranch. As soon as Grandpa got to the outskirts of town and out of eyeshot, he would reach under the seat of the pickup and retrieve his pint bottle of whiskey. Before he would take a drink, he would reach in his pocket and get his Bull Durham and a cigarette paper. To this day, I still don't know how he could roll a cigarette with one hand and then lick the paper shut and light the cigarette with book matches. All the while, Grandpa would be steering the ol' stick shift pickup straight as an arrow down the highway.

Once the cigarette was lit, he would pop the cork from the whiskey bottle and take a swig. He would let out an awful sound "aarugh" and recork the bottle. A few minutes later, he would again uncork the bottle, take a swig, and let out the same awful sound of "aarugh." I was about seven or eight years old and thought this must be so much fun, and I couldn't wait to try this myself.

"Grandpa, can I have a drink?" I asked. Grandpa looked at me and grinned and let out one of those great bellowing laughs of his.

"You want a drink?" he asked.

"Yes," I said, and Grandpa passed me the bottle. I took out the cork and took a swallow from the bottle. It tasted awful and burned like a fire in my mouth.

"Aarugh," I said.

I then knew why Grandpa made that terrible "aarugh" sound when he took a swig from that pint bottle of Four Roses. I also realized why the Indians in the Western movies called whiskey "firewater."

I'm just happy that I didn't ask for a cigarette. A few months ago, I walked into a local liquor store and asked if they had a whiskey called Four Roses. The fellow said he had never heard of it, and I think I may know why. I'm happy that Grandpa let me have that swig of whiskey. To this day, I'll have a beer or two but I don't care too much for firewater.

Joe Kent Roberts

Grandpa and the Snakes

Ever since I was a young boy, all my aunts, uncles, and relatives said to never mention "snakes" around Grandpa. Yet when I would ask them why, they would never give me an answer—they would just say, "Don't mention snakes." Naturally, I was curious after this response, and decided that someday I would ask him.

The summer I was fourteen, Grandpa and I were putting up a new fence on the ranch, and it was truly a thing of beauty. I would dig the posthole and Grandpa would set the post and the barbed wire. The new fence was just as straight and on line as it could be. Grandpa did great work.

Grandma would prepare our lunch every day that we would take to the ranch. My favorite was her fried seven steak. I bought some seven steak at the store a few months ago and fried it up, not quite as good as Grandma's, but it sure brought back some great memories. On this particular day, Grandma had prepared spaghetti and meatballs for our lunch. This was very unusual because Grandpa was pretty much a steak-and-potatoes man.

We would take our lunch out of the hot Texas sun and into the shed that Grandpa had built at the edge of the corral. The shed was about eight feet square, and Grandpa had built a little drop-down table that came out from the wall of the shed. Grandpa was on the other side of the table against the wall, and I was at the table next to the open doorway (fortunately, or I would not be relating this story today).

I was not aware that Grandma had prepared spaghetti, and when Grandpa uncovered the casserole dish, I was not expecting this big bowl of spaghetti. I looked at the spaghetti and thought "Well, it's pretty well now or never."

"Gee, Grandpa, this looks just like a big bunch of snakes," I said. Holy moly, did the fur fly! Grandpa let out with a shout as I was running out the door. He had slammed up the table to get at me and was chasing me out through the corral, down the fence, and through the brush and the trees. I really didn't know he could run that fast. He must have chased me for ten minutes or longer through the ranch.

After a bit, we both sat down on a fence post and Grandpa explained to me that as a teenager on the ranch he had fallen into a rattlesnake pit and that ever since he had been deathly afraid of snakes. I don't like rattlesnakes either and was happy to find that the snake pit was no longer there. I still don't know why my aunts and uncles never explained this to me. It sure would have saved Grandpa and me a lot of running.

Growing Up in Texas

Growing up in Texas was very confusing to me as a small child and even later as a young adult. My parents and all their friends had Texas accents, which are difficult to understand, plus my grandparents spoke German when they didn't want me to know what was going on. Whenever I had a question about anything, they would just tell me to go outside and play. I still don't know the answers to most of my childhood questions because I played outside an awful lot.

My childhood probably had quite a profound effect on my life as an adult. Whenever I'm at work and have a question, I just automatically go outside and play. When I was a young lad in Texas, everything was written in Texan and everyone spoke Texan—well, except for my grandparents, who spoke German around me an awful lot.

Everything was just peachy-dandy in Texas until the Texas legislature passed the English-only amendment. Then they had the entire state change all the signs everywhere from Texan to American English. They even changed all of our high school textbooks from Texan to American English. I don't know about the other kids, but I was totally confused. Perhaps, if I had attended high school in another city besides New Braunfels, the transition would have been a bit easier. At that time, nearly 90 percent of the town was German, so most of the kids and their parents spoke German.

My bride keeps telling me that I should act my age. My response to that is, I missed the vast majority of my childhood years and should be allowed a little bit more time to grow up. Perhaps I am becoming a bit more mature, because I no longer want to be a cowboy when I grow up. Now, when I go outside to play, I get to play with my children. I also get to playfully answer all of their questions and propose some of my own. I especially enjoy the evenings alone with my bride, after the kids are all safely tucked into bed. While growing up in Texas, all of my school report cards said that I played well with others, and my bride seems to think so. She'll even answer my questions, and I no longer have to go outside to play.

H

Dictionary

HA—No relation at all to ho.
    Ha means "hi."
    As in: Ha.
        "Hi."
        HA HA Yew - Nope, it's not HA HA University
        Ha Ha Yew means "Hi, how are you?"
        As in: "Ha Ha Yew"
        "Hi, how are you?"

HAFT—This haft is mine, you get the other haft.
    Haft means "have."
    As in: Aah half tuh fe-ux duh flay-yut tar.
    "I have to fix the flat tire."

HANE-SUM—If the women are purdy, then the men are . . .?
    Hane-sum means "handsome."
    As in: Ma, ain't hay hane-sum?
    "My, isn't he handsome?"

HAV-A-LEENA—No, Leena's not a type of beer in Texas.
    Hav-a-leena means "javelina."
    As in: Yew gonna hun sum hav-a-leena?
    "Are you going hunting for some javelina?"

HAY—Starts many questions and sentences.
    Hay means "hey."
    As in: Hay, ware yew ben?
    "Hey, where have you been?"

Hay is also a greeting. Sometimes Texans use "hay" as a telephone greeting instead of hello or "lo."

HAYS—They wuz, we wuz, she wuz, and now . . .
    Hays means "he is."
    As in: Hays muh bay-est fray-und.

"He's my best friend."
HAY-YER—A comb and a brush are helpful here.
    Hay-yer means "hair."
        As in: Naught nay-yo, alm warshing muh hay-yer.
            "Not now, I'm washing my hair."
HEP—Not to be confused with hip or with it.
    Hep means "help."
        As in: Aah cud nade uh lil hep.
            "I could use a little help."
HE-YAH—If it's not there, it must be . . .
    He-yah means "here."
        As in: Owl bay he-yah.
            "I'll be here."
HI-DEE—Just a nice friendly greeting.
    Hi-dee means a friendly and warm "Hi."
        As in: Hi-dee.
            "Hi."
HOWDY—A formal friendly greeting.
    Howdy means "Hi, how have you been doing?"
        As in: Howdy.
            "Hello."
HOWL—Wolves are not the only ones to howl at the moon.
    Howl means "how will."
        As in: Howl aah larn tew daince?
            "How will I learn to dance?"

Texan—English

Hail-e-yuts-vail—Hallettsville

Hallettsville is just a little south of Schulenburg, and I really enjoy stopping here on the way to Shiner or Victoria. The town has a population of around three thousand folks and is situated on the banks of the Lavaca River. The town is named after John Hallett, who was one of the area's first settlers. His wife, Margaret, was gracious enough to donate the land upon which Hallettsville was built.

The courthouse was built in 1897 and is listed in the National Register of Historic Places. This may sound a bit on the dull side to you, but folks will come from hundreds of miles away to film and photograph this courthouse each Christmas Season. The old five- or six-story courthouse is situated in the middle of the town square. The courthouse has the most awesome lighted decorations I've ever seen, and it must take them several months to prepare this display each year.

Through the years, I've taken dozens of photos of this courthouse and have not yet been able to do it the proper justice. Then again, I'm the same fellow who takes photos of my aunts, uncles, and other assorted relations, and am asked, "Where's the rest of them?" Well, some of my aunts are rather large women, and some of my uncles are rather tall gentlemen, so it's not easy getting all of each of them into a single photo. I think anytime a professional photographer takes a photo of a large lady and a tall gentleman and there are no parts of any of them missing, there should be a disclaimer on the photo—something like "This photo was taken by a professional. Please do not attempt to duplicate this on your own." Now, whenever we visit relatives who are not comparable in size, I leave my camera in the car trunk.

The town's water works are supplied by artesian wells. This is probably some of the best water that you would ever want to drink; it is clear, pure, and cold. This is probably one of the few places in Texas where you can have pure artesian water running from your water tap. The local folks are very fortunate to be able to bathe, shower, and wash their clothes in pure artesian water. The ladies traveling through Hallettsville from out of town probably wonder why the local ladies have such nice-looking hair. It's the water.

    Most folks can only buy artesian water in the stores. Anytime you ever want to have a water well dug on your property, ask an Artesian to do it. The Artesians are originally from Artesia, Germany, and are famous for their water wells. Be sure to look for their bottled water in the stores, and read the fine print on the bottle to be assured that this is indeed pure Artesian water.

Holidays in Texas

I guess I'll just list the Texas holidays in their order of occurrence rather than alphabetically, otherwise my favorite holiday would be listed first rather than last.

Valentine's Day

Valentine's Day is named after Saint Valentine, who must be the patron saint of love and romance. Most of the saints just made cheese and wine; apparently, this saint also made lots of candy. I always enjoyed his colorful little hearts with the stamped notes on the top of them. I think he was the one who said, "A loaf of bread, a little wine, and thou." I guess the candy, flowers, and greeting cards came much later.

It always seemed odd to me that we would give our sweethearts heart-shaped boxes filled with rich chocolates—especially when we know that later that year they're gonna ask us, "Honey, does this dress make me look fat?" It's probably best that we don't answer this question. Usually, I'll just pretend that I'm having a heart attack (hey, it is heart season) or I'll make a startling statement like "Hey, honey, I think the barn's on fire!"

Easter

Easter was always great fun at my great-grandfather's home outside of Hondo because he had so many children, grandchildren, and great-grandchildren. Great-Grandpa had a huge front yard that went way out into the woods, and all my aunts and uncles would hide hundreds of Easter eggs for all the children to find. Seemed to me that there must have been at least forty of us with baskets in hand all scrambling after these Easter eggs. The child who collected the most Easter eggs received a special prize from Great-Grandpa and Great-Grandma. The year I won, Great-Grandpa gave me a huge block of chocolate. I was hoping for a pet billy goat. The chocolate must have weighed several pounds, and I ate most of it that day. I was sick for several days. The billy goat would have lasted much longer and been a lot more fun.

The Fourth of July
    The Fourth of July was always great fun. As a kid, it seemed like we were celebrating the creation of fireworks. Grandpa would always buy me lots of the little tiny firecrackers that were fairly harmless. I would find a big anthill in the yard and place the firecrackers at the entrance, light them, and watch the ants be blown several feet into the air. These were the same fire ants that had stung me all summer, so it just seemed fair to return the favor.

    My uncles, who were older and apparently vastly more mature, would buy the bigger, better, more powerful fireworks, like TNT and cherry bombs. They would take one of Grandpa's milk pails, prop it up with a stick attached to a long string, and place one of the cherry bombs under it. Then one of them would light the cherry bomb and run off, while the other one pulled out the stick from under the milk pail. Ka-Blooey!!! The milk pail would go flying nearly a hundred feet into the night sky. My aunts and uncles would all be whooping and a hollering. Simple pleasures for simple people. They haven't changed much over the years, and neither have I. After about half a dozen cherry bombs, the bottom of the milk pail would be blown wide open. Then they would try a few more milk pails. Once the supply of milk pails was exhausted, they would try one of Grandma's washtubs. The washtub wouldn't fly nearly as high into the air, so there was not nearly as much whooping and hollering, but there were lots of oohs and aahs at what the cherry bombs could do to a washtub.

    For my aunts and uncles and myself, the Fourth of July was always lots of fun. Unfortunately, Grandpa was always unable to milk the cows the next day, and Grandma was unable to do the wash.

Halloween

    Halloween was a very special time while growing up in Texas. Shopping for and finding the right mask was almost as much fun as the night itself. When I was a kid, Halloween was "our" day, a special day just for kids. About all we needed were a mask and a pillowcase for all our loot. It was not unusual, after knocking on the door and yelling "trick or treat," to be invited inside for fresh-baked cookies or candied apples. None of the adults would scare us; they would just give us cookies, candy, and treats. Nowadays, in the unfriendly state where I now live, some adults seem to get some sort of a perverse pleasure in scaring the begeebers out of young children. I myself get a kick out of answering the door and seeing them in their costumes and giving them lots of candy. I enjoy them watching a big handful of candy loudly plop into the bottom of their bag and saying "Wow, thanks, Mister!"

I still lament the fact that I grew too tall too fast and had to stop trick-or-treating when I was about thirteen. My dad had a sweet tooth, and I guess the neighbors thought I was my dad whenever I knocked on their doors. The lucky kids were the ones who went on to become horse racing jockeys. They got to go trick-or-treating well into their sixties. Then again, because of their height, I suppose today's professional basketball players have to stop trick-or-treating when they are about six or seven years old.

Thanksgiving

Every Thanksgiving we would all gather at Great-Grandpa and Great-Grandma's house in the country. They had eight children, so I had lots and lots of aunts who would bring cakes, cookies, and pies to this feast. All of my uncles were farmers and ranchers so we always had all types of beef, pork, chicken, venison, and so on for this Thanksgiving feast. There would be two big tables about eight feet long just filled with food. One table would have meat, vegetables, and all sorts of salads that I was forced to eat some of. The other table was my favorite; this table was loaded with every delicious cake, pie, and cookie that a young child could ever dream about. All the aunts would ask me if I had tasted their cake, cookies, or pie. I did not wish to say no and see a look of disappointment in their eyes, so I would have a delightful taste of each and every item on this table. Sometimes it would take three or four platefuls, yet I would remain undeterred to bring a smile to each and every one of my aunts. As a young lad, getting sick every Thanksgiving became a yearly ritual that I greatly looked forward to. I think that's the reason I grew so tall so fast and missed several years of trick-or-treating.

Christmas

Talkin' Texan

For all the movies I've seen over the years, I can't ever remember seeing a Christmas movie about Christmas in Texas. All the Christmas movies show people all bundled up and laughing and playing while soft swirling snow lands gently on their shoulders. In the classic movie *White Christmas,* they're even singing about having a white Christmas while it's snowing. They rarely show people trying to shovel two feet of snow off their sidewalk, or cars slipping and sliding on the treacherous black ice on the city streets.

There is a nice hotel out in the middle of nowhere, way up in Wyoming. My youngest son and I were taking a father-son vacation and were caught in blizzard conditions while we were traveling. The story goes that the founder of this particular hotel was riding on horseback under similar conditions and decided to open this hotel after surviving his ordeal so that future travelers caught in the same circumstances wouldn't have to be unsheltered, cold, and hungry.

After checking into the hotel, we immediately went to the restaurant and each had chicken-fried steak with all the fixings. Later, we went and found our room for the night. The room was quite magnificent and larger than some folks' houses. The beautifully draped sliding glass doors would open to reveal a completely frozen swimming pool. We would have preferred being in such elegant circumstances in the summer and to not have experienced such a bitterly cold white Christmas that year.

Having a white Christmas in Texas is much warmer, because we have all the modern conveniences of "spray snow." Spray snow is on every available window in every home and business in town. It's very easy to spot the Grinch in town, because he's the one with no spray snow on the windows. For kids, Christmas in Texas is the best. We wake up on Christmas morning, run into the living room, and there under a white-flocked Christmas tree are our gifts. After we open them, we can go outside in the warm sun and play to our hearts' content. We don't have to bundle up or anything, and we won't be sliding our new bicycle into an icy cold snow bank. Plus, I think most of the kids up north have to shovel snow during a white Christmas.

It's always a great joy for me to have Christmas with my children. We always leave cookies and milk for Santa, and I always wrap the gifts from Santa in a special Santa paper. I started using a special Santa Claus paper some years ago when one of my young sons asked why Santa's presents were wrapped in the same paper as Mom and Dad's. I replied that Santa had run out of paper and woke me up to ask if he could use some of ours. I told him that I had known Santa from when I was a little kid and was very happy to let him use our extra paper.

Several weeks before the next Christmas, this same son, then six years old, was really behaving very badly, and I came up with a plan to hopefully get him back on track. One evening I called home, and using my best falsetto voice, I told him that I was Blinky, Santa's chief elf. I said that Santa was checking his Christmas list and had him listed in the naughty section. Naughty children would receive a big bag of horse poop from Santa, instead of beautifully wrapped Christmas toys. Blinky also explained that Santa was known for always checking his list twice, so he still had a chance to make the nice list. I wasn't too sure if he really believed me until I came home and he went racing up to me to say that Blinky had called, and he was shocked to learn that he was on Santa's naughty list. He was a complete angel, very helpful and well behaved until he had opened his presents that Christmas morning. I really don't know if he could have held out another day.

Since Santa loved milk and cookies, the children and I would always put out a nice cold glass of milk and a small plate of cookies for Santa. Some of the children thought Santa would probably like a bigger plate piled high with cookies. I explained that lots of other kids would also be leaving cookies and milk for

Santa and we really shouldn't delay him too much on his worldwide trip. Although everything looks bigger to a kid, the world is actually quite small, so each of my children would insist on leaving Santa at least two cookies each.

My sweetheart noticed that Santa seemed to be getting a little chubbier each year. I tried to explain to her that our children knew precisely how many cookies had been taken out of the cookie jar and that it was very difficult for me to put any of the cookies back in the jar. I either had to consume the milk and cookies myself or share them with the dog. The dog was pretty agreeable for the first few cookies or so but soon wanted something besides cookies.

Being a good Santa is probably one of the more difficult things a parent is required to do. When my youngest son was five years old, he went up to his mom and asked her for a very expensive Christmas gift. When she declined, he walked over to me and asked if I would buy him this gift for Christmas. Normally, I'm a pretty soft touch, and my kids can ask me for just about anything and I will agree. I still believe I should spoil my kids as much as I possibly can if it is within my means or ability to do so. They get enough "nos" while growing up that I can't possibly add any more through indifference. It was with great reluctance that I had to tell my five-year-old that this gift was well beyond my means. His reply was, "That's okay, I'll ask Santa—he'll get it for me." Sure enough, I was with him as he sat on Santa's lap that Christmas and innocently asked Santa for this most expensive gift.

I suppose it's a handy thing for Santa to have a credit card, for although I really didn't feel I had mastered the moment, I did get a little deeper in debt that Christmas. Each time I made a payment on this credit card, I'd remember how much my five-year-old was having while he used and enjoyed Santa's present.

A year later, my number one son wanted a certain skateboard for Christmas, and I told him I would be sure and get it for him that Christmas. My bride made a huge blunder that Christmas, because she took our six-year-old to see Santa on Christmas Eve. He idolized his older brother and asked Santa for the same exact skateboard. She mentioned this to me after all the stores were closed as we were wrapping Santa's gifts that night. I quickly wrote a note from Santa thanking the children for the milk and cookies and also explaining that the skateboard must have fallen off the sleigh and he would look for it on the way back to the North Pole.

My six-year-old was greatly disappointed that the skateboard had fallen off Santa's sleigh but was somewhat appeased by the fact that Santa would try to find it and bring it to him. The day after Christmas I was fortunate to find one of these skateboards remaining in the store. I bought it and busted up one corner of the container box so I could convince my youngest son that the skateboard had indeed fallen out of Santa's sleigh. As I presented him with the skateboard that evening, he was thrilled that Santa was able to locate the skateboard. I explained that since he had known me from the time I was a young child, Santa had simply called me on the telephone and we met at a secret location so as not to disturb the other children.

I get up early Christmas morning, and as soon as I notice the children awakening, I'll toss a few rocks up on the roof to imitate the reindeer and holler out in my best baritone Santa voice, "Ho, ho, ho! Merry Christmas!"

Sometimes I get so caught up in the Christmas spirit that I'll ask my sweetheart, "Honey, do we have any more spray snow?"

Horny Toads—Horned Toads

There are some things that really should be renamed because they are too difficult to pronounce and sound odd when we say them the way scholars tell us we should. Horned toads should be called horny toads; it just sounds more appropriate. I can remember as a child saying "ketchup" and always being corrected that I should call this gooey red stuff "catsup." Catsup always sounded like it was made from red cats or something. Since you'd have to pound on the bottom of the bottle to get the red stuff out of the bottle, you were always trying to "ketchup."

Looking like a miniature version of some ferocious dinosaur from our distant past, horny toads are really unique-looking creatures. They are only about five or six inches long, and you'll see them go leaping, running, and zipping along over the local Texas terrain. As a young lad, I was taught not to get too close to a horny toad because they would spit tobacco juice in your eye. It was only after I got older that I realized horny toads don't chew.

Both horny toads and chameleons belong to the lizard family. Chameleons can change colors according to their habitat and background and are sold in pet shops as pets—although in my case, the chameleons became playful cat food. Perhaps it was just another one of my wild ideas, but as I was visiting the pet shop one day buying some live crickets for one of my son's pet salamanders, I got to thinking about the chameleons that were for sale. Hmm, chameleons eat bugs, and we have a lot of bugs and mosquitoes at home. Gee, I was almost giddy as I left the store with a bag full of crickets and a half-dozen chameleons. With childhood memories of all the chameleons I used to play with in the backyards while growing up in Texas, I could barely wait to get home and release the chameleons into our garden.

Well, crud, I had forgotten about our four cats, one for each child. The children were all very enthused and interested in Dad's new experiment as I explained how beneficial and how much fun it would be to have chameleons in our garden. Our cats were all great "mousers" and the chameleons didn't last too long after I released them. I explained to the children that they had just witnessed a home version of "Wild Kingdom." And as I thought about how much money I had just spent on the chameleons, I had a fleeting thought of "catsup."

    I'll bet those cats wouldn't have caught horny toads, especially if I could somehow teach horny toads to chew tobacco.

Texan – English
Hew-stun—Houston
Houston is named after General Sam Houston, who defeated the Mexican army at the battle of San Jacinto. If Mister Houston were to visit his namesake today, I kinda wonder how he would feel about this honor. The good thing is that several schools and a university are named after Sam Houston and the university happens to be right here in town.

I suppose they could have named the town Samsville or Samsburg, but they decided that Houston was much more dignified. The town was originally called "the Holler" because people would holler across the bayous at each other. Now they just holler out their car windows at each other. Some things really don't change much over the years.

Houston has a population of over four million people, and if you happen to be driving through town, you'll think they are all on your same street. This is another "white flag" city, so I hope that you kept your white flag from Dallas. (If you don't know what I'm referring to, then don't proceed any further until you have read about Dallas.) And I hope you kept your flag white instead of letting it turn to gray or black, because those colors on a flag have a totally different meaning. A gray flag means that you are elderly and probably a member of "gray power," quite possibly senile, and that's why your left turn signal has been on for the last forty-three miles. A black flag signifies that you are staying in some really cheap motels on your tour of Texas and need some roach spray.

Houston is probably most famous for "the" Astrodome, the very first domed baseball park. Since grass doesn't grow without sunlight, they developed Astroturf, which is a light layer of carpet covering hardened concrete. The brown spots on the carpet are from the chewing tobacco used by the ball players. When the Astrodome was completed, it was billed as the "Eighth Wonder of the World." It still is, except now they're wondering what they're gonna do with it. It's way too big for a Taco Bell franchise or a theme restaurant. The Houston Astros moved to a beautiful new ballpark called Enron Field, but they had to change the name because of all the shenanigans at the Enron corporation, which once was but now isn't. Then they changed the name to Astros Field but had to change the name again, because folks thought that this is where all the astronauts were located.

The ballpark is now called Minute Maid Field. For those of you from New England, these are not the Minute Men's girlfriends. Minute Maid is actually a brand of fruit juices, and the new mascot for the baseball team is a lady all dressed up in a maid outfit, who gives out free samples of Minute Maid fruit juices. The Houston baseball fans are rapidly becoming some of the healthiest fans in all of baseball, because there are absolutely no beer sales at the ballpark. All of the beer outlets were converted to juice bars and smoothie bars.

This conversion has worked out very well at Minute Maid Field, because folks can now enjoy a ballgame without being annoyed by loudmouth drunks. Plus, now when someone is juiced up, they're not falling out of their seats and onto the playing field. This new "juice policy" has also reduced many of the beer-related accidents while fans are leaving the ballpark. DUIs have been drastically reduced. This has allowed the local police officers to give more time to their other duties, like preventing robberies and burglaries at the city's many doughnut shops.

The Houston Astros were originally called the Colt 45s, but the other teams in the league felt intimidated by the pistols on the Colt 45 jerseys, so they changed the name to the Houston Astronauts. Astronauts was difficult for the fans to pronounce, so they changed the name to the Astros, and now the fans call them the "Stros," which is actually a beer brewed up north somewhere, even though NASA still calls the men who fly spaceships astronauts.

Talkin' Texan

Houston is a pretty town with lots of great restaurants. My favorite is on the west side of Wayside Avenue just a few miles north of the interstate. It's a cozy little place with some of the best in Tex-Mex food—tacos, enchiladas, tamales, and so on. The tacos carbon is delicious.

Houston also has some very fancy hotels and motels, but I do have a word of caution: If you happen upon a motel and the desk clerk is behind bars and bulletproof glass, then perhaps you have wandered into a rough part of town. There is something a little disconcerting about a motel with bulletproof glass and signs in the parking lot that—instead of the normal "Not responsible for articles left in cars"—reads "Not responsible for lost cars." I suppose it's okay to stay in one of these motels if you have a death wish or something, because the rates are normally real cheap. But if you do have a death wish, why would you care about money? It's like my grandpa always said, "Sunny (he said he called me Sunny because I was so bright), you can't take it with you. I've never seen a hearse pulling a U-Haul." So go on ahead and stay in a real nice hotel or motel—after all, you are on vacation.

There are numerous gas and oil refineries in and around the Houston area; therefore, gasoline is quite plentiful and cheap. Houston is the home of Texaco, one of my favorite gasolines. My car just seems to run better on Texaco gasoline. Exxon is also situated in Houston, but they changed their name after the *Exxon Valdez* incident, and now I don't know what they are called. If you happen to see a gas station that just says "Gas," I think that's them.

Garfish make their habitat in and around the numerous bayous and rivers. The fish are sometimes called "alligator gar" because nearly half of this fish happens to be a triple row of razor-sharp teeth. At times, you may see some of the local women wearing these garfish teeth as necklaces and earrings. You can purchase some of these necklaces and earrings at any of the local stores and gift shops in town. I've seen garfish three, four, and five feet long just swimming and floating on top of the waters. Seems to me you don't even need fishing equipment at all—you could just use a pellet gun or a bow and arrow and pick off one or two. They say that garfish aren't good eating, but then again they say the same thing about pigeons.

Fact is, people eat pigeons all the time, and they just don't realize that they are eating pigeon because the restaurants call them "squab" on their menus. If they called them pigeons, then no one would eat them. The same pigeon that someone was feeding in the park this morning and was seen pooping on a famous statue this afternoon may be the "squab" on your dinner plate this evening.

Another example would be "escargot"; if restaurants called them snails, then very few of us would eat them. Since "escargot" sounds very exotic and continental, we go ahead and order them. Plus, escargot comes in a unique and cool-looking container, with each snail in its own little slot. We tell our children not to "play with their food" yet someone's kids may have been playing with your "escargot" this morning in their backyard. If the restaurants were to call garfish "alligator fish" or "bayou fish or "tasty fish" and use a specially shaped plate with some kind of unusual garnish or perhaps honey mustard or Grey Poupon, then garfish could become a very popular entrée.

I have an awful lot of relatives in the Houston area, or is it a lot of awful relatives in Houston? Either way, none of my sisters or brothers, nieces, cousins, or anybody else will talk to me. I really don't understand why, because I hardly ever say or do anything that offends anyone. Seems that I'm the striped sheep of the family. You will probably see them at my funeral—they'll be the ones with big ol' grins on their faces. Some people bring happiness wherever they go, others whenever they go. I just hope they don't leave me hanging off a tree or something. I did buy a burial plot one time from one of my nieces, sight unseen. I bought it long distance over the telephone. I just asked her to make sure that the burial plot wasn't anywhere close to squirrels, because squirrels collect nuts during the winter.

Joe Kent Roberts

Hunters and Hunting

Most of us have seen photos of hunters with their freshly killed deer, elk, bear, or whatever. They usually pose kneeling on the ground with their kill and a big ol' smile on their face, or they are standing next to their kill while it is hanging off a tree or something with a big ol' smile on their face; they are a proud lot indeed. Vast improvements have been made in the rifle industry since the "ball and powder" rifles of the eighteenth and nineteenth centuries. Today's rifles are greatly improved from the old Winchester 30-30 I used as a young lad during my hunting experiences.

My old scopeless Winchester 30-30 was pretty accurate, with a drop of only about six inches in a hundred yards. Today's rifles have this same accuracy within a half a mile and, combined with the modern scopes that can calculate wind velocity, time, temperature, and humidity, really do not offer any game that is being hunted much of a fighting chance any more.

My thoughts are that with today's modern rifles, just about any ol' slob can shoot prize-winning game from a window in the comfort of his cabin from half a mile away while watching cable TV and munching on microwave popcorn.

The most challenging hunting today and one of the best-kept secrets is chicken hunting. Sure, I know that many of you may scoff at the very idea that chicken hunting is difficult. You may rest assured that it is one of the most difficult hunts in this era, and I am most proud of the photos that have been taken of myself with my many kills after chicken hunts. There are several chicken heads and stuffed chickens over my mantle and adorning the walls and on the front entrance to my home.

I'm more into the commercialized chicken hunting rather than the mom-and-pop variety, just because the mom-and-pop farmers cannot afford the lost profits that a really good chicken hunter could inflict upon them.

    I hunt with my trusty old Winchester 30-30 at night rather than in the daylight hours, and without the aid of infrared. It's just more relaxing at night without all of the noise of the traffic and everything. I prefer to hunt from a high hill overlooking the chicken farm versus a tall tree because a hill is more stable than the tree if the weather conditions happen to be windy.
    Once I have taken my position on the hill overlooking the chicken farm, I select one of the teeny windows high up on the barn and take aim at one of the chickens. I relax and gently squeeze the trigger and Boom! The chicken is felled. Now, for the difficult part of the hunt: I run as fast as I can down the hill and around the barn to the door and dash inside to claim my prize. I open the door to the cage, grab the chicken, and scamper out as fast as I can before the chicken farmer comes racing after me. The chicken farmers are not too happy, and they always have a ready shotgun loaded with buckshot.

After I have escaped the farmer and avoided his barrage of buckshot, I can now return home and view my kill. If the chicken is large, then I have a photo opportunity. (You know, wearing my flannel shirt with the fluorescent orange bib, my "eat more chicken" cap, while holding the chicken up by the feet, and a big ol' grin on my face.) If the chicken is of prize-winning category, then I'll visit my taxidermist for either stuffing or wall mounting. If the chicken is small, then I'll just pluck it and roast it and eat it. The great thing about eating chicken is that it tastes just like chicken.

I-J

Dictionary
Texan - English

IFFIN—A long, strung-out wondering word.
    Iffin means "I was just wondering if . . ."
    As in: Iffin aah dew, wood ja?
        "I was just wondering that if I did, would you?"
INDY-ANN—Is this a lady who races in the Indy 500?
    Indy-ann means "one who is from India."
    As in: Izzy Indy-ann?
        "Is he from India?"
JAKE-IT—This is a garment that they wear.
    Jake-it means "jacket."
    As in: Wors muh jake-it? E-yuts colt.
        "Where's my jacket? It's gotten real cold."
JAUNT—Not any type of walking or running.
    Jaunt means "do you want?"
    As in: Jaunt sum tew ate?
        "Do you want something to eat?"
JAY-UM—Many people put it on toast.
    Jay-um means "jam."
    As in: Alm rally e-yun uh jay-um.
        "I'm really in a jam.
JEET JET —Look up in the sky, is that a Jeet Jet?
    This is a real time saver—a Texan can condense four words down to just two. Readers Digest hasn't tried this one yet.
    Jeet jet means "Did you eat yet?"
    As in: Alm ratty tew ate; jeet jet?
        "I'm ready to eat; did you eat yet?"

Texan—English

Er-vun—Irving
Welcome to Irving, "home" of the Dallas Cowboys football team. Yeah, I know, it sounds puzzling to me also. I guess if they called them the Irving Cowboys no one would know where they were from. And since there's already a Texas Rangers baseball team, if they were to call them the Texas Cowboys, it would be way too confusing. Geez, I'm starting to get a headache just thinking about the reasoning here. Well, it wouldn't be the first time the Dallas Cowboys gave someone a headache. I think that's why the Dallas Cowboy cheerleaders are so pretty and why they dress them in such revealing uniforms. And I figure all the cheerleaders must be named June. They do seem to be busting out all over and it seems to me that the Dallas Cowboys must have spent so much money on players that the budget was a little short when it came to spending some money for uniforms.

It just makes us happy to see such pretty girls dancing around, probably so we won't be thinking why they didn't call them the Irving Cowboy Cheerleaders. I think that's why the local Hooters restaurant is so popular, because few things make a man happier than a pretty, busty, scantily clad girl bringing us food. And the Dallas Cowboy cheerleaders take our mind off the game when the Cowboys play poorly.

I played second base, catcher, and pitcher for our local Plano softball team and was returning home from a game in Irving one night and turned on the radio to the game between the Dallas Cowboys and the 49ers. The Cowboys were trailing 34 to 21 with less than two and a half minutes left in the game, and as I passed the stadium there were droves of Cowboy fans leaving the game. If I had had a ticket to the game that night, I wouldn't have left because Roger "the Dodger" Staubach was the quarterback for Dallas.

Talkin' Texan

I'm still a big fan of both "Dandy" Don Meredith and Roger Staubach, and that night Roger brought the Cowboys back from what was called "certain defeat" to win in the last seconds of the game by 35 to 34. I still have not figured out why someone would spend a bunch of money for a baseball or football game and then leave the game early just to get a head start on traffic. I was giggling all the way home as I listened to the game and the interviews and recap of the game.

Because of his great daring and having had so many concussions, Roger had to retire early. Seems like the whole state gathered for his retirement ceremony, and they played the country-western song "Mama, Don't Let Your Babies Grow Up to Be Cowboys," which brought tears to my eyes. Roger ended up buying a controlling interest in Church's Fried Chicken. Church's always had these great big ol' pieces of fried chicken and homemade biscuits and stuff. However, I still prefer to go chicken hunting—I suppose that "forbidden fruit" still tastes best, even if it does taste just like chicken.

Joe Kent Roberts

Texan - English
Thigh-lun—The Island
Padre Juan del Gado was in charge of a local Spanish mission located in a small hamlet outside of Corpus Christi. Padre del Gado was very highly respected and loved by this rather large but very poor congregation. They wondered how they could show their great appreciation to the padre for they had very little money and wanted to honor him in some way. The congregation decided they would create a statue for him and name an island after him. They chose a slender strip of land off the coast that was over a hundred miles long.

    All of those in the mission were very enthused that they had found a way to greatly honor this man who had done so much for them. Each day after they had completed their normal work, they would gather and make plans for the design of the sculpture and for all of the carpentry work that would be required. The people built several wooden boats because many would be needed to carry the congregation across the bay for the day of the great unveiling to honor Padre Juan del Gado.

    The carpenters and painters had completed over a dozen signs proclaiming the name of the island; the sculptors lovingly created a statue of Juan del Gado that was over eight feet tall. Finally, after many months of hard work, the time came to surprise Juan del Gado with all their efforts. Early one Saturday morning, the congregation arrived at the padre's humble home to take him across the bay to the island. Great quantities of food had been prepared for all of the planned festivities.

    The village people had also prepared candy-filled piñatas for the children and had much fun and games planned for this occasion. Unfortunately, there were no trees on the island and it was most difficult to hang the piñatas. Several gentlemen and one really tall lady came forward and volunteered to hang the piñatas overhead using a very long and sturdy stick. Being customarily blindfolded during this game, the children pummeled these poor people unmercifully trying to open the candy-filled piñatas. There is where the term "stick people" came from.

    Finally, the time had come for the unveiling of the statue and the signs for the naming of the island after their beloved padre. The crowd cheered wildly and the padre smiled broadly as the veils were lifted from the statue and signs. And that's how Padre Island happened to get its name.

Texan - English
Jaz-purr—Jasper

Jasper is located on Highway 96 between Beaumont and Nacogdoches. At this writing, the population is a little under 8,000 friendly folks. Jasper claims to be deep in the heart of Texas and deep in the piney woods. The heart of a watermelon is normally in the center—but I've never enjoyed a Jasper watermelon, so maybe they're located far to one side of the melon.

Jasper is completely surrounded by forests and it really is quite pretty. For those of you who enjoy bass fishing, Jasper has some of the best bass in the state. The town is located less than a dozen miles from the second-largest man-made lake in the state. I don't know if the term man-made is politically correct, because it seems to me that quite a few ladies worked on this project. Perhaps I should refer to it as an artificial lake? No, I can't do that, because too many folks would think the water wasn't wet or the fish are fakes. I could call it an unnatural lake, but then some folks might figure that fishing was unnatural. Geez, I'm so confused—I'm really happy that I never got into politics. If you fish, they have a lake, with bass.

Jasper is known as the "Jewel of the Forest," and we went into the forest to see her one day. Jewel is really quite a striking woman, very tall, with sky-blue eyes, and long flowing red hair. She has a neat little rock shop on the banks of the creek where she sells all sorts of objects handcrafted from the local tourmaline mine. Her overhead is so low that she has some great deals on gemstone jewelry. I purchased a couple of matching earring and necklace sets for my bride. Whenever she wears one of them, she talks about our trip to Jasper and our visit to Jewel.

Jasper has one of the oldest newspapers in the state. This is true, because I went down to the museum and saw it one day. The newspaper is really, really old. It's back over against the far wall of the museum, and it's in a big glass case. The newspaper is all yellowed and covered with dust, so I was unable to see the original published date. If you ever want to see some really old stuff, then go to a local museum. If you want to see some old stuff that talks, then visit an old folks' home, or come visit me. Hopefully, it will be after one of my frequent naps, so I'll be all refreshed and ready to receive visitors. I really love to see visitors when they bring me Shiner Bock, Maeker's dried sausage, or pecan pie.

Texan – English
Jung-shun—Junction

The North Llano River and the South Llano River join together here to form the Llano River. Therefore, they formed a junction—and this town came to be named Junction, instead of Three Rivers, Fork, or Jjunction, Texas. In keeping with tradition, some of the more popular girls names are Llinda, Llucy, Llouise, Llucinda, Llaverne, and Llavone. The more popular boys names are Bbilly Bbob, Ddavid, Ddwight, Jjohn, Jjustin, and Ttom. Junction is known as the "Lland of Lliving Wwaters" and it really is quite pretty around here.

With three rivers and several lakes in the area, water sports are very popular in Junction. The local folks and visitors have a vast array of water activities from which to choose: bboating, ccamping, ffishing, sswimming, and wwater ssking—but of course, no ffishing from any of the bbridges in the area.

On a high hill overlooking the town of Junction, you will find "Llovers' Lleap." Each weekend, lovers from all over Texas gather together to leap off this high hill onto a trampoline down below. Since there have been a shortage of lovers at times, they changed the requirements just a bit so more folks could join in on the fun. You really don't have to be a lover to leap, as the only requirement is that you join hands as you leap off the hill.

In the early years of jumping off Llovers' Lleap, some folks would just holler out different stuff like their names, or yippie, yah-hoo, and stuff like that. Nowadays, lots of folks, as they join hands and jump off the hill, sing songs on their way down to the trampoline. The couple with the most romantic song wins a really nice prize; however, you don't really need to holler or sing on the way down to enjoy jumping off Llovers' Lleap.

Since Llovers' Lleap is now open to everyone, a lot of the kids like to leap off the hill with capes and umbrellas and stuff. Some of the older kids fashion all types of feathers and wings to wear as they make their jumps. You get extra bonus points for the jump if you can sing some sort of a bird song on your way down. So far, the most popular bird song has been "On the Wings of a Snow White Dove" by Ferlin Husky.

There is a snack bar and gift shop located near the trampoline that is well stocked with capes and umbrellas, should you and your family decide to participate in the festivities. There is also a really nice picnic area where you can see all the leapers and jumpers in shady comfort. Should you happen to be visiting Junction on the weekend, just ask any of the locals for directions to Llovers' Lleap. Enjoy your stay, or lleap!

K

Dictionary

KAINT—Something that we cannot do.
    Kaint means "can't."
    As in: Aah kaint drank muh caw-fay blay-uck.
        "I can't drink my coffee black."
KAY-UDS—They are expensive, time consuming, and fun.
    Kay-uds means "kids."
    As in: Y'all kay-uds quite day-oun.
        "You kids quiet down."
KEAR-FUL—Beware of dangers, take care.
    Kear-ful means "careful."
    As in: Y'all be kearful
        "You be careful."
KET-FAY-USH—Have you been fishing lately?
    Ket-fay-ush means "catfish."
    As in: Y'all, thay-us ket-fay-ush as day-lis-yus.
        "You all, this catfish is delicious."
KLANE—Cleanliness is next to godliness.
    Klane means "clean."
    As in: Y'all kay-uds, klane yore plaits.
        "You kids, clean your plates."

Texan—English

Kur-vail—Kerrville
Kerrville is located on Interstate 10, a little over sixty miles west of downtown San Antonio. I would love to be able to retire here someday, because Kerrville is one of the most beautiful areas of the state. Situated in the Texas Hill Country, Kerrville has many scenic roadways, rivers, streams, lakes, and lots of trees. Unfortunately, I'm not one of the few folks to know about this town, because there are over half a million folks visiting Kerrville every year.

    The town was named after a fellow named James Kerr, who was a famous shingle maker. He also is credited with coining the word "kerrplunk" whenever an errant shingle would happen to fall off a roof. Kerr shingles became very popular throughout the state and rapidly replaced the tin roofs found on many early Texas homes. It really saddens me, because there is really nothing better than falling asleep with the rain coming down on an old tin roof.

    Kerrville has become very famous for its beautiful scenery, friendliness, colleges, arts, artists, hunting, fishing, and exotic game preserves. In the early 1950s, Kerrville also became famous for having one of the very first fast-food restaurants in the country. A fellow by the name of Joseph Kerr, called Joe by his friends, and being in no way related to the Kerrs in and around Kerrville, opened a fast-food restaurant on a heavily trafficked downtown street.

    Joe's fast-food restaurant was an instant success, because his menu didn't feature chicken, hamburgers, French fries, fish, roast beef, or tacos. Instead, Joe Kerr's Fast Food Restaurant featured antelope, jackrabbit, javelina, roadrunner, venison, and a stuffed swift-flying bird known as a swift. Your kids will be thrilled to learn that there are no vegetables on the menu, because there really are no fast-moving vegetables, although they do like to hide under mounds of mashed potatoes. Joe's menu also features instant coffee, instant orange juice, instant oatmeal, instant rice, and instant Texas toast. The service is very fast and friendly.

    Just to whet your appetite for fast food, there is a little locally owned convenience store located just off the interstate that carries javelina jerky. Pick some up and then head towards downtown. Ask any of the locals and they'll let you know how to get to Joe Kerr's. If someone you happen to ask doesn't know, then you've probably asked another tourist. I do hope that you think fast and enjoy your stay.

Texan - English
Kangs-vail—Kingsville
Less than a day or two ride by horseback from Corpus Christi, you'll find the King Ranch and a town by the name of Kingsville. This is the largest ranch in the country, and it covers over 825,000 acres. The ranch is larger than some of the bitty states in northeast America and is so big that it has its own town. The ranch and the town are both listed on the National Historic Register. I'm not sure how one goes about being listed on this register. I suppose you have to be really, really old or really, really big, and the ranch and the town both qualify.

The ranch contains over 60,000 head of cattle, and there is also an abundance of wild game. There is a unique wild javelina pig that occupies the ranch, and I'm surprised the town wasn't named Javelinaville or something along those lines. If you've ever seen a photo of a javelina, then you'll realize that it took a pretty brave individual to make bacon from this animal. Even the roughest, toughest cafes outside of Texas don't have javelina bacon on their breakfast menu.

There are several local cafes in Kingsville that serve breakfast featuring javelina bacon. Go ahead and try some while you're here in town, because it tastes absolutely nothing like chicken. I personally like the mesquite-smoked, thick-sliced bacon the best. Javelina has sort of a mild, wild pig taste and is a great complement to eggs, grits, Texas toast, and jam. There are several locations in town where you will be able to purchase some javelina jerky, javelina roast, and my favorite, javelina chops. Javelina is an Indian word that means "ugly, vicious, tasty" and is pronounced "have-a-leena."

Several years ago, the ranch would allow tourists to visit the ranch and take tours in the area around Wild Horse Desert.

Sometimes, these out-of-state greenhorns were not too familiar with the dangers of this part of the state, such as diamondback rattlesnakes, javelinas, scorpions, and such. At times, there was even a bit of a language barrier, hence one of the purposes of this little book. Anyway, as several of them were riding out on the range, one of the local cowboys spotted some wild, crazed javelina charging out of the woods after them. The polite cowboy hollered out, "Hey, javelina!" Unfortunately, he didn't point, because his mom always said that it was not polite to point.

As the greenhorn was contemplating the supposed question, he responded by replying: "No thanks, I'll stay with my girlfriend here. My mom always told me to go home with the one that brung me." And he kissed his horse and bade the girl goodbye.

∪∪

L

Dictionary

LARN—It's one of the ways to higher education.
    Larn means "learn."
    As in: Y'all kay-uds, larn tham boo-uks nay-ow.
        "You kids, learn those books now."

LATTER—You need a ten-foot latter to hang those Christmas lights.
    Latter means "letter."
    As in: Muh bay-be sant may uh latter.
        "My baby sent me a letter."

LAY-DEE—And there are also gentlemen.
    Lay-dee means "lady."
    As in: Wut a naws lay-dee.
        "What a nice lady."

LAY-TUH—Why can't we do this now?
    Lay-tuh means "later."
    As in: Nought nay-ow, lay-tuh.
        "Not now, later."

LES—Sometimes there's less, sometimes there's more.
    Les means "let us."
    As in: Les goan tew da rainch.
        "Let's go on to the ranch."

LIL—Once there was a famous one with diamonds. This ain't her.
    Lil means "little."
    As in: Aah rally lof lil kay-uds.
        "I really love little kids."

LOCK—Foreigners put these on doors and gates.
    Lock means "like."
    As in: Aah rally lock yew.
        "I really like you."

LOT—Well, if you follow these directions, you'll surely get lost!
    Lot means "light."
    As in: Whale, y'all jus torn rot at da farst lot.
        "Well, you just turn right at the first light."
LOW—A not too enthusiastic greeting.
    Low means "hello."
    As in: Low
"Hello." (I'm really not interested in talking to you, I'm just letting you know that I'm still alive and breathing.)

Texan—English

Luh-ray-duh—Laredo
Laredo is located on Highway 87 less than a hundred miles from present-day Zapata, or about 180 miles west of San Antonio as the crow flies—although I really don't believe that a crow could fly this great a distance in a straight line. If you happen to be traveling by airplane, don't follow a crow, because it may or may not know the way to Laredo.

    The Spaniards didn't depend too much on crows during their exploration of the New World and pretty much followed the Rio Grande up to Laredo. Of course, it wasn't called Laredo back then, and the Rio Grande wasn't called the Rio Grande. This area of the country has been inhabited for over ten thousand years, and the Apache Indians called this great river "Tawantatakakawayahosay," which means, "sometimes roaring, peaceful, great river with many fish." The Spaniards felt that this was way too difficult to pronounce, and they renamed the river Rio Grande del Norte, which means Great River of the North. Texans decided that this also took too long to say, and they just call the river the Rio Grande.

    The Spaniards discovered that the Apache didn't have one leader in charge of everything as they themselves had, but had many male and female chiefs called bandleaders. This was probably one of the first committees in the Americas and would eventually lead to the downfall of the Indians. I guess the saying about learning from past history is true. If we don't learn from past history, then history may repeat itself. I kinda wonder why we still have committees.

    Of course, having bandleaders was a great idea and eventually resulted in the Big Band Era during the 1930s and '40s. The Indians had to relinquish their Indian names, such as Running Bear, Soaring Eagle, Crazy Cow, and stuff like that, for stage names. Many folks don't realize that quite a few of the most famous big band leaders were actually Indians. Then, once the Indians learned how to play the guitar, they added that great drumbeat, and country-western music was born. One of the most famous Indians mastered the saxophone and became a worldwide rock 'n' roll star. Of course, he did have a stage name that I'm not at liberty to divulge.

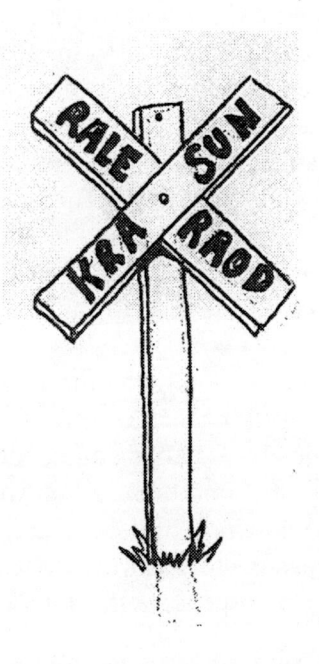

The Lone Star State
The state flag of Texas has a single gold star in a field of red, white, and blue. They decided on the star for two reasons. Normally, on any given evening in the big cities, when anyone looks up into the sky, they'll see just one single star. The star also represents all the most-traveled directions from San Antonio, the original capital of Texas: north, northwest, northeast, southwest, and southeast. Hardly anyone traveled from east to west or from west to east in Texas until recently. The state legislature is considering underlining the star to represent this type of travel.

I've asked several types of folks just exactly what the colors of the flag represent. To the farmer they mean one thing, to the rancher something else, to the cowboy something entirely different, to the sailor something to do with the seas, and to the city slicker something incomprehensible. I made the mistake of asking a politician, and he gave me the following response:

Red for his fiery speeches,
White for his wisdom and purity,
Blue for the color of the state flower, and
The Gold Star for the state's abundant treasures.

I also asked some common, ordinary folks like myself what the colors of the state flag represented and I kinda like their answers the best.

Red for the chili peppers in a good bowl of chili,
White for the virgins in Vestal, Texas,
Blue for having to work on Mondays, and
The Gold Star for the fillings in their teeth.

These folks also told me the true meaning for Texas being called the "Lone Star State." Seems that it's the beer. While most beer brewed in America is from rice, barley, and hops, Lone Star beer is brewed with corn, barley, and hops, using only the purest artesian spring water. They also pointed out the fact that Texas wanted to counter the claim made by the state of Wisconsin about beers that had made Milwaukee famous, because Lone Star just didn't make a single little city famous—Lone Star is the beer that made a whole humongous state famous. After all, that's why it's called the Lone Star State.

These folks also wondered why Wisconsin was supposed to be some sort of wholesome "dairy state" and why they would want to be brewing beer while milking dairy cattle. Who in the world would want to buy milk and cheese from someone who had also been brewing or drinking beer all day long? Beer, milk, and cheese just don't go very well together, whereas beer, chili, beef jerky, and tamales complement each other wonderfully.

A few years ago, I was traveling through central Texas and stopped at a convenience store to purchase some cold Lone Star beer. They didn't have any! For the next hundred miles or so, I continued to stop by convenience stores and look for some cold Lone Star—nope, nada, zip, nothing. I kept hearing a rumor that Lone Star Brewery had been bought out by a big conglomerate back East and soon would not be available anywhere in Texas. There were several beers in the stores that were Lone Star look-alikes, but no genuine Lone Star. I was very disappointed to find out that Lone Star would no longer be available, because Lone Star has a unique and original taste.

When I returned home, I sent off a letter to my congressman expressing my sadness at the passing and early demise of Lone Star beer. If Lone Star beer is no longer fully available statewide, then how could Texas possibly qualify for being called the "Lone Star State"? Recently, I was pleasantly surprised to learn that the Texas legislature is now considering changing the slogan from the "Lone Star State" to the "Shiner Bock State" in honor of the finest beer in the country.

Texan – English
Loang-vue—Longview
Just a few miles south of Marshall, on Interstate 20, you'll find the town of Longview. In the mid-1700s, a fellow by the name of Moses Thyme and his lovely wife, Mary, were traveling through this part of the country and were overwhelmed by the forested natural beauty of this area. They decided to halt their wagon and take a good long look at the countryside. They agreed that this would be a great location for a town and initially wanted to name it Longlook but finally agreed that Longview would be more readily accepted.

If you happen to be a hunter or a fisherman, Longview is a great place to make your headquarters because it's less than thirty miles north of the biggest lake in Texas. The lake is around a hundred miles long and nearly fifteen miles across in different places. The lake is loaded with trophy bass, brim, crappie, perch, Rio Grande, and catfish.

If the catfish aren't biting, don't be too concerned about not having any catfish for dinner, because there are several catfish restaurants in Longview. They have catfish fixed just about any way you could imagine. They have baked, grilled, poached, fried, barbecued, and etouffee catfish. Most of these restaurants will also have an all-you-can-eat catfish special. They'll just keep bringing you catfish and French fries to eat until the buttons on your clothes start popping.

If you happen to be a hunter and didn't have any luck or you're just a really poor shot, you can still have venison for dinner. There are a couple of exotic game restaurants in Longview. If Longview is still a dry county, as it was my last time through, then you won't be able to have a beer with your meal. You might just want to place a "to-go order" and then drive back to the lake and enjoy your dinner.

However, I think you can only consume beer while you are on shore, so you won't be able to have your dinner on board a boat. Seems that in past years there were too many folks who would have a bit too much beer with dinner, or while they were fishing, and fall overboard.

Years ago, I was asked to give a eulogy for Don Duet, a friend of mine who had passed away in this manner. Don had a shock of white hair as long as I had known him, and most of his friends called him Whitey. I resisted the request to speak because I didn't think I would be able to put a positive spin on the circumstances surrounding Whitey's passing. I suggested that they ask the new assistant pastor, who had just graduated from seminary.

I greeted Whitey's wife, Wendy, outside the church on the morning of the funeral, and she had been crying for days. I tried to console her and lift her spirits up a bit. She seemed to perk up a little and then turned to the young pastor to ask him how she looked. He may have blundered when he answered. He replied that she looked a lot better than Whitey.

The young pastor said some nice things about what a good man he was and something about the happy hunting grounds and that great fishing hole in the sky. He concluded the eulogy by stating, "Please don't eat, drink, and boat, because you may fall overboard and drown" and then someone might ask me to give YOUR eulogy.

Texan - English
Lob-uck—Lubbock
"When will we be arriving in Lubbock?" she asked flatly.
"In less than half an hour," he replied hurriedly.
"Are those rain clouds on the horizon?" she asked wetly.
"Yes, I believe they are," he thundered.

Lubbock is situated on the interstate just a few hours south of Amarillo. Will Rogers once traveled between Amarillo and Lubbock, proclaiming that this was the most "nothing" he had ever seen. Apparently, he had never traveled to some parts of Arizona, California, Colorado, Kansas, Nebraska, Nevada, New Mexico, or Utah. I find these areas rather enchanting and most unique. The folks who inhabit these areas of America are strong, quick-witted, and rather friendly. Their ancestors must have transferred these traits onto their offspring.

If you happen to enter Lubbock via the interstate, you may wonder where the city is located. The interstate is about sixty feet below the city so when you drive through it all you see are concrete walls, lots and lots of concrete walls. The interstate seems to be built in some sort of a canal, and I'm sure that if the Martians are looking through their telescopes at Earth, they're wondering why we are driving on canals.

Once you get off the interstate canal and start driving around town, it's really quite nice. Lubbock is also the hometown of a very famous rock 'n' roll star, and there is a building dedicated to his name in town. One of his song titles even became a much used response by Texans whenever they thought there was no way something would occur. My publisher wants me to appear young and handsome whenever I make a personal appearance at any of the bookstores throughout Texas; that'll be the day.

One of my cousins selected Texas Tech University to complete his college education. He had visited most of the major colleges in Texas, and I asked him why he chose Texas Tech over the many other fine colleges. He said that Texas Tech had the prettiest girls on campus. I tend to agree that Texas has the prettiest women, and this university may have a bit more than its fair share.

I have always loved the name of the school mascot. While other Texas colleges have more mundane names like Longhorns, Mustangs, Bears, Eagles, and so on, the Texas Tech team calls itself the Texas Tech Red Raiders. Unfortunately, the team has never been especially good; perhaps all those pretty girls on campus are too much of a distraction. I've always felt that their games would be a lot more entertaining if the play-by-play announcer sounded more like Elmer Fudd.

As an example, if Elmer were announcing, the commentary might go something like this:

It's a bweatuful day hewe at the staweum as we pway owr dweaded cwoss state wivals, Texas Wonghowns. The Wed Wadders have ewected to weceive the ball duwing the coin toss and eagewy await the kickoff.

The kick is high and deep and Weggie Walling weceives it at the twee yawd wine, wuns and weaves the ball past diving takwers and is finawly twakeled at the fawty fowa yawd wine.

It's fust and ten at the fawty fowa as Wandy Wennols weceves the snap fwom centa and dwops back to pass. Wow, folks, it's a statue of liwerty pway and the wide weceiver has weversed his diwection and gwabs the ball as he wuns by Wandy.

A friend of mine was unable to grasp the notion of Elmer Fudd as an announcer, so I thought that I'd just give an example for those of you who have the same inability to understand the concept.

There are many college and professional sports teams spending millions of dollars on their players and coaches. Texas Tech prefers to spend its money on professors and education;

therefore, their sports teams are rarely in first place. So, I just figured they could replace their present sports announcer with Elmer Fudd to spice up their games a bit.

Texan – English
Laf-ken—Lufkin

In the very early 1880s, the railroad was looking for a route between Houston and Shreveport and decided to send a survey crew into the piney woods of East Texas. The chief of the survey crew, a Mister Willie Fyndet, with his crewmen Seymore Streams and Rod Enchane, arrived in Homer on the afternoon of August 1881.

    On that hot Texas August afternoon, the men immediately located the Reginald Arms Hotel and Mister Reggie Sturr, the proprietor, welcomed them with open arms when they told him they were wanting to bring the new railroad through Homer. Reggie not only gave them a free room, he allowed them unlimited room service during their stay at the hotel, plus a coupon for a free bath for each of them at the Homer Bath House.

    After Willie and the boys took advantage of the baths and changed clothes, they agreed to forgo the room service and have a nice juicy T-bone steak at the hotel restaurant. Reggie once more graciously gave Willie and his crew this fine meal at no charge. At this time, the Reginald Arms did not possess a liquor license, so Reggie suggested that the men have an after-dinner drink over at the Dew Drop Inn. Reggie also gave the men several coupons for free drinks at this local tavern.

    Reggie had taken care of them very well, and they also had a room with a balcony and a great view of the surrounding countryside. After a week of surveying for the railroad in the hot Texas summer, Willie and the boys were feeling pretty good as they arrived at the tavern. They were debating whether they should have a couple of cold beers or perhaps a few vodka martinis with their coupons.

    As Willie and his crew arrived at the inn, the owner of this fine establishment greeted them near the swinging doors. Mister Al Kohol had received word from Reggie, by courier pigeon, that

Willie and his crew would be arriving shortly. The pigeon was resting comfortably on its perch as the men entered the tavern. The pigeon's name was Quick.

Willie and his crew had heard of courier pigeons before but had never seen one close up and in person. Al explained how courier pigeons could deliver messages and small amounts of money and stuff. Willie and the boys decided that having a pigeon like Quick would be very helpful to them while they were away from home and family.

During the evening, as the men's coupons were used up, Al continued to supply them with buckets of beer. The men were having buckets of beer because pitchers of beer hadn't been invented as yet. Al was so excited when Willie told him he was recommending that the railroad would be coming through Homer that Al offered to give him Quick, perch and all. Willie readily accepted Al's offer and looked forward to sending notes and messages to the folks back home.

Al probably shouldn't have so generous with supplying Willie and his crew with all those free buckets of beer, because the men became very drunk, belligerent, and rowdy. Since both Marshal Orel Forsez and Sheriff Denny Dewet were out of town attending a law enforcement convention, Al had to send Quick to fetch Howie Dunnet, the local constable.

When Howie arrived at the Dew Drop Inn and asked the boys to quiet down, Willie and the boys were highly insulted that they were asked to behave by a local constable. See, back then, a governor outranked a marshal, a marshal outranked a sheriff, a sheriff outranked a mayor, and a mayor outranked a constable. There were no state senators or congressmen back then, which is probably a good thing, and mayors weren't really elected, they were just the ladies or gentlemen who weren't very good at farming or ranching. I think that's why they were called the chosen few.

Anyway, Howie pulled his pair of pearl-handled six-guns on them and hauled them off to jail for the night. Howie put Quick and his perch in another cell to keep him protected from the drunken men. When Willie and the boys woke up the next morning, they not only had an awful hangover but also were furious that they had missed out on their free room at the Reginald Arms and the complimentary breakfast.

Willie and the boys picked up their belongings over at the hotel and, as they rode out of town towards Denman Springs with Quick, vowed that the railroad would never run through Homer. I was trying to come up with a moral to this story other than "Never give a drunken man a quick bird," but I couldn't think of one. Perhaps Ben D. Stroyd, the former mayor of Homer, or one of his offspring can come up with an appropriate moral.

Willie and his crew arrived at Denman Springs the very next day, and this is the present site of Lufkin. Willie sent Quick back to Houston with a note to inform them that Denman Springs would be a much better location for a train station than Homer because of the gentle terrain, the pine forest, and easy access to water. The name was changed from Denman Springs to Lufkin because one of the fellows who owned the railroad wanted his name on something besides a railroad car.

With the arrival of the train, Lufkin quickly became a thriving commercial area in this part of Texas. Shortly after the railroad came to Lufkin, Homer became a ghost town, because most everyone moved their homes and businesses there to be near the railroad. Lufkin became commercially famous for its sawmills, lumber mills, and timber industry. Unfortunately, when you turn on a television in Lufkin, you'll only see commercials for new cars, hamburgers, pizza, and beer.

Lufkin also became a cultural center for this part of the state because they have a library, a museum, a college, and two indoor malls. The malls add culture to the town because they have used book sales and art shows on the weekends. Lufkin has shown their appreciation to Willie and his crew for choosing this site for the railroad by erecting a statute to them in downtown Cotton Square.

When you visit Cotton Square, you'll not only be able to see this statue and the plaque honoring these men, you'll also be able to see some of Quick's descendants hovering around the statue. Pigeon-food vendors are available around the square should you wish to feed the pigeons. There are also plentiful park benches in the square for relaxing and writing notes to send the folks back home.

Every time I show this story to Professor Bob, he insists that I didn't fully explain what happened to Homer. While I do appreciate all of the great help and assistance from the professor for his insight in keeping me focused and on track, I can't understand why he doesn't understand what happened to Homer. So I'll add a short paragraph to the end of this story and hopefully fully explain Homer. For most of you, this will seem like déjà vu all over again.

After the railroad was built through Lufkin instead of Homer, Homer became a ghost town, because most everyone moved to Lufkin. Even today, the railroad is very important in moving products to market and entertaining travelers on scenic vacations.

The great thing about traveling on the train is having the dining car conveniently located in the center car of the train, and seeing things that just can't be seen by air travel. The dining car has everything from soup to nuts, coffee, soft drinks, beer and bratwurst, steak dinners, trout dinners, and spaghetti and meatballs. Plus you're not all squished up, like you are on an airplane, trying to reach over folks for something to eat. In the dining car, you can stretch out, relax, and chat with your friends, family, and other passengers while having a great meal.

Talkin' Texan

When my family and I travel first class by train, we have our own room and can pretty much wake up and go to sleep whenever we want. The aisles on the train are nice and wide, and I'm not falling over other passengers or disturbing anyone while walking up and down the train. When we travel by train, I don't have to go through those embarrassing security checks like they have on the airlines where I have to empty all my pockets, take off my watch, wedding ring, and necklace, take out my billfold, remove my belt, take off my suspenders, and hold my arms up in the air like a bird in flight while security personnel wand my entire body. I rarely feel like I live in "the land of the free and home of the brave" while my pants are falling down around my ankles.

Once, while in this position, I started making airplane noises and flapping my arms like a bird, but this seemed to irritate them. I've also learned that you should never say the word *bomb* around any airport security personnel. Even if the last movie you saw bombed, don't even think of mentioning anything about it when you are strolling about the airport with friends or family.

Anyway, with these last few paragraphs, I hope I've fully explained what happened to Homer without the advantages of having the railroad going through their town. Homer doesn't even have a bus depot in town, although you can still get there by car, truck, SUV, taxi, horseback, donkey, burro, pack mule, walking, hiking, or hitchhiking. I suppose you could crawl on your belly, like a Texas Rattlesnake, but that seems to be such a bother.

M

Dictionary

MAIN-YEW—Nothing to do with any main street.
    Main-yew means "menu."
    As in: Cay-yun aah hav uh main-yew?
        "Can I have a menu?"

MARE—Some in government are more like mules and donkeys.
    Mare means "mayor."
    As in: Awed lock yah ta mate are onnor-bull mare.
    Although it makes more sense the Texan way, it translates to:
        "I'd like you to meet our honorable mayor."

MATE—Could this be a peer on a ship?
    Mate means "meet."
    As in: Alm playzed tu mate chew (and perhaps they will be).
        "I'm pleased to meet you."

MAUDIE—There are also some ladies with this name.
    Maudie means "mighty."
    As in: E-yuts maudie naws tu mate cha.
        "It's mighty nice to meet you."

MAW-CROW—Be sure to hear this word in proper context.
    Maw-crow means "micro."
    As in: Duh guv-mant wonts may tew maw-crow-mange muh rainch.
        "The government wants me to micromanage my ranch."

MAW-NIN—After the night, there's dawn and then . . .
    Maw-nin means "morning."
    As in: Guh maw-nin, hiya dune?
        "Good morning, how are you doing?"

MAY—A month of the year, a girls name, a request?
May means "me."
As in: Shay luvs may, shay luvs may not.
"She loves me, she loves me not."
MAY-ELK—There are lots of deer in Texas, but the elk have all gone.
May-elk means "milk."
As in: Awl hay-uv sum may-elk.
"I'll have some milk."
MAY-RE—This can be a feeling or a greeting.
May-re means "merry."
As in: Y'all hava May-re Cray-us-mus!
"You all have a Merry Christmas!"
MAY-YELL—Could this be something to relieve the tension?
May-yell means "mail."
As in: E-yuts tom fur tha may-yell.
"It's time for the mail."
MAY-YUN—Little boys will grow up to be one of these.
May-yun means "man."
As in: Awl bay maudie prowed tew bay yore bay-ust may-yun.
"I'll be mighty proud to be your best man."
MEANYEW—A triple combo, three words in one.
Meanyew means "me and you."
As in: Hunny, is jes meanyew.
"Honey, it's just me and you."
MEE-DUL—Well, you certainly wouldn't want to be off center.
Mee-dul means "middle."
As in: Nought tewda rot, nor tewda lay-uft, bot rot inna mee-dul
"Not to the right, nor to the left, but right in the middle."
MIBBIE—Not yes or no or could be.

Mibbie means "maybe."

As in: Whale, awl chay-uk ayun aif way have tom, thay-un mibbe.

"Well, I'll check and if we have time, then maybe."

MINE—It's not yours, it's not theirs, it's not ours.

Mine means "mind."

As in: Uh mine e-yus uh tar-bull thang tuh wase.

"A mind is a terrible thing to waste."

MINT—The really classy places leave these under your pillow.

Mint means "minute."

As in: Holger hosses, awl bay thare inna mint.

"Hold your horses, I'll be there in a minute.

MON—Just a little French if you go to Paris, Texas, mon sheree.

Mon means "mine."

As in: Whale, wan ware marred, whuts mon e-yus yores.

"Well, when we're married, what's mine is yours."

Mamaw

My father-in-law is a tall, lanky gentleman with an easy smile and a soft laugh. He could easily play the part of an Indian chief in any Western movie or TV show. Ansel is about 90 percent Cherokee Indian, a very quiet distinguished gentleman and very family oriented. His favorite alcoholic beverage is Scotch, and each Christmas I'll get him a bottle of the most expensive Scotch available. He very rarely drinks, so the Scotch will last him all year. His favorite movie star and singer is Cher, and he thinks she is the sexiest woman who ever came down the pike, other than his lovely wife, Loretta.

I suppose it really is true that "opposites attract," for as quiet and subdued as he is, his wife is the complete opposite. Everyone calls her Mamaw. She is around five feet tall, slender, and a constant bundle of energy and chatter. Rarely will she sit still for more than a few moments, and she is absolutely the best cook in Texas. She taught my bride many of her cooking secrets, and I am a very fortunate man indeed. Whenever I'm around Mamaw, she always seems to be cooking.

I always look forward to being invited to Mamaw's house, because I know that she will grant any food request that I might ask. I married my sweetheart at a fairly young age, and I still possessed a rather large appetite, much to Mamaw's great delight. She would beam when I asked for seconds and almost jump for joy when I requested thirds. She seemed a bit disappointed when she had finally filled me up but would give me a large smile as she offered dessert. I always saved a little room for some of Mamaw's apple or pecan pie.

All of Mamaw's four children were married, and I was her newest son-in-law. After a few visits to Mamaw's, she decided she would make both apple and pecan pies whenever we were invited over. My ladylove and I arrived early one day, and I wandered into the kitchen while my sweet darling was chatting with her dad. The food in the kitchen was in various stages of preparation, and Mamaw said she had already prepared all my favorites, except for the pecan pie.

I don't know about y'all, but I must have had a rather sheltered life, because I had never seen a pecan pie being prepared before that day. I was always intrigued whenever I saw a completed pecan pie, because the pecans looked like they had been lovingly placed just so, on top of the pie, with no empty spaces at all. Mamaw had the pie pan with the graham cracker crust and the pie filling on top of the stove, about three or four feet away from where she was shelling the pecans. After she had shelled all the pecans, I fully expected her to gently place each one of the pecans in its assigned space on top of the filling.

I was completely shocked as she began tossing several of the pecans over to the pie pan from this range. She laughed hysterically as I explained to her how I thought a pecan pie was prepared.

One summer, my sweetheart and I were invited by my brother-in-law and his wife to watch their ranch for a week while they attended a rodeo up in Wyoming. I asked Mamaw if she would care to join us, and she quickly accepted. This 5,000-acre farm and ranch was located about ten miles north of Dilly, Texas. I was kinda hoping that I could explore and stomp around a bit while we were visiting the ranch. As we were approaching the main gate, we couldn't miss seeing a freshly killed diamondback rattlesnake hanging on the fence about four feet from the gatepost. A regular barbed wire fence is about four feet tall, and the snake's head was lying about a foot on the ground on one side, with the tail lying about a foot on the ground on the other side. I did some quick calculations: a ten-foot RATTLESNAKE!!!

After we reached the ranch house, I asked Sonny about the rattlesnake. Yep, he said he had shot it that morning as he was clearing some woodpiles around the main gate. I was kinda hoping that this wasn't the runt of the litter and its mom or dad wouldn't come a looking for the perpetrator of this crime against their offspring. I wondered if I would be able to reason with a rattlesnake: "Hey, I didn't do it! Sonny had the gun!" Plus, he had the only gun available on the ranch, and he took it with him when he left. I was left pretty much defenseless and never left the vicinity of the ranch house without a garden hoe.

A coiled rattlesnake can strike at a distance of two-thirds its total length. So an eight-footer would have a striking distance of around five feet. I had a five-foot-long garden hoe, with an additional arm reach of about a foot and a half, and figured that I'd be fairly safe from being bitten by any snake less than eight feet long. I think that's one of the main reasons they teach us math in school. I have absolutely no idea why they taught us plane geometry in high school, because I've rarely been able to prove anything. Anyway, I spent most of my time during this week hanging around the ranch house.

A short time after my brother-in-law left, Mamaw announced lunch. I ended up having three helpings of fried steak, mashed potatoes, gravy, hot buttered biscuits made from scratch, green beans, and apple and pecan pies. She was still beaming as she and my darling wife started clearing the table, and I slowly wandered out to the front porch to read the paper. After reading the newspaper for a while, Mamaw asked me what I'd like for dinner. Good grief, dinner! I had barely started to digest that huge lunch, and she was already thinking about dinner. Mamaw makes some of the greatest enchiladas I've ever tasted, and I requested some for dinner. She always referred to them as encha-lall-lees, and I would eat just about as many as she could prepare.

It seemed that hardly anytime at all had passed before Mamaw announced that the encha-lall-lees were ready. She neglected to mention that she had also prepared Spanish rice, pinto beans, and hot buttered tortillas. I can't remember how many enchiladas I consumed that evening, but I did make sure to have three helpings of them, plus one or two helpings of pecan pie with ice cream. Mamaw was absolutely thrilled to have this growing boy with such a fondness for her cooking in the family. Mamaw was actually a bonus that went along with having such a beautiful and loving bride.

As I was just finishing up from taking a shower the next morning, Mamaw hollered out that breakfast was ready. I quickly got dressed and joined her and my darling bride at the kitchen table. This breakfast was bigger and better than a famous restaurant's "Grand Slam" breakfast. Mamaw and my sweetheart had prepared eggs over easy, sunny side up, and scrambled, bacon, sausage, hash browns, grits, toast, gravy, buttered biscuits, strawberry preserves, peach preserves, pancakes, maple syrup, honey, coffee, and orange juice. Mamaw and my true love ate very dainty portions of this fabulous feast, so I accepted this challenge as an army of one to consume every last morsel of this enormous breakfast. Again, after having three helpings, I failed in my attempt to leave nothing uneaten. Mamaw just beamed, gave me a big hug, and went about cleaning up to prepare for the next meal.

After six days of Mamaw's cooking, my brother-in-law returned to the ranch with his family, and we prepared for the return trip back home to San Antonio. Although quite delicious, Mamaw's cooking had taken its toll on this growing boy, and I couldn't get my pants anywhere close to buttoning. I had gained twelve pounds in six days! As I was driving the car on the return trip home, my bride reached over and gently patted my protruding tummy and suggested several ways that I could get back into shape. I was so happy that we arrived in San Antonio after dark, because I didn't want to be seen in public wearing a pair of pants that wouldn't button. We dropped Mamaw off at her home and then proceeded to our own. I couldn't leave the house the next day, so my honeybunch went to the store and bought me five new pairs of thirty-six-inch-waist pants. I called them my fat pants and couldn't wait to start practicing my lover's suggestions for losing weight.

    Mamaw is probably the best cook I've ever known, and fortunately she passed on most of this great ability to my wonderful bride. Well, perhaps all but one, because my sugarplum still has trouble exactly matching Mamaw's pan-fried steak. I think they're the same, but my sweetheart continues to believe there are slight differences between the two. She mastered Mamaw's enchalall-lees and the first time the love of my life prepared them, she asked how many I wanted. I requested three. The next time she fixed enchiladas for dinner, I asked for six. Seems that I never could get enough of my lovely bride or her wonderful enchiladas. One day as she was preparing them for dinner, she asked, "How many enchiladas would you like?" and I responded, "How many will fit on the cookie sheet?"

    Mamaw wanted to see some of her relatives over in Houston, and we offered to drive her there and back over the weekend. When Mamaw wasn't cooking, she loved to chatter. I remember on the return trip from Houston, Mamaw had pretty much talked the both of us out. She was sitting in the back seat of the car and would start reading out loud any sign that had captured her attention. She would read the name and sometimes make a statement. We were passing a grocery store called Rice Food Store, and Mamaw's comment was: "Rice Food Store! Huh, they probably have the highest rice in town!"

    She also loved to read out loud any billboard or road sign along the highway. It was dark of night as we were driving back to San Antonio, and Mamaw would read the distance to the next town out loud to us. She would say things like Schulenburg, twenty-eight miles; Bastrop, forty-two miles. As we approached these various towns, she would again read aloud any particular sign that caught her eye and comment if she did or didn't like that particular town.

As we were traveling along the highway that night, she saw a road sign and stated, "Litter Barrel, one mile." After about ten minutes, Mamaw said: "You know, I never did see that town." I asked her, "What town was that, Mamaw?" She replied, "Litter Barrel." I always enjoy being around Mamaw, and I look forward to visiting her again. I probably have the most wonderful mother- and father-in-law anyone could ever hope for. My wonderful wife is a great delight, and her folks are an extra-special bonus.

Talkin' Texan

Texan - English
Mar-shul—Marshall

In the mid-1800s, this small East Texas town was continually being raided and ravaged by a mean, nasty, pesky, local outlaw, Gordon Pest, and his gang. The town folk were at their wits' end trying to figure out how they could stop Gordon from decimating their small town. After holding a town meeting, they decided there was only one man who could stop Gordon and his gang.

Marshal Clay Potts received an urgent telegram from the town folk begging him to come to their aid. The marshal responded quickly and arrived a few days later with his lovely wife, Cherri, and their ten kids. Like most kids, the Potts kids came in all sorts of different shapes and sizes. The town folk welcomed them warmly upon their arrival and cheered the Potts heartedly. Being such a large family, the Potts arrived in six covered wagons, four wagons for the family and two wagons full of Cherri's flowers, plants, and gardening supplies.

Well, it wasn't long before Gordon and his gang came into town to confront the marshal. They met at high noon on a bright summer day at the Bo-Kay Corral, and there was one heck of a shootout. The marshal defeated Gordon Pest and his gang that day and sent them a-running. The town folk were very happy that they had called upon the right man at the right time. They contemplated long and hard on how they could show their appreciation to the Potts family.

The town folk named the town after him and built a huge barn next to the Bo-Kay Corral to honor Marshal Clay Potts and his lovely wife, Cherri, and all the kids. Y'all can still visit there today and see where this mighty battle took place. Please be sure to sign the guest book and take a picture or two.

Joe Kent Roberts

Talkin' Texan

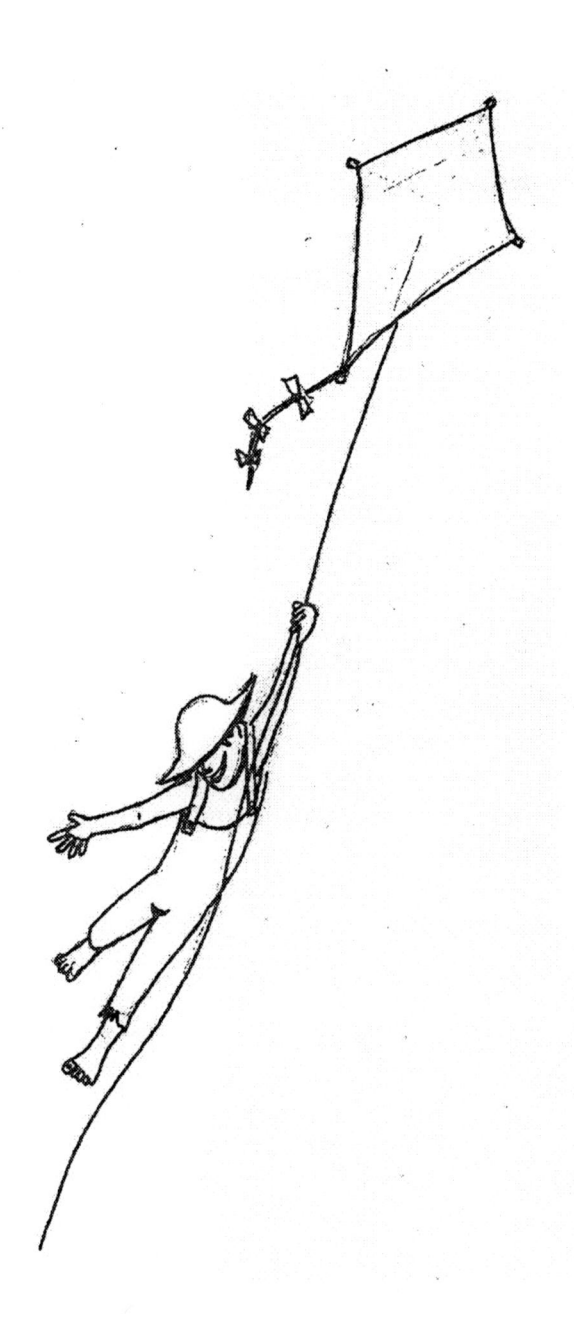

Texan – English
Med-lun—Midland

If you happen to be traveling on the interstate between Dallas and El Paso, you might want to stop over at Midland or its sister city, Odessa. If you have been traveling eastbound from El Paso, then you've been through some of the West Texas desert country—lots of cactus, scrub brush, and mesquite trees. There are several fine steakhouse restaurants in these two towns that are well known for cooking steaks over mesquite logs. Mesquite wood adds a unique flavor to steaks, and Texans export quite a bit of this wood to the rest of the country.

They also export quite a few tumbleweeds to other parts of the country to be used as decorations. Tumbleweeds can be colored, dyed, painted, and adorned with all kinds of things. Because of a shortage of spruce and fir trees in the area, some folks use tumbleweeds in place of traditional Christmas trees. Tumbleweeds make excellent Christmas trees because they never dry out or lose their needles. Some folks take their old tumbleweed Christmas tree and keep it in the garage or one of their outbuildings to reuse for the next Christmas season. Texans are very eager participants in the recycling programs that are currently sweeping the rest of the country and love to reuse things. (Note: Some of the more popular recycled items are used cars, pickups, and ex-spouses.)

Tumbleweeds are called tumbleweeds because they tumble along the ground while being blown by some mighty fierce West Texas winds. At times, there are very damaging sandstorms that will literally strip or sand the paint right off a car. My folks wouldn't let me go outside to play during a sandstorm, but once the winds subsided to the normal thirty or forty miles an hour, they would allow me to go outside and fly my kite. I loved flying a kite in Midland because I'd never have to run to get the kite up in the air. I'd just hold the kite out, let loose, and watch as up to ten rolls of kite string ripped off the reel while the kite soared nearly out of sight. I always wanted to race a sports car with my kite, because in about ten seconds the kite would be more than a quarter of a mile away.

After I had flown my kite for a while, sometimes my folks would call me in for dinner. My dinner was always cold, because it would take nearly an hour to rewind all ten rolls of kite string. I always lamented the fact that I wasn't a rich kid, because I could've just cut the string and let the kite fly off to California or some other strange country. I wanted to put my name and address on the kite and be the first kid to have a response to a kite, instead of the popular note in a bottle by way of the sea. I'm sure that if I were to check the *Guinness Book of World Records*, some rich kid from Midland probably holds the record for "First Pen-pal via Kite."

Along with the tumbleweeds comes blowing sand. This is the desert part of Texas, and there is sand everywhere—in your hair, your eyes, your clothes, and in your house. There was always sand inside our house, on the floor, on the furniture, and especially on the inside windowsills. It always seemed to be such a waste of sand to just dust it away. There was a lady in our neighborhood by the name of Sandy Soyall who felt the same way, and she would collect the sand from the windowsills in a glass jar, similar to the glass grease jar that Grandma always kept on her stove. Sandy would fill up her glass jar pretty quickly, then take food coloring, tint the sand, and create all types of elaborate designs in the sand.

Sandy showed her creations to some of the other ladies in town, and sand painting became a very popular pastime for these local women. Sand painting quickly caught on in the rest of the country, and most of the craft stores started selling sand-painting kits. Some of these ladies were very crafty, and their sand-painting designs were even better than the ones Sandy and the other ladies in Midland created. The craft shops sell their sand, but the sand in Midland is free, so the ladies in Midland are famous for being very thrifty, while the ladies in the other parts of the country are known for being very crafty.

I attended grade school in Midland, and the main reason they are called grade schools is most kids are not inclined to like school. They do try to sorta ease young children into school during first grade. They started us out with coloring pages and coloring books. We had to have a box of crayons with at least sixteen different colors of crayons; some kids had boxes of thirty-two, while still others had the giant box of sixty-four. I liked to color the sky all different shades of purple and orange, with rivers of red tinted with yellow. I also liked to add stuff to the pictures and characters. I was always in trouble for coloring outside the lines, and I didn't make very good grades in school. I didn't care much for cutting and pasting either, even though the glue tasted pretty good.

If I can, I'd like to digress for a moment, or is it regress? I don't know, because when the difference between the two was discussed, I think I was sick that day. Plus, my dictionary is way over on the other side of the room, and I don't want to lose my train of thought while I'm looking up a word. I'm hoping that my train has absolutely nothing in common with the Texas law concerning two trains meeting at the same time on the same track. Anyway, my first-grade teacher was Miss Steel, and she was very pretty.

Whenever we wanted to leave the room to go to the restroom or something, we would have to raise our hand and leave one or two fingers up, depending on our purpose for leaving. They never told us what holding up three or four fingers represented, but my children tell me that when they return from the restroom, they will slap hands for a "high five." I asked Miss Steel why they called it a restroom, since there was no place to rest—no couches, chairs, or comic books. I also asked her why some kids referred to it as the bathroom, since we couldn't take a bath in there or anything. Apparently, she really did take note of my questions, because I've noticed that when I visit my kids at school, these rooms are now named either "Boys" or "Girls." I suppose Miss Steel was correct when she said, "Don't be afraid to ask a stupid question." Gee, who would have thought that a first grader could have such an impact on such major changes?

While I was in grade school, I had a girlfriend who was a Girl Scout, and she always seemed to have lots of Girl Scout cookies. When I was asked to join the Boy Scouts, I was thrilled because I thought they would have something equally as good, possibly Boy Scout candy, or something along those lines. Geez, they didn't even have Boy Scout bratwurst or beef jerky or comic books or anything. All we did was learn about wild animals and tie all types of knots and stuff. I quickly became disenchanted, disillusioned, and retired at a very early age from the Boy Scouts. Being an Indian Scout had to be a lot more fun! However, my grandson is in the Eagle Scouts and loves it. They must have added a lot more fun stuff since I was a kid, and I guess it is a good idea to ask stupid questions, although I still haven't seen any Boy Scout candy or Boy Scout bratwurst around.

Months of the Year
Jan-yary—January
 Being the first month of the year, they named this month after both a boy and a girl—that way, both sexes can start the year off in parity. Way up in the northern states, there's probably snow on the ground; down here in Texas, it's nice and warm and the trees are starting to bloom.
Feb-yary—February
 I've often wondered who named all these months of the year and why they spelled them so oddly. I think it was some English teacher, so she could have a few trick words for her spelling bees. This is a fun month because it has Valentine's Day in it, and the flowers are in bloom. Well, maybe not in your neck of the woods, but the flowers are in bloom down here in Texas. However, I'm pretty sure that Valentine's Day is celebrated in other parts of America.
Marsh—March
 I never cared for this month too much; it always made me feel obligated. When I was in the military, we always had to march—forward march, to the rear march, sideways march. I prefer the Texan marsh, which is actually our rainy season. When we first got married, my bride went out and bought a loveseat instead of a couch. I rather enjoyed it back then, but later on it put way too much pressure on me. It's very difficult to stretch out and take a nap on a loveseat; I prefer napping on a couch.
A-prul—April
 I think the English teacher named this month after herself. She also came up with the saying, "April Showers, bring May flowers." Sometimes, Easter falls in April and at other times Easter falls in May. Easter always moved around quite a bit and I never knew when it was. Thankfully, the Easter Bunny always knew when Easter occurred, so I always received an Easter basket. Now that I no longer believe in the Easter Bunny, my wife lets me know

when Easter will occur. Therefore, I always have lots of treats for our children. Always marry a woman who can keep track of Easter, because she will be really smart.

Mae—May

This particular month was named after the English teacher's mom. It's probably better to have a month named after you than a school, street, or town. Some of those things will come and go, but a month pretty much lasts for all time. Which reminds me of when my bride was in her eighth month of pregnancy with little Gus, and I was up all hours of the night trying to satisfy her unusual food cravings. She had me running all over town getting stuff for her. I still don't understand her craving for peanut butter and pickles, because Gus won't eat this combination at all. Sometimes Easter would fall in May on the old Grecian or Egyptian calendar, but not on an Italian colander. Somehow, there's never been an American calendar and the Texan calendar is no longer observed because of the English-only amendment. If you were fortunate enough to marry a smart woman who can tell the difference between a Roman calendar and an Italian colander, then your kids won't be disappointed about the Easter Bunny forgetting about them.

Jew-une—June

The English teacher's mom had a sister. This is also the month that the teachers decided to let the kids out for summer vacation. Before the modern convenience of air conditioning, June, July, and August would get mighty hot in those old schoolhouses, so they would let the kids stay home during these hot summer months. I've noticed that since the schools now have air conditioning, the kids have to stay in school much longer, and summer vacations are shorter. They also have something called summer school, which most kids do not like to attend.

Jew-lie—July
One of my favorite riddles goes something like this: "If H-u-l-y is Hulie and M-u-l-y is Mulie, then what's J-u-l-y." Invariably, their answer is Julie and you have to say, "Nope, it's July." Actually, I think the English teacher named this month also, because English always has these tricky sorts of laws. Like "e" after "i" unless it's followed by the letter "p" or, in this particular case, "y" instead of "ie" if it's named after your sister.

Aw-gus—August
Miss April Showers, the English teacher, named this month after her boyfriend, Ben Augustber. They later got married; I think it was one of those April-August types of romances. They later changed their name to August because so many folks had trouble trying to pronounce Augustber. It's a good thing they changed it to August because Augustber would probably have been a much colder month. Ben decided that he didn't want to totally lose the last three letters to his family name, so he just used the "ber" on the last four months of the year.

Sap-tam-bur—September
Ben was also a well-known lumberjack in these parts of the world, and as the tree was falling, he would holler out "Timber!" September is not only the ninth month of the year, it's also the last month of most pregnancies. My bride always looked forward to the last month of carrying our newest child, because it was pretty much all over but the screaming. With six kids and twins on the way, she must love me an awful lot to attempt to give me my own baseball team. Plus, there's all the yelling and hollering in the delivery room. Sometimes she has to ask me to be quiet.

Ok-toe-bur—October
Ben had a brother named Octo, and Octo loved to bring in the fall season with lots of beer, bratwurst, songs, singing, and dancing. They were trying to come up with a name for this festival and decided on Octoberfest. Octo enjoyed this immensely, because

it was a lot more fun with a bunch of people, rather than dancing around by himself with a beer in one hand and a bratwurst in the other. I guess it just goes to show that good things can happen when lumberjacks fall in love with English teachers.

Noe-vam-bur—November

This is another oddly spelled month of the year. I like it because this is the month I get to open birthday presents. This is also the month we celebrate Thanksgiving. Thanksgiving is similar to Easter in that both holidays move around the calendar quite a bit. The reason they keep moving Thanksgiving around from year to year is so we can sneak up on the turkey. Turkeys and pigs are probably the smartest animals in the barnyard, and they really try to avoid this holiday. Try singing a "Happy Thanksgiving" song around a live turkey or pig and just see what happens. Then again, it could be the singer and not the song. I've never been invited to sing in any choir; once, I was even asked to leave. That's okay, because my bride lets me sing in the shower as long as I want.

Dae-sam-bur—December

The English teacher and her husband must have really loved kids, because they gave them several weeks off to enjoy Christmas. It's nice that they also kept Santa, the elves, Rudolph, and all the other reindeer up at the North Pole, along with all the cold weather and the snow. Santa and the elves have no cable TV at the North Pole because it's so bitter cold up there that the cables freeze. Plus, all they can ever get on their TV is snow. So they just drink a lot of hot chocolate and eat a lot of freshly baked cookies to stay warm. Mrs. Claus also bakes them lots of pecan pies because Santa brings her bags full of Texas pecans on his way back from Texas each Christmas.

Joe Kent Roberts

N

Dictionary

NACK-LUS—Not many years ago, only women wore these.
    Nack-lus means "necklace."
    As in: Shay war uh purdy parl nack-lus.
        "She wore a pretty pearl necklace."

NADE—Some have many of these, and others just a few.
    Nade means "need."
    As in: Aah nade un-nother drank.
        "I need another drink."

NAF-FEW—Just one of the many benefits of having a married sister or brother.
    Naf-few means "nephew."
    As in: He-yahs muh naf-few, Billy Bob.
        "Here's my nephew, Billy Bob."

NAG-LA-JAY—Some ladies wear these, so they won't become one; some of the most fun ones wear these even though they can't spell it.
    Nag-la-jay means "negligee."
    As in: Aah bot muh waf sum nag-la-jay fur har barth-dae.
        "I bought my wife some negligee for her birthday."

NAHM-LEE—If variety is the spice of life, then why do we have this word?
    Nahm-lee means "normally."
    As in: Nahm-lee, way wont hay-uv uh watt Cray-us-mus roun cheer.
        "Normally, we don't have a white Christmas around here."

NAH-MUL—We're all supposed to act this way when we are in the company of others.
    Nah-mul means "normal."

As in: Ats jes nah-mul.
"That's just normal."

NARA—Some of them are wide and broad, others are not.
Nara means "narrow."
As in: Ats uh rail nara strait.
"That's a real narrow street."

NARTH—Some of us prefer to be warm and cozy, instead of being from here.
Narth means "north."
As in: Awl bay warkin up narth e-yun Laskuh.
"I'll be working up north in Alaska."

NARVE—At times, this is made of steel; at other times, Jell-O.
Narve means "nerve."
As in: Hays rally goh sum narve.
"He's really got some nerve."
This can be a positive or negative statement, depending on the circumstances.

NAX—Sometimes, number machines can come in handy.
Nax means "next."
As in: Yore nax.
"You're next."

NAY-UCK—Seems that at times we have our head attached to it, and at other times we don't.
Nay-uck means "neck."
As in: Naw, aah jes keister ona nay-uck.
"No, I just kissed her on the neck."

NAY-UST—Sometimes you can look up in the trees and see one of these, and you can find them in most unusual places.
Nay-ust means "nest."
As in: Alm gone hom tuh muh lave nay-ust.
"I'm going home to my love nest."

NAY-UT—When you go fishing, you will need one of these.
Nay-ut means "net."

Talkin' Texan

    As in: Quack, Wilbur, whares duh nay-ut???
        "Quick, Wilbur, where's the net?"
NO-EASE—Yeah well, pretty much until after we retire, then perhaps we can sit back and not let things bother us. No-ease means "noise."
    As in: Y'all kay-uds stup awla no-ease.
        "You kids stop all the noise."
NOUGHT—Neither zero, nor below zero, nor bright. Nought means "night."
    As in: Wan somer nought way fail e-yun luv.
        "One summer night we fell in love."

Texan—English

Naga-dough-jez—Nacogdoches
Situated on a major highway about a hundred miles north of Beaumont, you will find the pretty little college town of Nacogdoches. The college campus is actually quite nice, because Nacogdoches is located in a beautiful forested valley in the eastern part of the state. One of the entrance requirements for applicants into Nacogdoches College is to be able to spell Nacogdoches. This is a very small college, and attendance will only increase when the entrance requirements are reduced.

The town of Nacogdoches was actually the first town established in Texas. The founding fathers and mothers figured that if most folks couldn't spell the name, it would help keep the riffraff out. It must have worked because there are some really smart people in town, and the majority of the state's spelling bee champions hail from here. Hail is another four-letter word that has about three different meanings and several different spellings. Sometimes, hail falling out of the sky is very harmful to crops, animals, and people. Then there is another spelling for hail, and most folks prefer not to go there. I think that's why they came up with the popular phrase, "Don't go there."

Spaniards discovered the town of Nacogdoches in the mid-1700s. Another thing they discovered were lots and lots of Indians. This tribe of Indians called themselves the Nacogdocheetos and called the Spaniards "Kemo sabe," which means "smells like wet chicken." The Nacogdocheetos Indians were probably the most intelligent and industrious Indian tribes in America.

The Indians were farmers, ranchers, manufacturers, and merchants. They grew barley, beans, hops, maize (which we call corn), oats, potatoes, squash, watermelons, and zucchini. The Indians showed the Spaniards how to grow these crops; the Spaniards showed the Indians how to make beer and sour mash whiskey. The Indians returned the favor by introducing the Spaniards to tobacco and peyote cactus.

One summer afternoon in the mid-1700s, the Spaniards held a party in honor of the Indians. After a feast of smoked buffalo, deer, elk, beans, corn on the cob, muffins, and honey, the Spaniards offered them some booze. Later on, the Spaniards asked the Indians, "Hey, would you like us to make you a reservation?" The Indians were thrilled because no one had ever offered to make reservations for them before. The Indians are still there today and have learned never to trust anyone who smells like a wet chicken. Even after all these years, the memory of the results of that day is very disturbing to the offspring of these Indians. So if you happen to have an Indian friend and want to describe the taste of an unfamiliar food to him, please don't say "It tastes just like chicken."

The Nacogdocheetos Indians were also goat ranchers, and their Indian monks made some of the finest goat cheeses in the land. The Indians were famous for blending maize and cheddar cheese into a product they called "cheetos." The monks would cook the cheetos down at the Indian Hot Springs, so called because they were the Indians who owned the "hot springs." The Indians also found out they could slice potatoes and toss them into the hot springs to make something called potato chips.

The Indians had a teepee down near the hot springs where they sold these items. The Spaniards discovered that these were some great things to snack on and went especially well with soft drinks or beer. About the only thing the Spaniards didn't like about the cheetos was the orange residue it would leave on their hands. The men would always have this orange powder all over their clothes and stuff. Their wives would get upset with them, because they would have to go down to the creek and beat these clothes with rocks just to get the orange out.

The Spaniards were dismayed by all the extra work they were causing for their wives and resolved to save them time from the many trips to the creek. They decided that whenever they had cheetos and beer, they would not wear their fine clothing. Therefore, they would strip down to their T-shirts whenever they consumed them. This Spanish tradition is still carried on today in many of our modern households. With all of the advances of modern science and technology, it's nice to see that some things just don't change.

○○

Texan - English
Nu Bra-fuls—New Braunfels

The once small, cozy town of New Braunfels is located on Interstate 35, less than forty miles north of San Antonio. The town is famous for the crystal-clear springs of Landa Park and the beautiful Guadalupe River. There are hundreds of these springs in and around Landa Park. One of the most dramatic springs can be seen gushing out of the side of a mountain at one end of the park. Most of the other springs can only be seen while you are taking a leisurely journey by paddleboat out on Landa Lake.

When I attended New Braunfels High School, the population was only about 20,000. The old vine-covered high school was located right behind a great carhop restaurant. The old high school is now a public school warehouse, and the restaurant is now a used car dealership. The high school had a huge building out back that was a great student hangout. There was a large stone fireplace on the east wall surrounded by all sorts of couches and plush chairs. We had a pool table, ping pong table, lots of soft drinks, and popcorn. I haven't seen the new high school built sometime in the '80s or '90s, but I would hope it's as nice for the kids as the old one was for us.

Right before my senior year, the town built a new high school and called it Canyon High. The high school was nowhere near a canyon, so I have no idea why they gave it this name. Then again, I suppose there is a certain amount of artistic freedom when folks are naming things. I live on a street called Jackrabbit Run, and there hasn't been a jackrabbit anywhere near here in a hundred years—although Jack, one of my neighbors, occasionally runs out to the edge of the street in his underwear to retrieve the newspaper, and he's pretty quick as he goes running back to the house. It would be much more fun living on a street named Jillrabbit Run, but there is probably some kind of a street-naming law against that.

Somehow, back when I was in Canyon High School, I ended up on the annual staff and also on the student committee involved in the naming of the school mascot. I suggested we call ourselves the Canyon Cougars, and I was thrilled when it was accepted. Flushed and dazed with victory, I also had a suggestion for the school colors. I suggested red and white. "Why red and white." they responded? "Red for our courage and white for our purity," I replied. I haven't checked lately, but I do hope the high school is still called the Canyon Cougars and the school colors have remained unchanged. They did balk at my suggestion that we have a live cougar on the sidelines during all sporting events and school functions.

During the first year of Canyon High, I was one of only twenty-three seniors. We knew we were seniors, but most of the other students didn't, because we were not to receive our senior rings until about a month before school was out during our senior year. The majority of the other students would comment, "I didn't know you were a senior!" At this time, I was a little disappointed that the other students hadn't realized I was a senior. After all, didn't I possess the wisdom and demeanor of a senior? Nowadays, I can walk into any retail store and I'm immediately recognized as a senior and offered a discount. As disappointed as I was not to be recognized as a senior in high school, my greatest disappointment is that the hair I never grew on my chest is now growing out of my ears.

New Braunfels was a farming and ranching community, and I remember the day we were measured for our rings. The fellow had one of these ring finger measuring devices, and, as he took each student's ring size, he would holler out the name of the individual with their exact ring size to his assistant. I had a size 8½; most of the girls had size 9 or 10; all of the guys had size 11, 12, and 13. For just a brief period of time, I considered taking up the piano. However, I didn't much care for bright lights, vast crowds, and tuxedos, so I joined the Air Force after graduation.

Fortunately, because of my height, the coach always wanted me to try out for the only sport we had at that time: basketball. I have a very fond dislike for basketball. I always enjoyed a game of HORSE, but I couldn't dribble at all. However, I was very adept at drooling over our five gorgeous cheerleaders who accompanied us to all our out-of-town games. On every fifteen-man basketball team, I was always sixteenth. I have no idea why I was allowed to ride on the team bus to each and every game. I always sat in the back of the bus with the cheerleaders. It was always a treat to be sitting and chatting with the girls on the return trip after the game. While the guys were all sweaty and smelly, the girls seemed to be energized. They were all soft, curvy, talkative, and smelled way better than the guys.

There is just something about Texas women that makes me all weak in the knees. I was fortunate enough to have dated a few of the cheerleaders, and at times I wonder how things are going for them. Our senior class was so small that I was never aware of us having any senior class reunions. I never cared much for family reunions as I got older because I knew my relatives much better by then. However, I think a senior reunion would be great fun; perhaps we could hold it in a Volkswagen.

Each fall, New Braunfels holds an Octoberfest for all the folks in and around town. Octoberfest is a very fine German tradition, brought over from the old country. They call it Octoberfest because they have it in October and it's very festive. The Germans have lost a few world wars, but they really know how to party. Octoberfest lasts for over a week, with lots of beer, bratwurst, polka music, and dancing. Octoberfest is a very exhausting festival, and I think that's one of the reasons Germany lost the last war. Hitler decided that the German people needed a big morale boost towards the end of 1944. He halted production of all the weapons-making factories and had the entire population of Germany working on the production of beer, bratwurst, and a new polka song for the occasion.

The scheme did have the desired results and Octoberfest was a huge success throughout the country. However, way too many German women became pregnant during this time, and the production of war machinery was drastically reduced. Plus, many of the German officers and soldiers could not give their full attention to their duties. They were wondering how their wives and sweethearts were doing back home. Hitler's great morale booster came to be known as the Blunderfest Octoberfest Blitz. Some folks just refer to it today as Bob. Quite a few German families ended up naming their sons Bob to mark the occasion.

If you enjoy some great bratwurst and happen to be heading out of New Braunfels towards Seguin, then over on the right side of the highway you'll notice a local establishment proclaiming "Our wurst is the best." I missed stopping there the last time through town, so if you happen to stop and visit, I'll be wishing you the best as you enjoy your wurst.

O

Dictionary

OB-SARVE—Sometimes we can learn a lot just by watching. Thanks, Yogi.
    Ob-sarve means "observe."
    As in: Y'all ob-sarve howtuh prop-ly slang thay-us cay-ow chay-up.
        "Please observe how to properly sling this cow chip."

ODE—Sometimes it refers to money, at other times to age.
    Ode means "old."
    As in: Shays maudie ode.
        "She's mighty old."

O-KAYS-YUN—At times, these are a surprise because they can occur most anytime.
    O-kays-yun means "occasion."
    As in: Y'all maught fawn ay-un o-kays-yun tew slang uh cay-ow chay-up bay-uck hoam.
        "You folks might find an occasion to sling a cow chip back home."

OP-SET—Most of us have a TV set, but how many of us have an op set?
    Op-set means "opposite."
    As in: Aahmona op-set sod.
        "I'm on the opposite side."

OR-GUN—Sometimes sounds like "Ore gun."
    Or-gun means "Oregon."
    As in: Way waynt tuh Or-gun.
        "We went to Oregon."

OR-NARY—Nary a one, or are they?

Or-nary means "ordinary."
As in: Sout uh duh or-nary.
 "It's out of the ordinary."
ORN-REE—Some are, some aren't.
Orn-ree means "ornery."
As in: Hays shore orn-ree.
 "He sure is ornery."

Texan—English

Oh-des-uh—Odessa

Odessa is located less than twenty miles from Midland. I've never been there personally, because I was just ten years old when I went to school in Midland. My folks allowed me to ride my bike to school, but I wasn't allowed to ride my bike anywhere outside of town and certainly not on the highway over to Odessa. Therefore, I had to rely on Internet search engines and the encyclopedia to be able to research this article about Odessa.

Odessa is very much different from what I could have possibly imagined. The town is famous for manufacturing huge amounts of petroleum products, airplanes, automobiles, and motion picture equipment. Odessa is also a popular destination because it has a health resort and a black sea. I suppose the sea is black because of all the huge amounts of oil in the area, and swimming in huge amounts of oil must be very healthy.

The Tartars conquered Odessa in the 1200s, and they were well known for making a special sauce for use on seafood. This sauce quite possibly was developed because the seafood that came out of this black sea had a somewhat oily taste and the sauce would make the seafood a bit tastier. The Ottomans ruled Odessa in the 1500s. The Ottomans were famous for bringing us those fancy little footstools that go in front of our chairs. Ottomans are still quite popular; however, nowadays most folks prefer recliners.

No one knows what the original name of the town was because the American Indians didn't keep any written records, but a bunch of Russians got together in 1795 and named the town Odessa. While I was in school in Texas, none of my Texas history books ever mentioned these Russians, so they must have come over to this part of Texas by way of the Alaskan land bridge or something. Anyway, tradition has it that Odessa was a very beautiful Indian maiden with long blonde hair and blue eyes. This was very unusual because most Indian maidens around this time were brunettes. Then again, every so often there is a white buffalo in Indian legend, so a blonde Indian maiden is pretty easy to believe.

    Another fascinating fact I discovered about Odessa is that it's very popular for supplying mail-order brides to the rest of America. Most of these brides speak only Russian, and very few of them speak English or Texan. Apparently, these Russian families won't allow their daughters to date any of the local boys around this part of the state, so they just ship them off to other parts of America.

    There is a saying in Texas that if you don't like the weather, just wait thirty minutes or travel twenty miles down the highway. This is a reality in Midland and Odessa because the difference in climate and temperature between these two towns is absolutely amazing. I checked with one of the weather channels the other day and Midland had a high temperature of 93 degrees, while Odessa was a balmy 73 degrees with gentle sea breezes. That oily black sea must really be something. I just wish that my folks could have stayed in Midland until I got my driver's license. Although I don't speak Russian, I sure would have liked to have visited that sea and perhaps tried one of their Tartar sauces.

Oo

Texan – English
R-unge—Orange

Orange is just about as far southeast as you can possibly be in Texas without being in another state. If you are in Orange, West Orange, or Orangefield, you are also in Orange County. Don't look for any orange trees here, because there ain't any. Which may make some folks wonder why they named it Orange. Why didn't they call it Red, Green, Yellow, or Chartreuse?

There are actually two different theories as to how this town received its name. One is that there was a cattle rancher who had an unusual way of naming all the different ranges on his vast acreage. Moe Barnfuls would keep track of all his different ranges by naming them after the alphabet. So there was the A range, B range, C range, and so on. Then one day a fellow approached Moe about purchasing his O range and building a nice little town where he could raise his family. Moe agreed to sell the gentleman this parcel of land as long as the name remained the same. Therefore, the town came to be called O Range.

The other theory is that a fellow by the name of Sunny Daze was watching a magnificent orange sunset one day and decided to call the place where he was standing Orange. It's probably a good thing it wasn't one of those multicolored sunsets that day or the town could have been called Red, Yellow, Blue, and Orange, or possibly just Sunset, Texas.

The area between the towns of Beaumont, Orange, and Port Arthur is called the "Golden Triangle." Just like Orange not having any orange trees, there is no gold in the Golden Triangle, unless you happen to visit a jewelry store or something. No one knows why they call it the Golden Triangle and no one dares ask anyone. I think it's kinda like being in Orange and asking where all the orange trees are located. When folks live here, they actually do have a "Home on the O Range."

Joe Kent Roberts

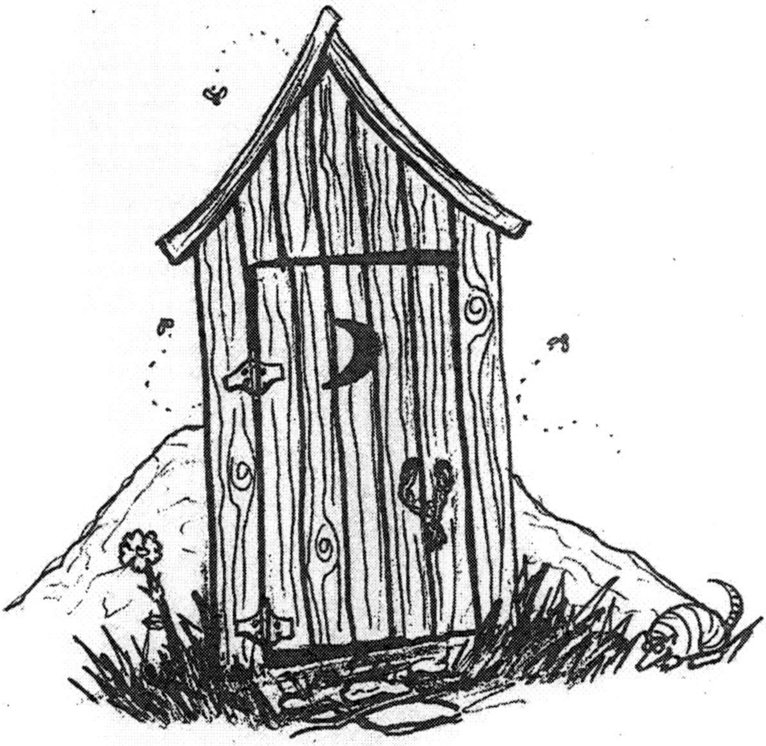

The Outhouse

It's always tickles me just a bit when someone proclaims, "I was born in the wrong place at the wrong time; I'd be more comfortable living in the 1800s or 1900s." While some may be nostalgic and yearn for things of the past, not only do I remember the Alamo, I also remember the outhouse; Especially on those cold winter mornings.

Normally, there was a well-worn path leading from the back door of the main house to a tiny little wooden structure called the outhouse. Nearly everyone I knew had an outhouse, unless they had the luxury of having their house surrounded by a bunch of trees and bushes. Outhouses were most useful before the days of indoor plumbing, air fresheners, ceiling fans, matches, and potpourri.

Grandpa's outhouse was situated in the far corner of the backyard, past the rain-barrels and his old Chevy pickup truck. Grandpa's outhouse was a two-holer, while most folks only had a one-holer, but some of the rich folks even had three-holers. No waiting! Well, not unless you were having a family reunion or something. With a three-holer, I suppose they could even get together and discuss the events of the day. Nowadays, we have houses with two and a half baths with not nearly as much togetherness. Indoor plumbing has pretty much eliminated the many "outhouse contests" that families enjoyed in the 1800 and 1900s: the biggest this, the loudest that, and so on and so forth.

Potty training was quite different with the ol' outhouse than it is today. Therefore, another advantage of the two-holer is revealed. Grandpa and Grandma taught me the proper outhouse etiquette when I was a young child, and my aunt helped me refine this art when I was about six years old.

As a very young child, I can remember being led to the outhouse for the proper instruction on how to use this necessary outdoor facility. Fortunately, Grandpa had installed some well-positioned handrails so the younger children like myself would not fall in. Nowadays, there are all types of gadgets on the market for small children so they can eliminate this fear of falling.

The outhouse never did smell too nice, even with using lye, matches, potpourri, and all kinds of different things to get rid of its pungent aroma. One of my few necessary duties around the house today is taking out the trash. This is a pretty simple task compared to Grandpa's duties of also having to move and clean out the outhouse. Nope, I was born in just the right time. I've been able to observe the waning use of the outhouse and applaud the modern convenience of indoor plumbing.

Rarely did we run out of paper in the ol' outhouse. If we did happen to run out of the handy stuff that came on rolls, we always had an old newspaper, sometimes called yesterday's news, or last year's Sears and Roebuck catalog.

The fellow who carved the first half-moon on his outhouse door did not realize he was starting a whole new trend in outhouse decorations. Decorator outhouses became quite popular, and lots of folks spent a great deal of time and effort in making sure that their outhouse was one of the best-looking in the neighborhood.

Folks would attempt almost anything to make sure they had the most up-to-date outhouse in the county. Some of the most innovative outhouses were painted with seasonal colors. Outhouses were painted with pastels during the springtime, and deep-tone colors for fall and winter. Some folks had built-in fireplaces, while others added skylights for a nice view of the moon and stars during their nighttime visits to these necessary facilities.

Today, finding these old decorator outhouses has become very popular for weekend outings for some of the city folks. They'll travel all over the countryside seeking out these old abandoned decorative outhouses to purchase for their backyards back home. Years ago, these decorator outhouses could be purchased quite cheaply from many of the local farmers and ranchers. It didn't take too long for the farmers and ranchers to catch on, and these antique decorator outhouses are very expensive nowadays.

If you happen to be in the market for a genuine antique decorator outhouse during your visit to Texas, you might want to be a little wary of the many cheap imported reproductions that are on the market today. These reproductions are available from Mexico, China, and Taiwan. Fortunately, all of these imports are labeled, so if you want to make sure that you're buying an original decorator outhouse just take a peek under the old outhouse hole to make sure there's not a "Made in China" label under there.

During your search, if there are no indoor plumbing facilities nearby and you are in need of actually having to use an ol' outhouse for a number two, I do hope that you remembered to bring in the paper and you'll enjoy a nice breeze on your cheeks while you catch up on the news.

P

Dictionary

PAINTS—Well, on certain women, these do look like they are painted on.
    Paints means "pants."
    As in: Aah tar muh paints.
    "I tore my pants."
PANNY-HOSE—Not at all related to a garden hose
    Panny hose means "panty hose."
    As in: Aah gotta run emma panny-hose.
    "I've got a run in my pantyhose."
PARSE—When the preacher says "for better or worse," this is one of the many "for worse" parts of the wedding vow.
    Parse means "purse."
    As in: Hunny, hole muh parse fur a mint.
    "Honey, hold my purse for a minute."
PAY-US—Sounds like it, but it ain't.
    Pay-us means "pass."
    As in: Y'all kaint pay-us onna rot.
    "You can't pass on the right."
PEAR-SHOOT—No, they don't shoot them off of trees.
    Pear shoot means "parachute."
    As in: Aah gotta pay-yuck muh pear-shoot.
    I've got to pack my parachute."
PLANE—Don't bother looking up into the sky for this.
    Plane means "playing."
    As in: Aahs jus plane.
    "I was just playing."
PLAYS—Using this word shows very good manners.
    Plays means "please."
    As in: May aah haff sa moor, plays?

"May I have some more, please?"
PO-LEASE—This has nothing to do with land or apartments.
    Po-lease means "police."
    As in: Aah gotta getta po-lease.
        "I've got to get the police."
PROLLY—Just another Texan timesaver.
    Prolly means "probably."
    As in: E-yut prolly wone rane.
        "It probably won't rain."
PURDY—There are lots of women like this in Texas.
    Purdy means "pretty."
    As in: Shay shore as purdy.
        "She sure is pretty."

Texan—English

Pay-nots—Peanuts
Texas is America's second largest producer of peanuts, harvesting over 290,000 acres of peanuts per year. Peanuts do not like hot and dry conditions, which may make you wonder why there are so many peanuts and peanut farmers in West Texas. Peanuts grow underground so it's very difficult to see how the peanut crop is doing; therefore, there are peanut experts who go from farm to farm inspecting the quality of the peanut crop. I have a friend of mine who is a peanut expert, and he makes bunches of money by doing this.

The Chacanought Indians, a native Indian tribe in West Texas, originally discovered peanuts. Several of the braves were just digging around in the dirt one day and discovered them. The braves brought them back to the tribe, and the chief and elders of the tribe liked them. After much deliberation, they decided that these nuts from the ground would taste better salted and roasted. The tribe never realized the true potential of their discovery because baseball and TV had not yet been invented.

Peanuts are a high-water-use crop and need from twenty to twenty-four inches of rain during their growing season. When West Texas does not have ample rainfall, you will see lots of irrigation going on. Plus peanuts, like other plants and crops, need lots of fertilizer—stuff like cow manure, sheep manure, and so on. They rarely use chicken manure; I guess it somehow affects the taste of the peanuts.

There is quite a bit of competition and rivalry among peanut farmers as to who can grow and harvest the choicest peanuts. One farmer will develop a water and fertilizer combination and the other farmers will want to go out and outdo him the next year. Then that prize-winning peanut farmer will come up with an even better water and fertilizer combination the next year. There is a lot of rivalry and jealousy among peanut farmers about who has the best peanuts. I guess that's where the term "peanuts envy" came from.

Some of the best peanuts are harvested just a little southwest of Lubbock. If you happen to be in the area around October and November, go ahead and buy a bunch or two. Peanuts can be purchased in their natural state or roasted and salted in the shell. Some of the peanut farmers are even coloring and flavoring their peanuts much like M&M candies. I like the purple ones the best.

Texan - English
Pick-um-ups—Pickups
There are several different types of pickups in Texas. One would be the classic "Ha thar, lil dor-lin, wunna daince?" (Translation: Hi there, little darling, do you want to dance?) The other type of pickup would be the workingman's best friend, his reliable ol' pickup truck. This pickup is also pretty easy to identify: the bed of the truck (well, it's called the bed, although most folks don't actually sleep on it, unless there are special circumstances involved) is usually all scratched up, with scuffs and dents. Normally, the outside of the truck also shows signs of hard work and lots of wear and tear.

Then there is the "city slicker" pickup truck. This truck is normally all shiny, waxed up, and decked out with all sorts of doodads that the workingman would consider as so much "fluff." The city slicker truck will have a special liner for the bed of the truck, so as not to get any scratches on it, just in case they ever put anything in the bed. Some city slickers even put a cover over the top of the pickup bed to keep out the dust and stuff. Of course, this truck also will have fancy wheels and tinted windows. This truck is all for "show and go" and is used for picking up sweet-smelling things rather than hay and stuff.

Then there is the rancher's pickup truck; this truck will be a bit more fancy than the farmer's truck. This truck will always have a gun rack in the back window and one or two high-priced rifles in the rack. This truck will also have an alarm system to protect these rifles and all the other fancy equipment inside, a very powerful engine, and a trailer pull on the back bumper for hauling horse trailers and things. Some of these trucks even have four wheels on the back instead of the normal two. These trucks are called "duelies," not to be confused with dueling because that's a whole different thing.

Another type of pickup truck is the monster pickup, so called because it is a monstrosity on the streets and highways. These trucks will be riding on the largest legally available tires on today's market. These tires are usually taller than most six-year-olds and their owners are not much brighter. The suspension has been dramatically modified to give the monster truck as much height as possible. Some of these trucks have several types of extension ladders available to enter or exit the truck. Others have an electronic lift gate installed to raise or lower the occupants of the truck.

Some folks with very poor memories have great difficulty finding their cars in many of the parking lots at malls, big box stores, sporting events, and places like that, so they have resorted to attaching all types of items to their car antennas to be able to find them again. Car alarm systems also worked fairly well, because they could just push a button on the remote, and their car or truck would beep at them. Even these tactics won't work for those with very limited mental abilities so, necessity being the mother of invention, the monster truck was born.

Texan - English
Plane-vue—Plainview
Located on the plains of West Texas just about thirteen miles northwest of the town of Barwise as the crow flies, or less than twenty miles as the pickup drives, you'll find the town of Plainview. Plainview is pretty much smack dab in the middle of the "Steaked Plains." In the early 1600s, Spanish explorers traveling through this area of the country would leave nice juicy steaks along the trail to help them find their way back and forth across the country. It gets mighty hot in this part of the country, and the Spaniards could cook some very tasty meals by leaving these steaks on flat rocks.

These "sun steaks" went very well with their "sun tea," "sun-baked potatoes," and "sun-baked beans." Lemons were not locally available around this area of the country and had to be imported from Spain. However, since they found no gold or treasure around here, they would just use their empty treasure chests as a box to keep their ice. These treasure chests later came to be known as "ice boxes" and we can thank the Spaniards for this valuable resource.

The tradition of having a nice juicy steak, baked potato, baked beans, and a nice cold glass of iced tea with a slice of lemon is still carried on today by many of the local restaurants. During your stay in Plainview, visit one of the local restaurants and join them in keeping this tradition ongoing.

The Spaniards also cooked "sun tortillas" on these flat stones and would have beans and tortillas as a snack. The Spaniards would trade with a few of the local Indian tribes in the area for other needed supplies. The Indians had a beautiful multicolored vegetable that they called maize, which we now call corn or sometimes Indian corn. This Indian corn is very popular during the fall holidays for decorations but most folks don't realize that it can also be used for a food.

The Spaniards were thrilled that they could have both flour and corn tortillas for making an item they called tacos. The most popular were the soft tacos, made with multicolored Indian corn. These tacos were very colorful, festive, and only available on very special occasions. True Spanish or Mexican tacos are soft, and the hard, fried taco shells are actually an invention by Texans because of their love for fried things. Chicken-fried steak is an example, although chicken-fried taco shells never really caught on. At times, you can find a Mexican restaurant owned by gringos and be able to order chicken-fried enchiladas, chicken-fried tamales, or chicken-fried burritos.

The main street leading into downtown is liberally decorated with life-size, fiberglass Hereford cattle. This is cattle country, although I'm a little disappointed about Herefords being the only type of cattle represented. No longhorns, Brahmans, Black Angus, or my grandfather's favorite breed, White Angus. Grandpa really enjoyed going out on his front porch at night and being able to count his herd in the dark.

In the 1800s, there were range wars all throughout Texas between cattle ranchers and sheepherders. Seems that one of the bones of contention between the two was that the cattlemen claimed that sheep would pull the grass out of the ground by the roots while they were grazing on the open range. When the sheepherders denied this charge, the cattlemen would counter with additional reasons as to why sheep should be driven from the land.

The cattlemen reasoned that most folks preferred steak and potatoes, rather than lamb chops and string beans. This is true, because you always hear about someone being called a steak-and-potato type of guy and never hear of anyone being called a lamb-chop-and-string-beans type of guy. Through restaurant records, the cattlemen also found out that baby back ribs outsold leg of lamb by twenty to one. Of the restaurants surveyed, all of them had chicken-fried steak on their menus, while none of them offered chicken-fried lamb. All of them had chicken-fried chicken, but that's a whole 'nother story.

The cattlemen further found that folks preferred leather jackets over wool coats by a large margin, and that the most popular rodeo event was bull riding (most folks would just be mildly amused by wild sheep riders). And they discovered that calf roping was much more popular because of its degree of difficulty than sheep roping was.

The cattlemen were a very organized bunch and formed an organization called the Texas Cattlemen's Association, whereas the sheepherders were pretty much loaners and formed no such organization. They would loan their shears, staffs, and feed to almost anyone who asked and were pretty mild-mannered and meek. The cattlemen didn't care too much for this attitude and developed a plan to drive the sheepherders from the land.

The two groups decided to get everything out in the open and had a get-together in plain view of everyone in the area, hence the name of the town. There is a bronze marker located right on the town square that marks the spot where this historic meeting took place. The cattlemen proposed that whichever of the two groups had the most animals would be the victor of these range wars. The sheepherders readily accepted this proposal and felt that victory would soon be in their grasp, because their sheep herds greatly outnumbered the cattle.

At high noon on a crisp November day, the counting began. The cattlemen began counting their cattle, and the sheepherders began counting their sheep. The sheepherders soon fell asleep, and the cattlemen continued to count their cattle. The sheepherders had always been wary of wolves in sheep's clothing, whereas they should have been concerned with the wily coyote ability of the Texas cattlemen. The cattleman won the contest and even today, when the children of cattleman have trouble falling asleep, they will suggest that the children count sheep in honor of this great occasion.

Texan – English
Play-no—Plano

Located just north of Dallas, the town of Plano was founded by two gentlemen in the mid-1800s. Misters Ben Dare and Don Datt decided that this would be a great place to build a church, farm, and raise their families. This giant metropolis that was once just a small little town on a dusty cattle trail still has its charming main street and the original church. The church, with its beautiful steeple and adjacent fishing pond, could easily be on any picture postcard. My children and I have experienced great joy catching crawfish in this pond many an afternoon after church on Sundays.

In the 1970s, the city fathers and city mothers cancelled their regular bar-b-que to hold a meeting to determine Plano's future. The population at this time was less than three thousand friendly folks, but after the meeting all this was about to change. In order to bring more business and revenue into the area, the city developed a new slogan. Plano came to be known as the "City of Meetings" and this slogan revolutionized this area of Texas.

All types of businesses flocked to Plano so they could hold their meetings, solve problems, and plan their future. One of the major ideas that came out of these meetings was that there should be more meetings. Plano was the first city to inaugurate the idea of a "power lunch," followed closely by the "power breakfast" and the "power dinner." At one of these power breakfast meetings, they came up with the idea of the "power coffee break." Most visitors to Plano will discover that there are a lot of hockey fans in town.

One of the greatest time-savers ever developed out of one of these meetings was voice mail. Seemed like they figured out they could hold meetings whenever they wanted, and their customers would never get a busy signal. All they had to do was to assign different instructions to each number on the telephone dial pad. Fortunately, the Texas school system is one of the best in the nation, and nearly all their customers had the ability to count to nine.

There is a proper etiquette to be used when leaving a message on a voice mail system. Keep your voice pleasant, and never, ever shout, holler, or cuss. Speak in distinct, easy-to-understand words and state your desire very plainly. Please remember that the person you are leaving the message for has probably just returned from a meeting.

Located to the west of the interstate and on the other side of the mall is a huge golden-domed building called "The Meeting Place." There are lots of folks who mistakenly think this is a singles bar. Nope, this is where companies and organizations come from all over Texas to hold meetings. There are podiums, stages, executive tables, red carpets, captain's chairs, genuine leather executive chairs, recliners, school bells, waiters, waitresses, and the finest in catering, including gourmet coffees and French pastries.

The Meeting Place is open from 6 A.M. until 12 midnight daily, and only closes on Sundays, major holidays, bank holidays, city holidays, state holidays, national holidays, three-day holidays, in observance of the sinking of the Spanish Armada, and Remember the Alamo Day. If you'd like to call ahead to schedule a meeting, just remember that everyone could be in a meeting planning the next meeting, or at the ball game. It may be a good idea to just leave them a message on their voice mail system and let them know that you'd like to make an appointment to hold a meeting. They will call you back, just as soon as the meeting is adjourned or the ball game is over.

∪∪

Q

Dictionary

QUARLY—Just about every three months.
    Quarly means "quarterly."
    As in: Y'alls quarly ray-parts ratty?
        "Are your quarterly reports ready?"
QUAY-YELL—When they're successful, there is a lot of whopping and hollering—hunting, that is.
    Quay-yell means "quail."
    As in: Y'all lak fraud quay-yell?
        "Do you like fried quail?"
QUEE-UT—Stop it, don't do that anymore, maybe.
    Quee-ut means "quit."
    As in: Y'all kay-uds quee-ut thay-ut.
        "You kids quit that."
QUEE-YUCK—Don't dawdle, hurry up.
    Quee-yuck means "quick."
    As in: Keer-ful, thay-uts quee-yuck-say-und.
        "Careful, that's quicksand."
QUEE-YUZ—Lots of teachers enjoy having these.
    Quee-yuz means "quiz."
    As in: Sa-praws, pop quee-yuz!
        "Surprise, pop quiz!"
QUES-SHUN—These are not allowed during a pop quiz
    Ques-shun means "question."
    As in: Sa-praws, pop quee-yuz! No ques-shuns loud.
        "Surprise, pop quiz! No questions allowed."
QUITE—One of the most difficult words for a kid to hear.
    Quite means "quiet."
    As in: Sa-praws, pop quee-yuz! No ques-shuns loud—y'all bay quite.

"Surprise, pop quiz! No questions allowed; please be quiet."

QWAIN—The next logical progression for a princess.

Qwain means "queen."

As in: Aaah bay-ud tew qwains.

"I bid two queens."

Texan – English
Quee-hee—Quihi

Less than six miles from Hondo, my ancestors settled the small town of Quihi in the 1860s. Quihi is an Indian word that translates to buzzard. I often wondered why my ancestors would name a town "Buzzard" instead of something a bit nicer. I asked one of my favorite uncles about this one day, and he explained the choice of this name to me. It seems that when the city fathers and mothers were naming the town, they had no idea that Quihi meant buzzard.

They really liked the sound of the name and thought that when the Indians were pointing towards the lake and exclaiming "Quihi, Quihi" that they were referring to the lake and not to the numerous buzzards roosting in the trees. This also explains why the lake is called Quihi Lake and not Buzzards Roost.

In the late 1800s, Quihi was a bustling, growing town; however, in the early 1900s, most of the inhabitants left because of the huge increase in the buzzard population. If buzzard tasted more like chicken, I think most folks would not have moved out of town. About the only time there is a big influx of people nowadays is during buzzard-hunting season. If you happen to be an avid dyed-in-the-feather buzzard hunter, there are quite a few trophy buzzards to be bagged here.

Moses Stuffen, the local taxidermist in town, does a thriving business during buzzard season. Most folks in town just call him Mo, so if you happen to bag a buzzard that you're especially proud of, Mo will be happy to mount it for you. You'll probably want to take your trophy buzzard and display it over your mantle place at home so all your friends will be impressed by your many skills. Some wives may protest your choice of such a prominent location in the home, so you may also want to bring her some flowers and candy.

Hopefully, you'll be driving a large SUV with lots of room for your mounted prize and won't make the mistake of transporting your prize on top of your car. With today's highway speeds, your prized buzzard might arrive at your destination minus all its feathers, and even the most accommodating wife will rarely allow her husband to display a naked buzzard over the mantle. If you don't have an SUV, you might want to ask a friend for help. If none of your friends have ample space in any of their vehicles, you may just want to hitchhike back home. There are lots of SUVs traveling on the road nowadays, so you shouldn't have any problem hitching a ride. Just be sure you are still wearing your buzzard-hunting gear because you'll want to blend in with some of the other happy hunters hitching a ride back home.

R

Dictionary

RAH-MAN-ECK—Some folks are, some folks aren't.
    Rah-man-eck means "romantic."
    As in: Hay shores rah-man-eck.
        "He sure is romantic."

RAID—Cars, trucks, signs, and even rainbows.
    Raid means "red."
    As in: Zat chore raid trok?
        "Is that your red truck?"

RAIL—Rhymes with ale.
    Rail means "real."
    As in: Yore raid trok shore ays rail purdy.
        "Your red truck sure is real pretty."

RAINCE—A washing machine normally goes through this cycle.
    Raince means "rinse."
    As in: Worsh, raince, spee-yun
        "Wash, rinse, spin."

RAINCH—Occasionally some are small, but most of them are large.
    Rainch means "ranch."
    As in: Muh rainch e-yus rail be-ugh.
        "My ranch is real big."

RARE—Something old, something new, something curvy, something cute.
    Rare means "rear."
    As in: Muh rare tar luks loe.
        "My rear tire looks low."

RAY-UNT—Some rave, some rant, some don't.
    Ray unt means "rent."
    As in: Wut moo-vee yall wunna ray-unt?

"What movie do you want to rent?"
RES-RUNT—Most are actually quite big.
>Res-runt means "restaurant."
>As in: Wunna goatuh res-runt?
>>"Do you want to go to a restaurant?"
ROT—Just like the word "fine" has one spelling and several different meanings.
>Rot means "right."
>As in: Thaits nought rot.
>>"That's not right."
ROT—Some really like to, while others don't.
>Rot means "write."
>As in: Aah doan rot tew whale.
>>"I don't write too well."
ROTTEN—This one goes with raid-in and rith-muh-tac.
>Rotten means "writing."
>As in: Rotten Tex-cun snot uh dee-raw-gee-toree tarm.
>>"Writing Texan is not a derogatory term."

Romancing the Cow

My great-grandfather, who stood over six foot two, was long and lanky with white hair, a big white mustache, and twinkling blue eyes. He was a kindly old gentleman with a perfect Santa Claus face and an easy smile. Being his first great-grandchild, I was also his favorite. It's good to be the first; it's almost like being the king, and being a king must be great fun.

When I was four, five, and six years old, it was a real treat to accompany my great-grandfather as he went to the barn to milk the cows. While Great-Grandpa slowly shuffled along with his milk pails, I would be happily skipping alongside him swinging my own milk pail.

Once inside the barn, Grandpa would set down one of the milk pails and reach over and take his milking stool off the wall. We would then walk up to Betsy and pat her on the rump and ask her how she was doing. He would do the same to Shirley. This morning, he would be milking Veronica and I would listen intently as Grandpa started romancing the cow.

Grandpa would speak soft soothing words to her as he placed his stool under her full udders. Occasionally, she would turn her head to look at him as he milked her; all the while, Grandpa spoke to her in his soft gentle voice.

He would say things like:
"Veronica, how are you today?"
"Do you have some milk for me?"
"Have you been eating some good hay?"
"Veronica, you are such a pretty girl."
"You give the sweetest milk."
"Your milk makes me strong and healthy."
" You have such a nice big belly."
"Your fur is nice and soft."
"You have such big pretty eyes."

Listening to Grandpa romancing the cow was a great help to me as I was growing up and dating. However, I did have to change the greetings and a few of the words as I spoke to my girlfriends and my bride-to-be. It must have worked though, because I'm very happily married with six children and twins on the way. Thanks, Grandpa!

Texan – English
Raown Rok—Round Rock
Travel north of Austin for just a bit and you'll find the historic town of Round Rock. The town was established in the early 1800s by a group of weary travelers in search of gourmet Indian cuisine. These travelers were led by a scholarly gentleman named Edward Dewcate; most folks just called him Ed. He and his group camped by the banks of the river in the early evening of October, 1823 in hopes of meeting a local band of Indians the next day.

The Rockcuhbye Indians inhabited this particular part of the Texas frontier, and were most well known for the soothing Indian lullabies they sang to their young children. The Rockcuhbye Indians would keep their infants in cradles high above the ground in the treetops. This procedure would keep their young children well protected from coyotes, wolves, javelinas, other marauding Indian tribes, and any traveling circus that happened to be in the area.

Occasionally, the bough of the tree would break, and the Indians would have to catch several of their falling babies. This made the Indians adept at running and catching falling objects. Legend has it that they later started several baseball franchises in the Americas.

The Dewcate travelers were delighted when the Rockcuhbye Indians arrived early the next morning bearing gifts. The Indians brought all sorts of smoked and dried meats, plus many exotic local vegetables. This bounty included buffalo, bear, catfish, elk, javelina, prairie dog, squirrel, venison, cantaloupe, grits, hominy, fried okra, maize, peaches, peanuts, and watermelon. The Dewcate travelers were delighted to forgo their traditional breakfast of bacon and eggs that morning so as to enjoy this exotic Indian cuisine.

After enjoying a huge feast, lasting well into the afternoon, the Indians decided to show the travelers around the area. Chief

Ten Arrows and his medicine man, whom the Indians just called Doc, showed the travelers one of their most prized objects. The travelers were greatly amazed and astounded when the Indians showed them a perfectly round, twenty-four-foot diameter rock. The Indians had painted a world map upon this globe that included the Americas, Africa, Australia, Europe, and the Far East. The travelers felt that this world globe was rather primitive, because it didn't include Greenland or the Hawaiian Islands.

The Dewcate travelers fell in love with this area of the country and were determined to make a trade with the Indians for this land. Fortunately, a Mister Woodrow Cue, and his lovely wife, Barbara (most folks just called them Curly and Barbie), were in the company of the Dewcate travelers. Curly had received his nickname because of his long, curly red hair. Over the years, Barbie had developed a design made of brick and iron grates that was great for slow cooking various meats in a very unique way. Woody and Barbie called this type of cooking "Barbie Cue." The brick-and-iron structure was called a Barbie Cue grill. Years later, so as not to confuse the numerous billiards players in Texas, the Cues changed the name to bar-b-que.

Not far from the giant round rock, the Cues and the Dewcate travelers built the first Barbie Cue grill in Texas. Upon completion of the project, they invited the Indians to a neighborhood Barbie Cue. The Indians were greatly impressed by this unique way of cooking and requested a Barbie Cue grill for themselves. After much singing, dancing, and smoking of the peace pipe, it was agreed that the travelers would build the Indians a Barbie Cue grill, in exchange for the land around the giant round rock.

The Barbie Cue grill the travelers built for the Indians was the very first of its kind to have wheels. The Indians were very happy to have a mobile Barbie Cue grill and traveled all over Texas selling these delicious smoked meats to hungry travelers.

When you happen to visit one of these mobile bar-b-que units, please do not raise your hand and ask "How." The Rockcuhbye Indians are very protective of not only their children but of their secret bar-b-que recipe.

Initially, when the Rockcuhbye Indians and their braves took their traveling brand of baseball with bar-b-que on the road; there were a few minor problems. The fans greatly enjoyed the Indians' way of playing baseball, but the bar-b-que, being quite delicious, was also very messy to eat. The fans would use numerous napkins to get the bar-b-que sauce off their hands and faces and then toss them onto the baseball field. With all these bar-b-que-stained napkins fluttering all over the field, it was most difficult to play baseball.

The Indians decided to offer the bar-b-que on a "to go" only basis and have something else for the fans to eat at the game. The Indians were fortunate enough to meet a gentleman by the name of Franklin Furter, who had recently developed a hand-held food that he called a Frank Furter. The Frank Furters became the solution to the problem of the messy napkins; however, when the vendors would holler out "cold drinks and Frank Furters," it would confuse way too many of the fans. Plus, when the vendors would holler out "cold drinks and Franks," almost everyone named Frank would raise their hand.

The Indians decided that they would have to change the name of the Frank Furters to something else. Initially, since the Frank Furters were red in color and served hot, they called them "red hots"; however, since it gets mighty hot in Texas during baseball season, when the vendors would holler out "red hots," it would just make the fans more uncomfortable. So the Indians decided that since dogs were much more popular in Texas than cats, they would call them "hot dogs"—which is a good thing, because "hot cats" came to be associated with jazz musicians and saxophones.

Joe Kent Roberts

    What's really great is that nowadays you can attend just about any baseball park in Texas, enjoy a baseball game, sing a song, have some cold drinks, a few hot dogs, and get some bar-b-que to go. At times, you may even come upon one of these mobile bar-b-que wagons where the Rockcuhbye Indians and the Indians from Seguin have collaborated to offer bar-b-que and pecan pie to go.
    While you are in Round Rock taking in all the sights, please be sure to have your picture taken beside the giant round rock. Just about a block away, the original, immaculately restored, Barbie Cue grill is still in operation and on display. Be sure to enjoy some Texas bar-b-que while you are here, or order some to go. If you happen to glance up into the treetops and notice any cradles, then you'll know that the Indians are back in town.

S

Dictionary

SAG-NUL—Some folks use them, some folks don't.
    Sag-nul means "signal."
        As in: Yore torn sag-nals own.
            "Your turn signal is on."
SANE—Some are, some aren't, some are new, some are old.
    Sane means "saying."
        As in: Aah uner-stan yore olt sane.
            "I understand your old saying."
SAY-UND—There's lots of this on the Gulf Coast.
    Say-und means "sand."
        As in: Doan ge-yut stalk inna say-und.
            "Don't get stuck in the sand."
SAY-UT—You don't have to say "ut" if you don't want to.
    Say-ut means "set."
        As in: Aahm ul say-ut.
            " I'm all set."
SAY-YELL—They even have them in Yell, Texas.
    Say-yell means "sale" or "sail."
        As in: Yore was-uls own say-yell?
            "Are your whistles on sale?"
SHART—Some or these are worn with paints.
    Shart means "shirt."
        As in: At shore e-yus uh purdy shart.
            "That sure is a pretty shirt."
SHORE—Yes, there is sand and shore.
    Shore means "sure."
        As in: Aah shore dew.
            "I sure do."
SPALE—Sorta rhymes with pail.

Spale means "spell."
    As in: Aah kaint spale tew wail.
        "I can't spell too well."

SPROT—Another soft drink in the Coke family.
Sprot means "Sprite."
    As in: Wegut Sum-Up er Sprot.
        "We have Seven-Up or Sprite."

STARM—They did this to castles in England.
Starm means "storm"
    As in: Way shore hay-ud uh bay-ud starm.
        "We sure had a bad storm."

STAUB—Any object that happens to be sticking up from the ground that you could possibly hit or trip on; not found in the English dictionary.
Staub means "staub."
    As in: Aah he-yut uh staub wif muh moah.
        "I hit a staub with my lawnmower."

STAY-UMP—Why would we want them to stay?
Stay-ump means "stamp."
    As in: Y'all nade uh stay-ump?
        "Do you need a stamp?"

SUM-UP—We briefly discussed this before. I just wanted to see if you were paying attention.
Sum-Up means "Seven-Up."
    As in: Wegut Sum-Up er Sprot.
        "We have Seven-Up or Sprite."

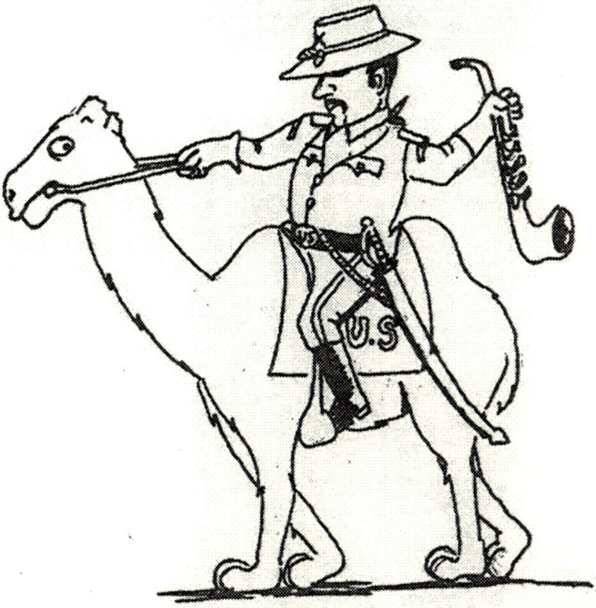
U.S

Texan—English

Sane Angie-lo—San Angelo
Located pretty much in the center of the state, San Angelo is about 220 miles northwest of San Antonio and midway between San Antonio and Lubbock. The town began as a trading post across the Concho River from the old Fort Concho military post. The town was originally called San Angela in honor of Mister Bart DeWitt's beautiful wife Angela, but the post office rejected the name saying that San Angela was incorrect Spanish.

    I had the same problem years ago when I was trying to name a town Muley. The post office informed me that Muley was an incorrect spelling. I countered by suggesting Muly, but the post office replied that it was too close to July, although I received their response in January. I suggested Mulie, and they informed me that this was too close to Mollie. I finally decided to go on ahead and call the town Muley, Texas, and to send and receive all my mail through a close friend living in a nearby town.

    Fort Concho was established in the 1860s and is listed in the National Historic Register as the most well preserved fort in all of North America. There is always something going on at old Fort Concho just about anytime you visit San Angelo, and it's a very entertaining place to take your children. The fort is completely restored to its original condition and there are all sorts of old cavalry activities and tours almost any season of the year. The conditions at military posts have improved quite a bit over the years because these fellows didn't have access to air-conditioning, cable TV, telephones, radio, the Internet, movies, or fast cars. They did have ready access to fast women and this tradition continues even today in our modern military.

    In the 1860s, the Fort Concho cavalry post was commanded by Colonel Benjamin (Benny) Jeneral and his second-in-command was an officer by the name of Major Shaykes. Next in command of the rank and file was Captain Woodrow (Woody) Kernel. (Note: They called them the rank and file because the nearest river was nearly three miles away, they rode in single file, and they seldom took baths.) The token lieutenant at Fort Concho was Lieutenant Moses (Moe) Sargent. The ranking noncommissioned officer was Sergeant Lou Tennant, and the only corporal at the fort was Corporal Juan la Capitán.

Since Fort Concho was located way out in the Texas frontier and the American Civil War was being fought back east, supplies for the fort were very difficult to obtain because most military supplies were being used for the war effort. When the supply wagons finally arrived from Fort Worth, the officers and men at the fort were disappointed that many of their supply requests had gone unheeded. Instead of ten wagonloads of supplies, they received only two. There were not enough supplies for a supply sergeant, so Colonel Jeneral appointed a supply private.

Private Lester (Les) Stokk arranged all the supplies in the supply shed and began taking inventory. One of the first things that Private Stokk discovered missing from the supply request was a bugle. The private immediately informed his immediate superior Corporal la Capitán, who informed Sergeant Lou Tennant, who informed Lieutenant Sargent, who informed Captain Kernel, who informed Major Shaykes, who informed Colonel Jeneral. This story would probably move a little quicker if I didn't have to follow the chain of command so I'll try to skip past it in the future. Plus, lots of folks and especially new recruits have a bit of difficulty in understanding military ranks and titles. I'll also avoid any reference whatsoever to military time, because that will generally confuse way too many folks.

A sign was posted near the open door of Colonel Jeneral (Note: Colonel Jeneral was one of the first officers in the U. S. Cavalry to have an open-door policy. It seems that the supply wagons also contained no doors for the fort and it is most difficult to fashion any type of a door from Texas cactus.) The colonel's sign requested all officers and men to conduct a search of their belongings and see if they could find a bugle. After an exhaustive search, the only musical instruments the men could find were an accordion, a guitar, a harmonica, and a saxophone.

Major Shaykes suggested that they use the saxophone for morning reveille and the guitar for taps (the evening lowering of the flag ceremony). The harmonica would be used on those sad occasions when someone from Fort Concho had passed on to that great cavalry up in the sky. It was most difficult to give a three-, seven-, or twenty-one-gun salute, because the supply wagons contained rifles and pistols but no ammunition or bullets. Therefore, on those rare and dignified occasions, the men would just aim their rifles towards the sky and holler, "Bang." Since no one cared too much for the accordion, they decided to keep this musical instrument in the supply shed.

Colonel Jeneral was greatly dismayed to discover that the supply wagons did not contain the Fort Concho flag, so he commissioned one of the officers' wives to make a flag. Mrs. Captain Kernel fashioned a very nice flag for the flag bearer and the troops at Fort Concho by using one of her silk petticoats. The ruffles on the flag fluttered quite nicely as the cavalry would go charging out of the fort led by the sounds of the saxophone.

Colonel Jeneral always wanted the fort to be in tip-top condition, just in case there were any surprise inspections from out of town, or in this case, from out of fort. Everything at Fort Concho was to be "spit and polish" but, unfortunately, the supply wagons contained no polish so it was mostly spit.

There wasn't too much for the men to do around the area because there were no Indians to be found around such a hot, dreary, desolate, treeless prairie. There was one incident in the fall of 1866 when a disoriented Mohican Indian by the name of

Lonesome Eagle wandered into Fort Concho asking for directions. Seems that most men are afraid to stop and ask for directions, but Indians always do because they want to know exactly where they are going. After receiving directions, Lonesome Eagle, "The Lost of the Mohicans," became the "Unlost of the Mohicans."

    The men of Fort Concho also didn't receive any horses on their supply train from Fort Worth, so Colonel Jeneral sent Major Shaykes into San Angelo to see if he could find seventy or eighty sweet rides for the men. Upon arriving at the O.K. Used Horse Dealer, he met Don Trustum and Moe Kruked, the used horse salesmen. The Used Horse Dealer had lots of free hot dogs and soda pop and was having a giant used horse sale. They informed Major Shaykes that they had just sold the last giant horse in stock and were completely sold out of used horses because that had just made an unusually large trade for eighty mules from a group of four gentlemen retiring from their twenty-mule-team Borax careers. The used horse salesmen knew that Major Shaykes was in a big bind, so they sold him all eighty mules for about five times the normal asking price.

    Major Shaykes consoled himself with the fact that the mules were completely loaded and came fully equipped with saddles, bridles, stirrups, rattlesnake repellant, mosquito repellent, topcoating, undercoating, and conditioning shampoo. The total price for each mule nearly doubled with the additional charges for new mule shoes, dealer transportation, dealer handling, dealer preparation, dealer acquisition fee, dealer registration, dealer extended warranty, and title charges, although each mule purchased came with a free bucket of oats and free mule shoe inspections.

    There was also another bit of a snafu on the supply shipment from Fort Worth because the men had requisitioned ten cases of Camels but the fort received ten real-live camels instead of cigarettes. It actually worked out pretty well because all the officers and noncommissioned officers rode camels while the enlisted men rode mules. There were no directions that came with the camels, so the men pretty much had to learn how to ride and care for them by trial and error. Fortunately, since this part of Texas was so much like Saudi Arabia, the camels felt right at home and hardly got homesick at all.

Several months later, Major Shaykes happened to meet these same used horse salesmen at the local Sit 'n Spit Saloon and confronted them about their gouging the military fort in its time of need. A heated and violent argument ensued and guns were drawn. Because of his superior military training, Major Shaykes was the fastest on the draw—but because of having no bullets, he only had "Bang" for his gun. Alas, because of the lack of supplies and proper military funding, there was no more Major Shaykes.

Colonel Jeneral contracted the local husband-and-wife team of coffin makers, Rusty and Penny Nayles, to make a proper coffin for Major Shaykes. The major was buried with full military honors, complete with taps being played on the harmonica and a full twenty-one-bang salute. Mrs. Shaykes was presented with the Fort Concho petticoat flag, Major Shaykes's saddle, and the camp accordion.

Legend has it that you can look up into the heavens on quiet silent nights and see the ghost cavalry from old Fort Concho charging across the moonlit night sky in full force, flag waving, camels burping, mules snorting, hoofs thundering, rifles glistening, with the gentle sound of a saxophone leading their ghostly brigade and the occasional shouts of "Bang, bang, you're dead."

Texan – English
San Un-tone (or San Ann-tone, by very happy residents)—San Antonio
Each of us has a special place in our heart for our hometown, and I will always have a flame that burns within my heart for mine. Whenever and wherever I have traveled, I have always compared other large and similar cities to San Antone. There is really no comparison. San Antone is the most beautiful big city I have ever seen or visited. Perhaps I'm just a teeny bit partial to the history and beauty of this city, this river, this culture, this architecture of a town built around the Alamo and the San Antonio River.

Take a leisurely stroll downtown to the Alamo where— were it not for the tremendous bravery of 186 men—there would be not only no Texas, there would be no San Antone. And perhaps no me. There would certainly not be the soft lilting Southern voice of those beautiful Texas ladies that I so love.

Just across from the Alamo is the Crockett Hotel. Samuel Clemens (a.k.a. Mark Twain) stayed here for a while and made some worthwhile statements, so I am told. Here, right across the small park from the hotel, the street is closed for ten days each April for the "Night in Old San Antone" festival. It's fiesta!!! If you have ever literally wanted to dance in the streets, you can do it here. Well, at least you can during fiesta; I really wouldn't recommend dancing in the streets any other time, unless you are trying to test the benefits of your health insurance.

San Antonio was named after Padre Antonio del Rio, the much-beloved pastor of many of the local missions. The padre was a saint, and saint and san are pretty much interchangeable words in that both mean "saint." Whether we use san or saint depends on how the words roll off the tongue. For instance, Saint Louis and Saint Joe sound much better than San Louis or San Joe.

There are over seven different Spanish missions in the San Antonio area designed and named by Padre Antonio. Each mission was state of the art; upon competition, the Spaniards would say to Padre Antonio, "This is your mission, should you choose to accept it." The padre would graciously accept each mission and put up a large "Grand Opening" banner for all to see.

Each grand opening would feature a tour of the grounds, padre quarters, pews, confessionals, cafeteria, cheese-making, wine-making, and tamale-making facilities. There were no balloons at the grand openings, but there was lots of music, wine, cheese, and tamales. The "ride-up-window" was usually closed during the grand opening, because the padres really wanted folks to get off their horses and come inside.

The city fathers and city mothers had considered naming the town Padre Antonio for a while and were very happy when the padre attained sainthood because they didn't want any confusion between Padre Island and Padre Antonio. That's why, even today, you will seldom hear the expression "Surfs up!" in San Antonio.

There are several festivals in San Antonio each year. One of the most beautiful and sweetest-smelling festivals is the "Battle of Roses" parade that is performed each year, thankfully after the roses have bloomed. This festival was originally called the "Battle of Roses and Cactus Blossoms" but was shortened after the first festival because there were way too many casualties between the rose people and the cactus people. The city doctors tried to keep the festival because it was good for their business but were outvoted by the Chamber of Commerce.

My great-grandparents actually attended the first festival and said that it was great fun because Grandma could sling a cactus pad farther than she could throw a cow chip. Grandpa got her a big bouquet of roses and cactus blossoms and Grandma got him some cactus jelly. Grandpa said he tried eating a "cactus dog" at the festival that wasn't too good—but that the cactus needles they used to fasten the cactus to the flour tortilla came in pretty handy as toothpicks.

Each Saint Patrick's Day there is a recreation of Saint Patrick driving the snakes out of Ireland. Since there are no snakes in the greater San Antonio area, they use many of the local politicians. Unlike the snakes in Ireland, the politicians always return. It's kinda like the swallows always returning to Capistrano, but not as joyously received.

During the Saint Patrick's Day celebration, the local folks dye the San Antonio River green. There are all sorts of parades and elaborately decorated floats along the river in the evening. For weeks and weeks after the parade, anytime you happen to catch a fish in the river, it will be green—green catfish, green perch, and green bass. They say that rainbow trout will not live in the river because it's not cold enough. Then again, it could be because they'd be way too embarrassed.

Texan - English
Say-un Mar-cuss—San Marcos
Just about sixty miles north of San Antonio lies San Marcos, a beautiful little town situated on a high hill surrounded by crystal-clear springs. Downtown is actually up on the high hill with a prominent university steeple that acts like a beacon to beckon you to come on up. (Well, yeah, I thought I'd try a play on words. Didn't work, did it?) You can spend several pleasant hours as you meander on up the hill and visit many unique shops and cafes.

What really makes San Marcos famous are its crystal-clear springs. Could be my Texas pride, but I think these springs are a ton better than the Silver Springs in Florida. Clear Springs has these glass-bottom boats that hold about sixteen or twenty-four people, you know, depending upon the size of the people. You just hop onboard and they take you on a tour of all of the springs that come gushing up from the bottom of the lake floor. You can look down through the bottom of the boat for forty, fifty, sixty feet, or more.

At the bottom of the springs are these big ol' catfish about four, five, or six feet long. They gave 'em all names like "Charlie," "Rob Roy," "Whitey," stuff like that. Therefore, they won't let you go fishing for them. I think if they hadn't named them, you would probably be able to do a little fishing.

Hope that you brought your swim trunks because at the edge of this crystal-clear lake, you can go swimming. Be sure to get some goggles for seeing underwater. If there are some beautiful women swimming while you are here, you might be able to spend several pleasant hours in the water. If there is a bunch of not-too-pretty women swimming during your time in the water, you can always keep your head above water and look down and count your toes, or look down and count the hairs around your belly button, whichever applies.

Texan – English
Shoo-lan-borg—Schulenburg
Located on the interstate smack dab in between San Antonio and Houston is the historic town of Schulenburg. *Schulen* is a German word that translates into sundown. *Burg* translates into small town, while *berg* would translate into very small town with a local brewery. Schulenburg was established around sundown in the early 1800s by German and Czech settlers. Two of the settlers were very disappointed that the town would not be allowed to have a local brewery.

The Czech fellow went about twenty miles southwest of Schulenburg to establish a brewery in the town of Shiner. The German fellow went several miles north and established a small brewery in the town of La Grange. La Grange is a very beautiful town with a state park dedicated to the now-defunct German brewery. The park is located just south of the town on a high hill. Drive north on a winding, forested, steep road down the hill to the town of La Grange. Just before you get to the main street, there is a really nice, friendly couple who operate a very comfortable motel on the right side of the road. This is a very enjoyable place to stay, and if my memory serves me correctly, the motel colors are predominately blue tones.

One of the Schulenburg settlers later built one of the first cotton gins in the state. The cotton gin is no longer there because so many folks were disappointed to discover that there was only cotton at this establishment and no gin. There is, however, a big muffler manufacturing company on the site of the old cotton gin, so if you need a muffler while you're in town, be sure to stop by. There is also a huge factory in town that makes cheese dip, so after you get a new muffler, be sure and stop by to pick up several cans of cheese dip. The cheese dip factory doesn't carry any sort of chips for dipping, so you'll need to visit the grocery store or something if you want to dip the cheese. Believe me, its way too messy to just use your fingers. Plus, your steering wheel will get all sticky from the cheese dip, and the hot Texas sun will dry the cheese dip on the steering wheel. Then you'll have cheese flakes fluttering all over the inside of your car.

If you get hungry while you are in town, there are a few places I might suggest. Located on the main street just across from the railroad tracks is a nice little place with an original soda fountain. They will fix you a milk shake or malt the old fashioned way, with all the extras. The proprietors and their staff are all very helpful and friendly; be sure to talk some Texan with them while you are there.

Another of my favorite stops is located on the southwest corner of the street, just off the interstate. This restaurant has all my favorites, including a giant hamburger with all the fixings. The owner and the staff are a great delight as they are most friendly. All of the waitresses greet me with a "Hi, hun" or a "Hi, sugar," instead of the most distasteful "Hi, sir." At my age, I much prefer to be called "hun," "shug," or "sugar" than "sir." This restaurant also has a very nice gift shop with all sorts of local jams, jellies, and baked goods. I like the pecan pie the best. They also have books about the local area and lots of Texas cookbooks.

Just about a block south on the right-hand side of the street is the Visitors Center. These ladies are all volunteers, so please don't ask them any dumb questions like, "Does anyone in town speak English?" They just don't get paid enough to answer silly questions like this. In fact, they don't get paid anything; that's why they call them volunteers. So if you don't want to make any money at all, it would probably be a good idea to volunteer for everything.

Please be on your best behavior, and be nice to these ladies because they may be one of my distant relatives or something. Compliment them on their hair or clothing, and say something like "Joe says you really make a great pecan pie" or "We'd like to buy everything in your gift department" because all of the proceeds from the Visitors Center remain in the community to buy stuff like baseball equipment and pecan pie recipes.

    My favorite American pastime—other than enjoying my beautiful bride and my children—is going to a local ballpark and enjoying a baseball game. There's just nothing better than being in the stands with a warm beer in one hand and a cold hot dog in the other. Probably the only thing better would be if the snack bar also served hot pecan pie à la mode.

Joe Kent Roberts

Texan – English
See-geen—Seguin
A nice little town just down the road from San Antonio along the banks of the Guadalupe River, Seguin is named after the Indian chief of the Tonkawa tribe. Seguin, in the Tonkawa language, means "loves pecan pie." Chief Seguin and his Indian princess Sewahaguin, which means "great pecan pie maker" in the native Tonkawa Indian language, were leaders of this peaceful Indian tribe that ranged for several hundred square miles in the Texas Hill Country.

The hundreds and thousands of pecan trees in and around this area of the country attest to the fact that Chief Seguin was born in the right place at the right time and had correctly chosen Sewahaguin to be his Indian princess. You may want to visit the museum here in town and discover additional facts about Chief Seguin and Princess Sewahaguin. The museum has a vast collection of artifacts about the Tonkawa Indians and the early Texas settlers who traded and intermingled with this tribe.

One of the most interesting facts that I came across was that Chief Seguin and the Tonkawa Indians actually used these sweet Texas pecans as currency, a.k.a. "wampum." After you have tasted a few of these Texas pecans, you will understand why. You may purchase a sack or two at one of the local grocery stores or buy a pound or two at any of the numerous pecan stands around town.

If you want to go the cheap route, you could just shake a few pecan trees and those sweet pecans will come tumbling down to the ground. Be sure to wear a hardhat. If you don't have a hardhat, just rinse the potato salad or beans out of one of your Tupperware bowls. Put the Tupperware bowl on your head, and while you shake the pecan tree you will be fully protected from any errant falling pecans. Gather up your pecans and store them in the bowl. The pecan is the Texas State Tree. There was a very heated debate in the state senate about whether the pecan tree or the mesquite tree should be the Texas State Tree and the pecan tree won. I'm really happy that it did, because I don't think I'd care much for mesquite pie.

Seguin is a great place for a family picnic, swimming, or for just a lazy afternoon resting in the cool shade of a huge oak tree and fishing along the banks of the river. Go native and use a cane pole and a bobber. There are lots of perch, crappie (pronounced craw-pea; who the heck would want to eat a crappie fish?), and the occasional catfish. Add a couple of Lone Star longnecks and a bar-b-que grill and this is really the life.

Later, you can stroll over to the downtown area and see a humongous bronze-encased pecan just a few steps from the old courthouse. Grab a camera and strap a saddle on this pecan and take a picture. Seguin is one of many Texas towns vying for the Pecan Capital of Texas. There's nothing better than a slice of Texas pecan pie and good hot cup of coffee. You will find several cafes in town where you can enjoy both. Upon leaving the cafe, you may hear: "Y'all kam bay-uck now, ya he-yah?" (Translation: You all come back now, you hear?).

Texan – English
Shy-ner—Shiner
Take a thirty-minute leisurely drive southwest from Schulenburg and discover my most favorite town in the whole state. Shiner has the two things that I most love in the whole world, well, besides my bride and children. Maeker's sausage and Shiner Brewery are conveniently located in this picturesque little town, nestled in the rolling hills of southeast Texas. With its meandering river, green grass, large oak trees, and pecan trees, Shiner is one of the most beautiful towns in Texas.

I don't know how he does it, but Mister Maeker has the finest sausage, dried sausage, and smoked bacon in America. Ever since we discovered Maeker's several years ago, we look forward to visiting Shiner each winter and purchasing around a hundred dollars' worth of the finest sausages in the land. His dried sausage is the absolute best that I've ever had the pleasure of tasting. His smoked bacon is thick sliced and fabulous. Nothing comes close to the taste of bacon and eggs with Mister Maeker's smoked bacon.

Mister Maeker is a very tall gentleman, usually seen wearing a white Stetson hat while overseeing his businesses. His wife is a very attractive, petite, friendly blonde, who helps us with our purchases and answers any questions we might have. It's unfortunate that we live so far away from Maeker's, because we can only enjoy his sausages and bacon for such a short time while we are in this area of the state. His sausages and bacon are only available within a sixty-mile radius of Shiner. I've asked him and his wife several times if they would please adopt me so I could enjoy Maeker's all year. They would agree, but there is some sorta state law that says a parent cannot be younger than the adoptee.

My other most favorite thing in town is Shiner Bock beer. The Shiner Brewery was established in 1909 by German and Czech immigrants that were thirsting for the good stuff back home, which proves that sometimes it's good to be homesick, and I'm so happy that they were. The brewery makes about four different kinds of beer. There is Shiner Blonde, Kosmos, one I forget, and my most favorite, Shiner Bock. There, I think that's all four, plus they make a special winter brew that is most delicious.

I don't know if the brewery was named after the town or the town was named after the brewery, but Shiner is a very special place. There is a really nice bronze statue of Kosmos Spoetzl, the original Shiner brew master, located in the town square—as well there should be. I just wish the bronze beer stein in the town square were in action, with cold Shiner flowing from it.

Each October, the town and the brewery host Boctoberfest. It's sort of a play on words, combining Bock beer with October. Anyway, there are over 100,000 people at this event every year. There will be lots of music, singing, dancing, bratwurst, and Shiner beer during this event. If you happen to have some beer spilled on you, don't dismay, just grab an empty glass and wring this golden nectar out of your clothes into the empty glass.

What I love about Boctoberfest—besides the singing, dancing, and stuff—is having a nice cold Shiner Bock with a link or two of Maeker's dried sausage. It's like a little bit of heaven on earth, and if I can't enjoy a Shiner Bock with some Maeker's dried sausage in heaven, then WHY would they call it heaven?

T

Dictionary

TAME—In certain realms, being docile is not a great attribute.
> Tame means "team."
> As in: Way nade moah tame-wark.
>> "We need more teamwork."

TAR-BULL—Well, once there was a children's book about a tar baby.
> Tar-bull means "terrible."
> As in: Yore tame-wark e-yus tar-bull.
>> "Your teamwork is terrible."

TARRED—Just as long as they leave out the feathers.
> Tarred means "tired."
> As in: Alm sic un tarred.
>> "I'm sick and tired."

Normally this is a mother's lament followed by many multiple thousands of things that we as children innocently do, and that somehow get on her nerves.

TAY-UBS—At one time, this was several soft drinks.
> Tay-ubs means "tabs."
> As in: Alm kapin tay-ubs own y'all.
>> "I'm keeping tabs on all of you."

TAXES—We should all pay homage to this great place.
> Taxes means "Texas."
> As in: Them's the bay-ust tame in Taxes.
>> "They're the best team in Texas."

TAY-YUN—Folks attempt to get one of these in one day at the beach.
> Tay-yun means "tan."
> As in: Alm gona barn e-yun-steada tay-yun.
>> "I'm going to burn, instead of tan."

TEE-YUN—Nothing to do with golf or a tee time, or tea time.
>Tee-yun means "ten."
>>As in: Aah gut uh tweeny anna tee-yun.
>>>"I've got a twenty and a ten."

THAY-ER—Well certainly not ours, or here.
>Thay-er means "there."
>>As in: Yup, e-yuts ore thay-er.
>>>"Yes, it's over there."

TOM—Our three children, Sage, Rosemary, and Tom.
>Tom means "time."
>>As in: Wut tom yew hay-uf?
>>>"What time do you have?"

TOT—No, because they call their children kay-uds.
>Tot means "tight."
>>As in: Aah lock uh gale e-yun tot paints.
>>>"I like a girl in tight pants."

TRON—Nope, it ain't one of the ancient Greek gods.
>Tron means "trying."
>>As in: Alm rally tron.
>>>"I'm really trying."

TUH—Well, there was a King Tut but not a King Tuh.
>Tuh means "to."
>>As in: Alm goan tuh or Alm fixin tuh.
>>>"I'm going to" or "I'm fixing to"

TUMPED—Another word unique to the Texas language.
>Tumped means "spilled."
>>As in: Aah tumped ore muh malk.
>>>"I'm spilled my milk.

Or it could also mean that they totally turned over a glass of liquid and it is currently running all over the table and down onto the floor.

Texan—English

A Texan's Map of Texas

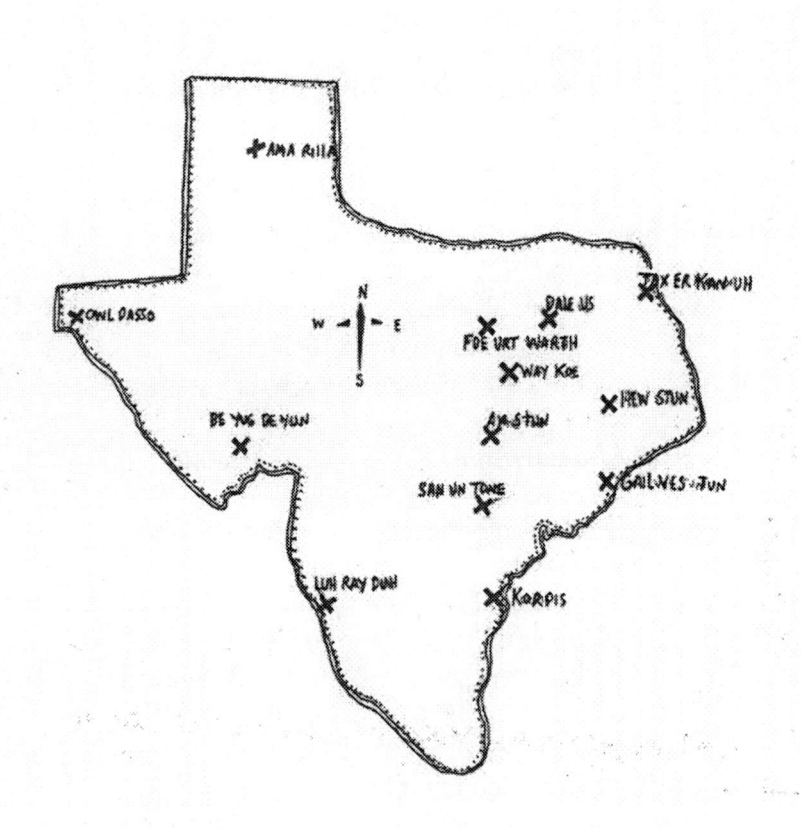

Texan - English
Tax-er-kan-uh—Texarkana
Texarkana is a combination of three different state names, Texas, Arkansas, and Louisiana. Texarkana is about as far east as you can get in Texas without being in Arkansas, and if you happen to drive across Maine Street, you are. The main street in town runs north to south; the west side of the street is Texas and the east side of the street is Arkansas.

The primary industries in Texarkana are agriculture, metals, minerals, mobile homes, and timber. The community is very well educated and is also very mobile. The majority of the folks in town live in mobile homes and for a very good reason. If they happen to get upset with one type of state government, they'll just pull up stakes, hook up their home, and cross Main Street. One week they might be living in Texas, and the next week they might be living in Arkansas.

Sometimes it's not state politics that determines if they will be living in Texas or Arkansas but whatever sports team they happen to be following, sometimes it's college or professional football, and at other times it could be a baseball or basketball team. Mobile homes give these folks a certain flexibility that most of us don't enjoy because our homes don't have wheels. A few of these folks may not be "movers and shakers" but they certainly are "movers and packers." The next time you have to move somewhere, you might want to contact a few of the locals here in town and get some moving and packing tips.

There are quite a few fine shops, cafes, and restaurants down on Main Street, and I like to be able to say that a certain shop or cafe is located on either the east or west side of town, but I can't. If you look closely, you'll notice that all of these places have giant wheels concealed beneath the buildings. Any time one of the local businesses moves from one state to the other, the whole town shows up and throws a party. That's why Texarkana is known as a big party town.

There was a lady who sang a very popular song about being downtown, and this town must have been the inspiration for her song, because with all the mobile homes rolling all across town and businesses moving around all the time, Texarkana is a beehive of activity. Most of the local folks are bilingual, and although you are in Far East Texas, they don't understand Chinese or Japanese.

Texan – English
Taxes Beg Tay-ouns—Texas Big Towns
Just like the other states in America, Texas has its big towns. Perhaps the biggest difference between these other states and Texas is that Texans are considerate enough to name these big towns. The following towns are the big towns in Texas. Then again, I've heard that Texans have a tendency to exaggerate just a teeny bit.

Big Foot, Texas, is located southwest of San Antonio on Highway 35. Well, it's not actually on the highway, but you can get there via Highway 35. You can't miss Big Foot—there is a giant foot painted on the town's water tower that is visible for miles around. Big Foot is probably one of the most famous towns in the world, because this is where the elusive "big foot" was first spotted. Elmer "Big Feet" Haingnell was cross-country skiing one day (Elmer's feet were so big that he didn't need skis) and came across some of the biggest footprints in the snow that he had ever seen. Elmer was in awe of these giant footprints and was bent over looking at them when he suddenly heard a shout of "Howdy" coming from the nearby woods.

Elmer looked up to see a giant of a man, nearly eight feet tall. Elmer, of course, said "Howdy" back to the gentleman, and they began to talk. When asked about this incident later, Elmer said that he didn't remember their exact conversation, but that they just chatted about the regular guy stuff, things like the ski conditions, what they had for dinner last night, the high price of horse fodder, and why bars don't have longer happy hours.

After several hours of talking and getting to know each other, the two men agreed that they had several things in common, the most notable being their enormous feet. They agreed that this was a really nice area and that it would be a great place to raise their families and start a town. After scratching their heads and pondering several hours on what to name the town, both men happened to glance down at the same moment. Therefore, the town is now called Big Foot and not Four Feet, as some would imagine. Elmer later opened up the town hardware store, and the other gentleman just sorta drifted off into the woods to become a legend of his own kind.

Southwest of San Angelo on Highway 67, you will find the town of Big Lake. The story goes that "Big Red" Lake and Corky Bartles, while traveling in this part of the country in the early 1800s, discovered a large lake in this area. Big Red was called Big Red because of his red hair and large size. Anyway, Corky's first reaction upon seeing this large lake was "Wow, that sure is a big lake!" Red looked at the lake and replied: "That *is* a big lake." They decided to name the lake Big Lake, instead of Big Red Lake, because they had already named a river after Red. Then they decided to break out their fishing gear and see what was biting. They landed some giant bass and decided to call these Big Lake Bass, instead of Big Red Lake Bass, because these fish weren't red and they didn't want to confuse anyone. Some people today just call them Lake Bass.

Since the fishing was so great, they agreed to build a bait and tackle shop near the lake. During their travels through the Oklahoma territory, Corky was given the honor of naming a town after himself, so Red got to name the bait and tackle shop Big Red Lake Bait and Tackle Shop. They later decided to call the bait shop Big Lake Bait and Tackle Shop, because they didn't want anyone to expect the lake to be red. The fishing was so great that they soon had a thriving little town. Many years later, Big Red's grandchildren decided to name a soft drink after him. You will be able to find this soft drink in many of the local establishments in town. It's my favorite soft drink; try one while you're in town and perhaps one day it will be yours also.

Big Spring is located on a major interstate highway between Lubbock and San Angelo. Most folks call it Big Springs instead of Big Spring. There is just one spring; therefore, it is called Big Spring. Some folks think the town is called Big Spring because of a single, giant underground spring in the area but this is not so. Others think it's called Big Spring because of the giant, thirty-foot-tall suspension spring on display downtown. Some folks surmise that space travelers left this big spring from the distant past. If so, that was a mighty big space ship, and it should have left rather large indentations in the soft earth around here.

The town actually received its name from a casual comment—or I should say an excited exclamation? Claude Hopper was a sorghum farmer in this vicinity of the state. Claude, along with his wife, Wendy, became sorghum farmers primarily because 90 percent of all Americans had no idea what sorghum was, and it also sounded very mysterious. When they told the other farmers in the area that they raised sorghum for a living, the cotton and corn farmers just shook their heads and said, "Yup," while the milo and cane farmers gave them a knowing nod. While raising milo is a bit mysterious, some folks find it more difficult to raise cane.

In the winter of 1833, this area of the state received nearly perfect weather conditions and just the right amount of rain needed for a perfect sorghum crop. Claude and Wendy harvested an enormous amount of sorghum in the spring of '34. Wendy was so happy about the harvest that she exclaimed to Clyde, "What a big spring!"

Claude replied, "Wendy, we have had a big spring! Perhaps our biggest spring ever."

They decided to name the area around their farm "Big Spring" instead of Wendy, Claude, or Biggest Spring in hopes that they would continue to have a big spring each and every year.

Texas is known throughout the world for its cattle and oil production. Big Wells became the town with the biggest oil wells in the state. There are oil wells nearly everywhere you happen to look all over town. These are some really big wells, perhaps even bigger than some of the ones in Saudi Arabia. Some folks in town even have more money than those Saudi Arabian sheiks. The local folks don't flaunt their riches with a lot of castles, harems, Mercedes Benzes, diamonds, emeralds, rubies, and stuff. You'll see most of these folks sitting on the front porch of their modest home just smiling and waving.

About the only "shake" in these parts is down at the local Dairy Queen; about the only castle is on a chess set; about the only emerald is the color of the river; about the only diamond is at the local ballpark; about the only Mercedes is on the FTD florist sign. There are several Rubys: Ruby Miller comes to mind. And, of course, there is a lot of stuff. There is also lots of stuff in the local cafes and retail establishments—you know, like food, souvenirs, and stuff. Be sure and have your picture taken beside one of the big wells. Just smile, wave, and say sheik.

Texas Cactus

A very severe drought had enveloped the Hondo area, and Grandpa and I went out to Great-Grandpa's ranch to help feed his cattle. We were out there for several days, using blowtorches to burn the thorns off of cactus so the cattle could have something to eat. It was a very hot summer and the heat from the blowtorches made it even hotter. Cattle don't eat hot foods, so it was very rewarding to see them munching on cactus a day or two later. The prickly pears were quite tasty and the cactus leaves tasted a little like green peas.

Not too long ago, my bride reluctantly asked me to visit the produce department and pick up some needed ingredient for the dinner she was preparing that evening. She wrote the item down on a piece of paper, gave me a kiss goodbye, and off I went to the grocery store. As I wandered around the produce department looking for the item, I tried to act knowledgeable by squeezing the tomatoes, thumping things, and holding an orange up to my ear and shaking it.

Satisfied that I had convinced most of the folks that I indeed knew my way around the produce department, I continued to wander the isles. If anyone would ever ask me, "Hey, have you been to the isles?" I'd be able to proudly say, "Well, yes I have!" I eventually found the item my bride desired and was turning to leave the produce department when I happened to spot some cactus leaves in the gourmet section. I was in complete surprise and blew my cover by exclaiming, "Hey, we used to burn these for cattle food."

Upon my return home, my bride consoled me by explaining that because of my love for bratwurst and pecan pie, I shouldn't be expected to know about all the various uses for cactus. I'm happy that my sweetheart has never put a damper on my childlike innocence, and still allows me to do things for her at the grocery store. I'll probably try to avoid the produce department at all costs the next time. I wonder what's new in the cookie isle? I'll have to ask the kids if they want to tag along.

Talkin' Texan

Texas Chili

I've often wondered why I've had such a great love for chili. Ever since I can remember, I've enjoyed a big bowl of chili, topped with diced onions and covered with crumbled Fritos. It wasn't until just recently I learned that chili was first brought to us from San Antonio. Chili is just another item given to us by the Indians, for they were masters at making and preparing chili.

Texas chili is some of the very best in the nation and Texas chili cook-offs are some of the most popular weekend activities in the state. Folks will come from all over the state to show off their most prized secret chili recipes. Some of the canned chili in the grocery stores isn't too bad; however, if you have been accustomed to eating these, then boy howdy! are you in for a real treat by attending a chili cook-off. Real Texas chili can be prepared from almost any kind of meat, beef, pork, chicken, turkey, buffalo, rabbit, javelina, jackalope, jackrabbit, venison, squirrel, dove, pheasant, or rattlesnake.

Chili can come with or without beans, although there are a few purists who insist that true chili contains absolutely no beans. I'm far from being a purist and perhaps have mellowed a bit with age, so I kinda like venison chili with pinto beans. I was quite shocked one day when an out-of-state friend invited me over for some chili and their chili contained kidney beans. Geez, what's next, refried kidney beans, refried navy beans, and refried black-eyed peas? Perhaps, I'm a chili-bean purist.

The Spaniards had persuaded some of the Indians to act as scouts during their exploration of the New World and they noticed that the Indians seemed very cool and comfortable, even on the hottest summer days. On one scorching hot July day, the Spaniards were sweltering under the hot Texas sun and decided to ask the Indians how they remained oblivious to the heat. As they approached the Indian scouts, they noticed that the Indians were cooking something mighty tasty looking in a big, black pot.

The Indians looked up from their spicy jackrabbit chili and said, "Hey, want some chili?" Well, the Spaniards were overjoyed that the Indians were willing to share their secret for staying so cool and comfortable. It must be the chili! Each of the Spaniards accepted a big, heaping bowl of chili and started gobbling up the chili, immediately after saying grace. The Spaniards started yelping and hollering that the chili was hotter than the sun. The Indians began laughing and giggling, because the Spaniards had supposed that chili would be cold. The Indians then offered them several habañeros and jalapeños and explained that these were New World peppers. The Spaniards were familiar with black pepper back in Spain, so they thought they would try some.

This was the start of the great Chili War of the New World, and it lasted for several hundred years. This was also the beginning of the famous Spanish sayings "Don't eat the chili" and "Hold the peppers."

Texas Insects

There are quite a few insects in Texas, but I'm just gonna mention a couple of the most notorious from my early childhood years.

Fire ants range far and wide throughout Texas and are an unwelcome guest at any outdoor get-together. Fire ants are about half an inch long and are cinnamon colored. They get great pleasure in stinging the daylights out of anyone within range, especially little kids. Their sting burns like fire, so you'll be wise to keep a bottle of whiskey handy. Because of its high alcohol content, the whiskey makes an excellent antiseptic. You can just dab some on the fire ant bite and drink a little to ease the pain. Every so often, you might see someone who was really badly bitten by fire ants sitting on a curb, or leaning up against a building in a somewhat painless condition.

There's probably about a million fire ants living in a visible mound that rises several inches above the ground. Occasionally, a fire ant colony will get another queen, and there ain't room anywhere for more than one queen at a time, so they will hold a big going away party for this new queen and fly off to form a new colony among the unstung.

Sugar ants are a lot more fun to watch and be around than fire ants, especially for a little kid, since little kids aren't allowed to drink whiskey. Sugar ants will travel all throughout the house in single file, just like an African safari, looking for something sweet. As soon as they find something sweet, they swarm all over it and do a little dance. They then send several of the dancers back to their anthill to tell the rest of the colony.

I liked the sugar ants because they didn't sting and, just like me, they also liked sugar. They seemed to really like lemon drops and Nabisco peanut butter cookies. They also seemed to like Hershey bars but didn't care too much for M&Ms. Because of the hard candy shell, the M&Ms were difficult for the sugar ants to get into and carry off. I felt sorry when the sugar ants couldn't find anything in our house to eat, so I'd put out some candy for them. I was always in trouble, because my folks were always saying, "Quit feeding the sugar ants." Apparently, because of their "adult tastes," adults didn't care too much for sugar, and because of my childish tastes, I didn't care too much for whiskey.

I always knew when it was summer in Texas because there was no school and everyone smelled like mosquito repellant. No one went outside in the summer without being rubbed down or sprayed down with lots of mosquito repellant. Most folks in Texas don't wear any colognes or perfumes in the summertime because the mosquito repellant kinda diminishes the effects of these expensive fragrances.

Once, when I was about ten years old, I was playing outfield during a Little League game and had forgotten to apply any mosquito repellant at all. I was scratching, swatting, and dancing around for the whole game. The coach said he really appreciated my enthusiasm, and I got to coach third base later in the game. Although some of the other kids seemed to be a bit confused by some of my signals and signs, I think we set some sort of a league record for bunts during bases-loaded situations.

Texas mosquitoes are anywhere from a half an inch to an inch long and come out in droves during the summer. It gets so bad that most all of the towns in Texas have city trucks spraying mosquito repellant on any standing body of water during mosquito season. They might kill nine trillion out of ten trillion of them, but the remaining trillion are gonna get their fair share of anyone not slathered in mosquito repellant. Mosquito repellant is sorta like garlic, because you really can't smell it too much on yourself. However, if you have been inside for most of the day and someone comes into the house who's been outside for a while, then the fragrance of mosquito repellant is very strong.

There was some fellow who discovered that mosquitoes were repelled by the smell of citronella oil and suggested that folks use citronella to keep mosquitoes away during their summer outings. Apparently, this gentleman had a very poor sense of smell himself but did notice that citronella oil would repel mosquitoes. Citronella certainly does repel mosquitoes and is widely used and suffered by folks who would rather smell the nauseous aroma of citronella than be bitten by mosquitoes. There are also citronella soaps available for folks who wish to repel mosquitoes and want to be totally undisturbed most evenings outdoors.

When I was about six years old, I discovered a very wonderful mosquito repellent completely by accident as I was walking out in the woods one day and startled a skunk. The skunk seemed to be ready to turn and run but decided to give me a spray instead. Skunk works even better than citronella and perhaps smells a bit nicer, because the mosquitoes didn't bother me for at least ten days. The only bad side effect to skunk was I had to take a lot of baths.

If you happen to know of any people who are really bothered by mosquitoes and don't seem to play well with others, you might consider giving them a citronella candle, a bar of citronella soap, or a pet skunk. If they are really antisocial, you might just take up a collection and give them all three. That way, they won't be bothered by mosquitoes and you won't be bothered by them. You'll be able to smell them coming, and this is where we get the saying "Getting rid of one rotten apple with three gifts."

Talkin' Texan

Texas Rabbits

Cottontail rabbits are probably the most popular and well known of the various rabbits that inhabit Texas. The cottontail is so named because its tail resembles a ball of cotton. Most of the plush animals that are available in most stores today are patterned after the cottontail. These animals are soft and cuddly, and many children like to keep them as pets. Perhaps these cottontails remind children of the Easter Bunny.

    Along with the chickens on the ranch, my grandma also kept a rabbit hutch. Sundays were usually the day we had fried chicken for dinner. I don't remember what day we had rabbit for dinner, but I do remember that I really liked it—although during dinner, I kept thinking about how cute and cuddly they were. I suppose this is why Kentucky Fried Chicken became a worldwide success, while Kentucky Fried Rabbit faltered. It seems that Texans and most people of the world prefer something that is pretty ugly, compared to something that is awfully cute, to eat. As an example, bacon and eggs are quite popular. So are ham and eggs, pork sausage and eggs, and foods like that. Pigs and chickens are not very pretty—therefore, they are very popular as foods.

    The hunting of jackrabbits is quite popular in Texas, because it allows men who are poor at golf to get out of the house on the weekends. Most jackrabbit hunters are extremely poor shots; therefore, they use shotguns to bring down their game. There are several different types of shotgun pellets, and the most popular pellets are made from salt and pepper—that way, the jackrabbit is already flavored for cooking after being shot.

    Nearly everything is bigger and better in Texas, and rabbits are no exception to the rule. Perhaps you have seen photos, pictures, or postcards of the giant rabbits that inhabit Texas. Maybe you were fortunate enough to have seen one or more of these giant rabbits in one of the local Texas rodeos. If so, then you have seen how the rabbitboys saddle up a rabbit while performing their various tricks and stunts on these giant rabbits. These giant rabbits are rarely seen during the daylight hours, as they are nocturnal creatures. Every so often, you can catch a glimpse of one of these giant rabbits while it is sleeping during the day. If the scrub brush or the trees are not too tall, you'll be able to see the tips of the rabbits' ears just above the forest. The best way to see a giant rabbit is to visit a petting zoo or attend one of the local rodeos.

Another of the varieties of rabbits where the deer and the antelope play is the jackalope. The jackalope has the appearance of a regular jackrabbit but is endowed with horns resembling an antelope. These rabbits are also nocturnal creatures and are rarely seen during daylight hours unless you happen to see one that's been run over by a car or something. The majority of the most recent jackalope sightings have been reported by bar patrons while walking home late at night. Should you happen to see jackalope available on any of the local restaurant menus, be sure and try some because jackalope tastes nothing like chicken.

Talkin' Texan

Texas Road Signs

Spade Limpt—Speed Limit

Yelled—Yield

Stahp—Stop

Karves A Haid—Curves Ahead

Gay Us—Gas

Joe Kent Roberts

Ate—Eat

Res Runt—Restaurant

Moe Tails—Motels

Law Jun—Lodging

Faln Rox—Falling Rocks

Soeft Sho Ders—Soft Shoulders

Rale Raod Kra Sun—Rail Road Crossing

May Yun War Kun—Men Working

Pac Nak Err Yuh—Picnic Area

Now Fashun Frum Bradge—No Fishing From Bridge

Tourist Season

I was working as a traveling salesman for Fritz, my most favorite boss ever. His company was based in the Dallas metropolitan area, and I would travel all over the country for him, anywhere he wanted me to go. When he offered me this position, he asked if I loved my wife. I told him yes, that I loved her very much. He said that my first traveling assignment would last three weeks, but since I truly loved my wife, he would let me fly back into town each weekend at his expense. Other than a famous Jewish boy who was born in the year zero, I think Fritz is the greatest man who ever walked on this planet.

For those of you who have already read my description of San Antonio, you'll know that this is my hometown. I was born at Fort Sam Houston, and we moved to Midland when I was about eight years old. I've lived in over a dozen different towns in the state. I joined the fighting Air Force while living in San Antonio, and I was restricted to base for some slight infraction of the rules while the rest of my squadron visited town during the weekends.

I had traveled to San Antonio several times before this particular summer sales trip into town. Before this trip, I had never had a problem finding a comfortable motel room but this time was an exception, as I tried motel after motel in search of an available room. Finally, several hours and about twenty motels later, I managed to find an empty room. The motel was way out on Austin Highway and about ten miles from where I usually stayed.

I began lamenting the difficulty of finding a room, as I was filling out the motel register. The gentleman commented to me, that I must not be from around these parts, because San Antonio was the most popular tourist destination in all of Texas. Starting with the Alamo, he rattled off a list of the most popular attractions in the area. After describing several of the Spanish Missions, he ended his vocal tour of the town with a questioning tone of voice. I responded by saying that I was from back east, and this was my first visit into San Antonio. I assured him that I would take in some of the local sights while I was in town.

As I was taking my luggage into the motel room, I was kicking mentally kicking myself for not knowing that my hometown was a famous tourist town, especially in the summer. I determined that my powers of observation and reason must be absolutely zero. No wonder, I always got into trouble when my bride would ask: "Hi honey, notice anything different about me?" I decided that from now on whenever she would ask this question, I'd just fake a heart attack or something. I suppose that I could just suck my thumb, but that wouldn't be the adult thing to do.

The Texas public school system is supposed to be one of the best in the nation, however they have installed some rather puzzling new concepts lately. One is that none of the teachers can no longer spank anyone. When I was in high school, there was nothing more embarrassing than being asked to the front of the class, grabbing my ankles, and being spanked. It did ruin my date-ability for one cute young thing I was trying to impress one day. The other thing that the school system is doing nowadays is passing anyone who is breathing, to the next highest grade. It's against the rules to flunk anyone in this age of enlightenment, because it may affect their self worth. So, when you are old enough they just say: "Hey, want a diploma?"

One such young lad named Russel Brane, and called Rusty by his friends was confused by the term, "tourist season". Rusty reasoned that since there was a "Deer Season", "Dove Season", "Pheasant Season", etc., that during "tourist season", the tourists were pretty much fair game. He spotted a family of four with out of state license plates, traveling in a Winnebago, up in the Texas hill country. I won't mention the name of the town, because I don't want to hurt their tourist business anymore that it already has been by this incident. Anyway, Rusty managed to subdue this family, hogtied them in the back of his pickup, and was headed back into town with a big ol' grin on his face, while pulling their Winnebago behind him.

The local Sheriffs department was not too impressed, with Rusty's "tourist season" story and the young lad went to trial. His lawyer got him off scott-free, because he argued that his client's predicament was the result of the lax public school system. The judge ruled that the young man should not be allowed to attend any of the higher learning facilities in the country, and also explained the term "wedding season" to him.

U-V

Dictionary

UN—Rhymes with bun, gun, run, and tun.
    Un means "and."
    As in: Yew un may, fer-aver.
        "You and me, forever."

UNNER-STAN—Some folks do, and some folks don't.
    Unner-stan means "understand."
    As in: Yew unner-stan wut alm sane?
        "Do you understand what I'm saying?"

VAIN-OUS—The fourth planet from the sun.
    Vain-ous means "Venus."
    As in: Shays purt-yer thay-un Vain-ous day mah-loe.
        "She's prettier than Venus de Milo."

VAR-STEE—You'll win a letter for doing this.
    Var-stee means "varsity."
    As in: Y'all wunna jon duh var-stee?
        "Do you want to join the varsity?"

VAY-UST—Add one of these to a suit and suddenly it's a three piece.
    Vay-ust means "vest."
    As in: Ats uh rail naws vay-ust.
        "That's a real nice vest."

VAY-YUN—A sign of being married, with family.
    Vay-yun means "van."
    As in: Uh many-vay-yun wif te-yun cop hollers.
        "A mini-van with ten cup holders."

VIE-LUT—A really popular flower from Africa.
    Vie-lut means "violet."
    As in: Zatta Affer-cun vie-lut?
        "Is that an African violet?"

VITE-MUNS—Some folks don't get enough of these, some get too many.
    Vite-muns means "vitamins."
    As in: Wares yalls vite-muns?
        "Where are your vitamins?"

VUL-SHUR—I'm looking for a really big cage for my pet.
    Vul-shur means "vulture."
    As in: Aah doan lak boz-urs ur vul-shurs.
        "I don't like buzzards or vultures."

Texan—English

Una-var-sal Siddy—Universal City
In the early 1900s, Universal City was home to the very successful Texas Moving Picture Company. In the early days of moving pictures, Texas had ideal scenery, horses, cattle, actors, and actresses for making many of the more popular Western movies. These early movies produced by the Texas Moving Picture Company were "silent films" with subtitles. These "silent films" became very popular throughout America and the rest of the world. The Texas Moving Picture Company was making lots of money with these movies, and all of their stockholders were quite happy with the results of their investments.

The future looked quite bright, and the company couldn't wait to produce one of its new "talkie" movies. The company had spent large sums of money to advertise its new talkie movie and planned a simultaneous premier throughout the whole country. The company executives were quite shocked by the audience's response to their new movie. Instead of the movie viewers being thrilled by actually hearing the actors and actresses' talk, they couldn't understand them. Unfortunately, the executives didn't realize that most of America just doesn't understand Texan.

The company did try to reintroduce the movie with English subtitles, but the movie was unsuccessful. This very dramatic movie became a comedy of errors, and people were laughing more than they were crying. The company attempted to return to their formerly successful "silent movies" but the people now wanted the talkies—not in Texan or with English subtitles. The company pulled up stakes and moved to California and opened up a brand new Universal City.

There are still a few remnants of the old Texas Moving Picture Company in town. The local high school students hold live stage productions of some of the old silent movies, complete with the piano player. The students occasionally perform the last talkie produced by the Texas Moving Picture Company. These high school students are really smart and quite talented. Years ago, they found out that it's a lot more fun to have stage plays than wash cars to earn the money needed for their senior trip.

These high school kids also did a remake of one of the old silent films, and occasionally this movie is shown down at the local theater. During your stay in Universal City, you may be lucky enough to take in one of these moving picture shows or stage productions. If not, perhaps one of the junior highs is having a car wash—then at least you'll be able to leave town in a clean car.

Joe Kent Roberts

Texan – English
Yuh-val-dee—Uvalde

Uvalde is located either south-southwest or south-southeast of San Antonio; I left my Texas map out in the car, so I'm not really positive and I'm having to rely on my memory. Forgetfulness and senility are actually wonderful things; because of my having these great abilities, I was able to plan my own "surprise" birthday party. I can't remember if I've planned one for this year or next year, but I'll really be surprised when it does occur.

Uvalde is a Spanish word that means box canyon and is so named because of being located in a heavily forested valley among literally millions of boxes on the north side of the canyon. The Spaniards were thrilled to discover all these wooden boxes in various shapes and sizes, because they were able to store gold, silver, and other valuables inside them. Over the years, these boxes have also evolved into corrugated and cardboard boxes. The owner of this box canyon, a Miss Eva Loushun, and her staff ship these boxes all over the country. She will let the local folks in Texas have any of these boxes free of charge, so you may want to brush up on your Texan if you want wrangle one or more of these boxes to take back home.

Even though there was a town named Uvalde back in Spain, the Spaniards decided not to name this town New Uvalde, because it was nothing like their beloved Uvalde, Spain. Plus there were already lots of towns in the New World named New This or New That, and the Spaniards thought it was kind of silly to have a town with a mailing address of New Uvalde, New World. There were lots of things that were totally different between Uvalde and Uvalde. For one thing, there were no Indians in Uvalde, nor were there any antelope, armadillos, white-tailed deer, elk, diamondback rattlesnakes, horned toads, jackrabbits, jackalope, or Apache Indians. Uvalde had all these things, but Uvalde didn't. Uvalde also had all these really unique wooden boxes, and Uvalde didn't.

At times, it's very difficult for me to believe that Spain once ruled this part of America. It must have been a very confusing era.

Uvalde had quite a few wild cattle in the region—not Uvalde, Spain, but Uvalde, New World. Most of these cattle are now domesticated; however, several of these wild cattle are seen wandering around the various roads and highways in the region at times. Please be sure to watch for "Wild Cattle Crossing" signs while you are in this region of the state, and please obey all traffic laws. If you happen to see any of these wild cattle during your tour of Texas, you might want to grab a rope and try your hand at being a real cowboy. Be sure that any cattle you happen to see are not branded.

Cattle brands are located on the right rear of the cow as you are facing the cow. It's probably best not to approach the cow from the rear because of cow residue, backfires, and things. Sometimes, the ranch brand will be a tag on the cow's left ear, and if you happen to see a tag on the right ear, it means that this particular cow has a calf. Every so often you'll see a cow with a bell attached to a strap around her neck. These are called cowbells and are used by the owner to keep track of where this particular cow is located in the pasture.

These cows eventually go crazy from the constant clanging of the cowbell whenever they move or walk. If this cow happens to be particularly valuable to her owner, she might be sent to a cow psychologist to help remedy the situation. There was one incident several years ago where a rich, young cow psychologist was seriously trampled by a cow because he had one of those very popular Italian leather couches in his office. Upon being asked to lie down on the couch, this crazy cow went into an absolute rage. She was eventually sedated and is presently being rehabilitated in one of the many cow asylums throughout the state. I would also advise that if you want to approach a cow that is wearing a cowbell, please don't wear leather shoes or a leather coat. Unless you happen to be dressed like a cowboy, it's probably best to be wearing sneakers. Um, dressed like a Western cowboy, not a Dallas Cowboy.

In the 1860s, a local outlaw named R. Barry Kruked was a notorious cattle rustler, train robber, and highwayman who terrorized almost everyone in this area of the state. He was just an all-around crooked, corrupt, despicable individual and was therefore appointed deputy sheriff in 1861. Barry was a smooth-talking fellow, quick on the draw, with a charming personality and friendly smile. His past experiences gave him the extra edge and ammunition he needed to succeed in politics, and Barry was soon elected sheriff. He then went on to have a very rewarding career in politics by robbing from everyone and giving to himself. Stuffing turkeys and stuffing ballot boxes are very similar, because they each give someone that full, satisfied feeling. Some politicians are real turkeys while still others are elected by real turkeys.

Since the 1990s, Uvalde has been recognized for its abundance of pecans, because there are over 2,500 acres containing over 30,000 pecan trees, watered by the largest artesian well in the state. So if you love pecans and pecan pies, this is another great place to visit during your travels in Texas. With all these billions of pecans, there were mountains of pecan shells left over after processing. The local folks decided to crush these shells, add glue, and make all sorts of figurines out of them. They are also able to manufacture pecan siding, pecan wallboard, pecan furniture, and even pecan houses from this process.

You'll probably notice the many pecan shell recycling centers throughout the state. Please be sure to save all your pecan shells and take them to one of these centers. If you love pecans and pecan pie as much as I do, then you'll be able to make lots of extra money during your tour of Texas. Some folks have even been able to pay for their entire holiday in Texas by recycling pecan shells.

Talkin' Texan

Texas is known for being cattle country but goats outnumber cattle by more than 50 percent. Each year in the 1990s, the local goat ranchers were able to bring in over $1.7 million by leasing their ranches for hunting purposes. Although most deer hunters would prefer a buck with a rack of horns, a young buck with two horns is perfectly acceptable to most novice hunters. Armed with this knowledge, the goat ranchers would just paint the word "deer" on the side of any expendable goat they might happen to have. The deer hunters were very happy for the assistance the goat ranchers had given them, and the ranchers were happy to cull their less desirable goats from their herds. It was a win/win situation, so everyone was quite happy, because most city folks can't taste the difference between venison and goat.

Joe Kent Roberts

Texan - English
Vic-tor-ya—Victoria
Victoria is situated halfway between Corpus Christi and Houston. I've often wondered why so many people are preoccupied with things that are halfway or in the center of or in the middle of something. There is a Center, Centerville, and Midland, Texas, but so far there is not a Halfway, Texas. Perhaps someday when we run out of names for towns or streets there will be a town or a street called Halfway. Hopefully, we're halfway there.

Newcomers to Texas just assume that Victoria was named after one of the queens of England, but this is not the case at all. Texas women are some of the most beautiful in the entire world, and the Texas men would often name a new city or town after their wives or sweethearts. Victoria was not only a beautiful woman; she also developed some great recipes for cooking armadillo.

If you happen to be in the area during Victoria's annual Armadillo Festival, be sure and visit for a while. Not only is there a genuine Texas rodeo complete with buffalo, longhorn steers, and clowns, there are also many stands and booths featuring the local ethnic foods. Of course, there are the popular and well-known foods such as chili, tamales, tacos, and bar-b-que; there are also the numerous stands and booths that feature many of Victoria's Secret recipes for armadillo.

You may choose from armadillo burgers, armadillo chili, armadillo tacos, bar-b-qued armadillo, armadillo etouffee, and my favorite: armadillo on a stick. Be sure to see the harvesting of the armadillos at the armadillo rodeo roundup. After the cowboys have herded the armadillos into the big corral at the rodeo, then the cooks come into the corral to select the choicest of the armadillos to prepare for some good ol' armadillo stew and other unique entrées.

After the cooks have harvested the armadillos and cleaned out the shells, they'll give 'em to some other fellows who add a few doodads to them and sell 'em as hats. Maybe the Wisconsin folks think their cheese heads are unique, but there is nothing cooler than an armadillo hat. The last time I was at the Armadillo Festival, these armadillo hats were selling for about $40 to $50. If you'd like to save a little money, you can just pick up an armadillo from the side of the highway. It's illegal to shoot armadillo from the side of the road in Texas, and I think the same law also applies to shooting husbands and wives. It's easy to determine a live illegal armadillo from the dead ones—the dead armadillos will be lying on their back with their feet sticking up in the air.

    Just pull off the side of the road and pick up the armadillo. If you're hungry, it's probably not a good idea to eat an armadillo that's been lying on the side of the road for too long. However, if you just ran over the armadillo with your car, then it's nice and fresh and mostly grilled. Then you can buy a copy of Victoria's Secret Recipes for armadillo for less than ten bucks and have a nice meal and a really cool hat.

W

Dictionary

WARDS—This one is pronounced the same as the now-defunct Montgomery-Wards.
    Wards means "words."
    As in: Thay-ums fott-un wards.
        "Them's fighting words."

WARK—There should be an easier way to earn a living.
    Wark means "work."
    As in: Aah godd uh goad tuh wark.
        "I have to go to work."

WASE—Sometimes we have too little, sometimes we have too much.
    Wase means "waste" or "waist."
    As in: Uh mine e-yus uh tar-bull thang tuh wase.
        "A mind is a terrible thing to waste."

WEARED—Nope, this is not the past tense of wear.
    Weared means "weird."
    As in: Jaunta hair sum-pen weared?
        "Do you want to hear something weird?"

WHALE—A spoken word rather than something in the sea.
    Whale means "well."
    As in: Whale, blass yore hort.
        "Well, bless your heart."

WHIZ-KEY—Sometimes this opens doors, sometimes this closes doors.
    Whiz-key means "whiskey."
    As in: Whiz-key Raver doan ron dri.
        "Whiskey River don't run dry."
        (Thanks, Willie.)

WILE—Some of us are, some of us aren't.

Wile means "wild."
	As in: Shay shoe e-yus uh wile thang.
		"She sure is a wild thing."
WORSH—At times, it seems that every day is this day.
	Worsh means "wash."
	As in: Aah godd uh worsh muh paints un sharts.
		"I've got to wash my pants and shirts."
WART-ER—Summertime is more fun with a wart-er pistol.
	Wart-er means "water."
	As in: Aah godd uh wart-er muh godd-un.
		"I have to water my garden.

Joe Kent Roberts

Texan—English

Way-koe—Waco
Situated in central Texas on the banks of the beautiful Brazos River, Waco is an exciting and interesting town. Riverboat rides and day trips are available each and every day in the spring and summer seasons. Naturally, you can have lunch or dinner aboard these various riverboats. The riverboat fare includes the more popular riverboat items like catfish, perch, brim, and so forth, and since Texas is so well known for livestock, they also serve various cuts of beefsteak, lamb chops, leg of lamb, roast lamb, pork chops, leg of pig, and a roasted pig, complete with an apple in its mouth.

Many out-of-state tourists have requested that the riverboats also serve rattlesnake, jackrabbit, jackalope, coyote, roadrunner, and armadillo. These items are under consideration but are not available on the menus at this time. While many tourists on their riverboat trips observe these animals along the riverbanks, some of these animals are very difficult for the crew to capture and prepare for lunch or dinner. The armadillo is fairly easy to catch, but some of the others are a lot more difficult. Rattlesnake bites are sometimes fatal, and riverboat crews are difficult to replace. Therefore, you will probably not see rattlesnake on the menu anytime soon. Although they quickly scurry about the boat, most of the crew cannot outrun a jackrabbit or a roadrunner. The ever-elusive coyote and jackalope are nocturnal creatures and therefore very hard to see in the dark.

Just a few blocks south of the riverboat docks, you will find the Texas Ranger Museum. This museum features all sorts of historical artifacts and information about the Texas Rangers. Please do not confuse this museum with the hysterical Texas Rangers baseball team and their ballpark mausoleum. The Texas Rangers baseball team is actually the old Washington Senators with a new name. The performances of the old Washington

Senators baseball team and the actual Washington senators were very similar. Things haven't changed much, so I guess history really does repeat itself.

The Texas Rangers are the finest law enforcement agency in the nation. Only the cream of the crop and the very finest that Texas has to offer are allowed to even be applicants. These men and women are the most friendly, intelligent, witty, and gracious individuals you would ever want to meet. Throughout the ebb and flow of Texas history, the ranks of the Texas Rangers have either been decimated or enlarged depending on the number of bad guys in the state. During times of great lawlessness, the ranks of the Texas Rangers were increased, but because of their great efficiency in getting rid of the bad guys, these ranks were soon reduced. Fortunately, the Texas Rangers are currently active and continue to protect Texans from the notorious.

This Texas Ranger Museum has some of the most fascinating documents and photos of early Texas history. While doing some ancestral research, I discovered that my great-great-great-grandfather was once a Texas Ranger. Naturally, I figured he had to have been a colonel, or at the very least a captain or something. So my family and I started to dig through the old documents in the museum to see what we could find out about this old gentleman. We were thrilled to discover that he had indeed served as a Texas Ranger in the early 1800s. The brief paragraph about him stated that he had served for three years, had two horses, two pistols, and a rifle.

As excited as we were to find this information about my great-great-great-grandfather, my sons and I were greatly disappointed to find barely a mention of the Lone Ranger and Tonto. I explained to my sons that it was probably because the Lone Ranger wore a mask and the other rangers figured only outlaws wore masks. Plus, the Lone Ranger's best and most trusted friend was an Indian, and the rangers were fighting Indians at this particular time in Texas history. Not only did the Lone Ranger hang out with Tonto, he was also a bit too eccentric to be totally accepted by the other Texas Rangers. Sorta like Rudolph the Red-Nosed Reindeer and the other reindeers.

The Lone Ranger was really hung up on silver, not only the color but also the metal. The Lone Ranger called his beautiful white horse Silver instead of Whitey or something like that. Plus, the Lone Ranger used only very expensive silver bullets and had no apparent source of income. The other rangers musta figured that the Lone Ranger was up to no good. I suppose anytime someone marches to the beat of a different drummer, he should probably not flaunt it so much or should be a little bit more low profile. My boys seem to have understood the lesson I was trying to teach them, for all of them have good jobs and they don't wear masks or anything—although one of my boys does have a white car that he calls Silver.

In the late 1700s, the Munney brothers and their wives arrived on the banks of the Brazos River. The brothers Grant, Les, and Bill, along with their wives Alice (Ali), Cindy, and Linda, traded a few trinkets to the local Swapngoe Indians for a parcel of land on the banks of the river. The Munney clan felt they had made a tidy little profit from this transaction and decided to open up a bank near this river because the Indians were so giving. The members of the Munney clan were financial wizards and initiated a pay-as-you-go plan called "financing." Basically, folks could buy just about anything they wanted with a little money as a down payment and finance the remainder, which was called a loan. The Munneys would lend you the balance of this loan if you had what they called collateral.

Collateral could be just about anything as long as it had value. However, it had to be valuable to them and just not to you. Therefore, they would loan you money on livestock, land, or property, but not on stuff like cookies, apple pies, pecan pies, egg sandwiches, or extra rolls of toilet paper. The Munneys would loan you money only if they approved of your collateral. All of their loan applications had some letters on the bottom of the application that read W.A.C.O., which meant "with approved collateral only."

The Munney clan had initially named their bank the Munney Bank; however, this had caused them a few problems with the locals and one of the notorious outlaw gangs in the area. One Wednesday afternoon in the summer of 1812, the Banks Gang rode into town with their usual scalawag intentions. Robert Banks (a.k.a. Rob) was the leader of the gang, and the other outlaws were his brother Richard (Rich), James Locks (Jimmy), Jackson Hammer (Jack), Hyrum Jenks (Hy), and Rob's girlfriend, Wanda Lute.

The bank guard that morning was an elderly gentleman by the name of Douglas (Doug) Cupp. Mister Cupp was very tall, thin, and lanky; most people had nicknamed him "Stick." The bank tellers on duty that afternoon were a Miss Nell Byter and Mrs. Delores Posit, a.k.a. Dee. The Banks Gang barged into the bank and announced to everyone that this was a "stick up." After much commotion, shooting, and shouting, the gang took the loot, departed the premises with guns a-blazing, mounted their horses, and rode off into the sunset, never to be seen in these parts again.

Some folks say they went up to Montana Territory; others said they went up to Alaska Territory, and still others say they went down to South America. Personally, I feel that none of these places were options, because with their Texas accents and slow Southern drawl, they would have been most difficult to understand. I think they went to Mississippi, became familiar with the riverboats, changed their names, and then returned years later to open up the Brazos River Riverboat Rides. After all, W.A.C.O. is a very friendly town.

Texan - English
Wart-er-mel-uns—Watermelons

Shortly after watermelons are first harvested each summer, they are loaded onto six-by trucks and covered with a tarp for the trip to market. These trucks will come zooming past you doing about ninety-eleven miles per hour, kicking up the roadside dust, tarps flapping in the wind. It's a beautiful sight. Some of these trucks are on their way to the numerous watermelon stands that seemingly spring up overnight throughout the state.

There are just a few things better than a visit to a watermelon stand on a hot Texas day. There are tubs full of ice-cold watermelons, and you can either buy some watermelon by the slice or buy several to take home. You can pick out the watermelon of your choice, and one of the folks at the stand will plug the watermelon so you can taste it. After you have made your selection, just sit down at a table under the canopy and enjoy some ice-cold watermelon.

Some of the most fun is spitting out the watermelon seeds, just to see how far they will go. The fancier watermelon stands even have seed-spitting contests for their customers. Some of the more popular watermelon stands have shooting galleries set up with all sorts of stationary and moving targets. You'll probably see quite a few experts at these galleries. I've seen some fantastic shots performed by these experts. Some folks might suppose that only men can become experts at seed spitting. This is not so—I've seen quite a few ladies who are expert shots. An expert will be able to shoot more than a dozen seeds at a moving target in just a few seconds.

One thing that you might be wary of at these watermelon stands is the seed-spitting "hustler." These folks will actually be working a circuit throughout the state at various watermelon stands. You may think you are a pretty good shot, but don't get suckered in by one of these experts. These folks are very, very good and will play for thousands of dollars, depending on the difficulty of the shot or the competition involved. I once saw a fellow shoot three flies out of midair in a split second to win a $5,000 bet. Another time I saw a fellow arrive in fancy duds, driving a Cadillac, and flashing lots of money. He left the watermelon stand wearing a barrel and hitchhiking. The good thing is, he did have some ice-cold watermelon before he bet one of the hustlers, lost his car and all his cash.

Texan - English
Wish-et-ah Faws—Wichita Falls

Located on Highway 287 between Amarillo and Dallas, Wichita Falls was named after the Wichita Indians, the Wichita River, and the beautiful Wichita Falls. This thriving community of over 50,000 friendly folks is a must-see stop during your visit to Texas. There is also a great park, located right off the highway on the north side of town complete with a roller coaster and all sorts of rides for you and your kids to enjoy

Other than the Alamo, the falls of Wichita are probably one of the most visited parts of Texas. The Wichita River drops over fifty feet into a beautiful horseshoe-shaped basin containing crystal-clear waters. The Spanish explorers were very excited to discover these falls during their travels from El Paso to what is now Dallas. The falls were a welcomed oasis to these hot and thirsty explorers in the 1700s.

The Wichita Indians had inhabited this part of Texas for over 10,000 years. The Indians were warm, friendly, hospitable, and welcomed the Spaniards to Kitikiti'sh Falls with open arms. The Spaniards were thrilled by such a warm welcome and were greatly intrigued by the Indian maidens. Seems that these Indian women traditionally wore nothing above the waist and very little below. Much to the delight of men from all over the country, this tradition continues to this day among these gorgeous Indian maidens. There are times when I'm a bit puzzled as to why the Alamo continues to draw more visitors than Wichita Falls. Perhaps it's because more folks are interested in history that I thought.

The Wichita Indians called themselves the Kitikiti'sh Indians, because of the abundance of cats that traveled with them. The Spaniards discovered these Indians because of their constant shouts of "Here kiti, kiti! Here kiti kiti!" The Spaniards had never seen so many cats traveling with an Indian tribe before. When the Spaniards approached the Indians, they asked them what they called themselves and the Indians replied that they called themselves the Kitikiti'sh Indians.

Not only did the Spaniards feel it was beneath their dignity to be constantly saying Kiti, Kiti but also they didn't want to be writing back home about the Kiti, Kiti Indians. Plus, the king and queen of Spain would probably figure that these Spaniards had discovered something other than gold, silver, and jewels. The Spaniards didn't want to lose their funding, nor did they want to appear less than macho to the folks back home, so they had to come up with another name for these Indians.

The Spaniards decided they would hold a feast for the Kitikiti'sh Indians at the Kitikiti'sh Falls. The Spaniards brought the Indians all the latest in swimsuit fashions from Spain, beautifully gift-wrapped, and the Indians brought the Spaniards some tamales so that they also would have something to unwrap. The Spaniards were delighted that the Indian braves loved their swimsuits and that the Indian maidens promptly discarded their bikini tops. The Indians also were overjoyed that the Spaniards unwrapped their tamales before eating them.

During the feast, the Spaniards proclaimed that the Indians would hereafter be called the Wichita Indians instead of the Kitikiti'sh Indians. The Spaniards explained that Wichita was an anagram that represented:

- W for witty
- I for intelligent
- C for cute
- H for handsome
- I for indigenous
- T for talented and
- A for affable

The Indians didn't really understand indigenous and affable but decided to go along with the Spaniards because they did understand all the other words. The Indians also didn't understand why the Spaniards kept calling them Indians, because India was way over on the other side of the world. The Indians decided that although the Spaniards didn't seem too bright, they at least made some pretty nice swimsuits and rode some really nice horses.

Wichita Falls is one of the few places in America where the Indians were allowed to remain on their original lands. The falls truly are beautiful and are fully maintained by the Wichita Indians. You may want to have Grandpa and Grandma take the kids over to the roller coaster park when you visit, because the falls are one of the few places in Texas that allows topless swimming. They do not allow cameras at the falls, so that's why you seldom see a photo of the falls of Wichita. Texans are also quite secretive about these falls, because they pretty much want to keep the falls to themselves.

During your visit to the falls, please refrain from calling the Indians *Indians*. Although we call the Indians *Indians*, they prefer to be called Kitikiti'sh. They are pretty easy to find in Wichita Falls. Just call out "Kitikiti'sh, Kitikiti'sh" and wait for a few moments; they should arrive shortly. Wichita Falls still has the largest amount of cats per person in the state, so you may want to carry a nice supply of cat treats during your stay, just in case the cats arrive first.

It's pretty difficult for non-Texans to be allowed to visit the falls unless they happen to be of Spanish decent. Texans want to keep the location of the falls a secret, so if you don't happen to be able to speak flawless Texan, you may not be able to visit the falls. The local folks may even say that these gorgeous falls of Wichita don't exist. Try using some of the Texan words in this little book and tuning your radio to a country-western station. If you are still unable to pass for Texan by speaking perfect Texan, driving a pickup, wearing Levis, boots, and a Stetson or Resistol hat, then there is just one other option available.

    Legend has it that when the Spaniards left the Wichita Falls area, they promised the Indians that one day they would return. Therefore, if you and your friends can obtain some Spanish conquistador outfits, you should have no problem visiting the falls. Just be sure you have a couple of dozen tamales with you. You'll probably see other Spaniards walking down the street eating tamales, so just tag along with them to the falls.

X-Y-Z

Dictionary

X-REE—A very important and expensive medical procedure.
    X-ree means "X-ray."
        As in: Y'all nade uh X-ree.
            "You need an X ray."
X-UT - You ain't supposed to go in here.
    X ut means "exit"
        As in: Muh ax dun x ut.
            "My ex made an exit."
Y'ALL—A word that can mean one person or a stadium full.
    Y'all means "you."
        As in: Ha, ha y'all dune?
            "Hi, how are you doing?"
YEAR—Not for just a year, but always.
    Year means "Do you hear?"
        As in: Y'all quee-ut thay-ut, year?
            "You all quit doing that, do you hear?"
YELLA—A popular color in a box of crayons.
    Yella means "yellow."
        As in: Shay wara yella ree-bon inner hay-air.
            "She wore a yellow ribbon in her hair."
YEW—A rarely used tense referring to a singular person.
    Yew means "you."
        As in: Aah luuv yew.
            "I love you."
YONG—When we're really yong, we get another type of discount.
    Yong means "young."
        As in: Aah wunna bay fer-aver yong.
            "I want to be forever young."
    Actually we don't, we just want to *look* young.

YORE—Seems that I started this project a long time ago.
>   Yore means "your."
>   As in: Wuts yore naim?
>   > "What's your name?"

ZEE—I think I'll get some z's.
>   Zee means "is he."
>   As in: Zee goanna aster tuh daince?
>   > "Is he going to ask her to dance?"

ZIT—Not relative to Texas teenagers.
>   Zit means "is it."
>   As in: Zit tom fer launch?
>   > "Is it time for lunch?"

Z-UT—A teenager's lament.
>   Z-ut means "zit."
>   As in: Yew godd uh nothar z ut?
>   > "Do you have another zit?"

Joe Kent Roberts

Texan—English

Ax-et—X IT
When the Texas legislature proposed the "English only" amendment, they didn't realize how confusing and costly this amendment would be to its citizens and to the state of Texas. This amendment forced the people to write and speak only in American English. Therefore, all the Texan names, signs, and road signs had to be changed from Texan to American English. Please see the chapter on Texas road signs as an example of the great turmoil that this amendment created.

Actually, it's a good thing that one of the bright legislators in the capitol building suggested that the English only amendment should be changed to the "American English only" amendment. Otherwise, Texans would be saying things like "Tally ho, the fox!" or "Tally ho, the armadillo!" If Texans had to call French fries "chips," what would potato chips be called? Then if they had to call the hood of a car a "bonnet," what would they call a ladies Easter hat? I guess I'll ask an Englishman some day. The English call an apartment a "flat"; what could the Texan possibly say when his car has a "flat"? Wow, talk about confusing! Then again, Texans have some of the biggest cars on the highway, so I suppose a Texan could have a car with an apartment.

Whereas most towns are founded, the town of X IT has been mostly losted. This town is one of the few mobile communities in the United States. The inhabitants of X IT are nomadic and are constantly roaming throughout the great state of Texas. Some fragments of the population of X IT have even been observed in other states of the union. The citizens of X IT were violently opposed to the English only amendment and decided they would speak in any language they preferred.

Therefore, the citizens of X IT speak a potpourri of languages in a wide range of all sorts of various accents. If you happen to come across one of the citizens of X IT while traveling through Texas, just say "howdy." Sometimes you will encounter some of the citizens of X IT in other parts of the nation, and you can just say "hi" to them in their local jargon.

The people of X IT also dress in vast array of different clothing, anywhere from casual to formal to downright tacky. They are a proud people and have a great desire to preserve their freedoms. I suppose you could call them the mavericks of the country.

The next time you are traveling down the highway and see a road sign that says X IT, just pull off the road and visit for a while. Pick up a few souvenirs and maybe buy a few postcards to send back home. Just jot a note on the back of the card, something like "From the heart of X IT, having a wonderful time, wish you were here." Just remember that with the English only amendment being in effect, the name of the town is now spelled EXIT. Hope y'all had a great time there, I know I did.

Texan - English
Yale—Yell
Nestled in forested woods just a few miles from Seguin, you'll find the town of Yell. Yell was named after its founder, William Yell, in the late 1800s. The town was originally called Yell Settlement and eventually called Yell when the town applied for a post office. Initially, all was well in Yell until the post office complained that there was a Tell, Texas, and it was too confusing to deliver mail to Yell and Tell.

The folks in Yell changed the name to Good, Texas, and again all seemed well. However, the post office complained that, since Texas was such a wonderful state, there had to be something better than Good. So the good folks of Yell and Good once again changed their town name from Good to Best. The folks at the post office were thrilled that Good had become Best.

Even to this day, the folks living in Best still refer to their town as Yell Settlement. The kids in Yell love it because they aren't scolded for being Good or for not being on their Best behavior; they're from Yell. Kids will be kids and do what they do best, which is yell and holler.

Not too long ago, there was a request from Best to have the town name changed from Best to Yell and Holler. The post office is currently taking this request under consideration. So, if you happen to be traveling around these parts and see a small town with Yell, Good, and Best all scratched out on business signs, road signs, and stuff, then you've probably found Yell. Please feel free to holler and yell, or yell and holler, whichever the new name is gonna be.

Joe Kent Roberts

Texan – English
Yoh-kum—Yoakum
Each May, thousands of folks follow the "wildflower trail" from Cuero northeast up to Yoakum for the annual Tom-Tom Festival. This walking and hiking trail literally flourishes with over three hundred native Texas wildflowers during this time of the year. The most recognized flowers are the bluebonnets, Texas's State Flower. Photographers have a field day with so many wildflowers to photograph and they compete in the Texas State Wildflower Contest held in Yoakum, coinciding with the Tom-Tom Festival.

 The photographers compete for many fabulous prizes to be awarded for winning Best Picture, Best Composition, Best Lighting, Best Wildflower at Sunset, Best Wildflower at Sunrise, Best Wildflower Including a Person, Best Wildflower Including a Celebrity, Best Wildflower Including a Grandpa, Best Wildflower Including a Grandma, Best Wildflower Including a Baby, Best Bluebonnet, and Best Rare Wildflower. The winners in each category will receive a $10.00 bill, an artificial wildflower, a no-expense-paid trip to Dime Box, Texas, and discount coupons for a large order of French fries or a free drink with a purchase of any size hamburger at the Yoakum Hamburger Barn.

 Just in case you're not a world-class photographer or don't own a camera, can't borrow a camera, or can't figure out how to find the photo button on a camera, there are other categories in which you may compete. These same fabulous prizes are also offered in other forms of competition. You may enter the Best Wildflower Painting, Best Wildflower in Watercolor, Best Wildflower in Pencil, Best Wildflower in Pen and Ink, Best Wildflower in Crayon, Best Wildflower in Oil, or Best Wildflower in Texas Crude Oil. (Note: The promoters of the Wildflower Contest are considering adding a Best Wildflower in Refined Oil category as soon as there are some classy, high falootin' folks in attendance.)

Since the Wildflower Contest and the Tom-Tom Festival are held in conjunction each year, you'll hear the constant beating of the tom-toms while you are walking along the Wildflower Trail. All day, all night, there is the continuous pounding and beating of the drums. Morning, noon, and night, the drums echo from the hills and valleys along the Wildflower Trail—always pounding, always beating, the ceaseless constant sounds of the tom-toms. Most folks will walk, hike, or stroll along the trail, but rarely march, because whenever they change tom-tom drummers, no one ever wants to be marching to the sound of a different drummer.

Some folks asked me, "Hey Joe, how did tom-toms come to be?" Well, I started doing some research. I searched high and I searched low; I searched over hill and I searched over dale. I logged on to the Internet, I went to the library, and I even consulted the banned-in-Texas *Encyclopedia Britannica*. I discovered no new information whatsoever. So I decided to consult an Indian, also known as an Indian consultant.

My journey began on a cool August day as I embarked on my quest to discover the inventor of the original tom-tom. I ventured into the deep piney woods of East Texas seeking information from Wiley Enjun, chief of the little known Wannadaince Indian tribe. Unfortunately, the chief wasn't listed in the Yellow Pages, so I couldn't let my fingers do the walking, plus the chief was of the old school and didn't own a telephone. The chief and I communicated by smoke signals until we could meet face to face. Fortunately, during my brief stint in the Boy Scouts as a youth, the only thing I remembered was how to send, receive, and understand smoke signals.

Crossing cold raging rivers, swimming across catfish-laden streams (fortunately, the chief didn't live across the sea, or I would have had to cross shark-infested waters.), and ignoring all the "No Trespassing," "No Hunting," No Solicitors," "No Tourists," and the frequent "No Deposit, No Return" signs, I finally arrived at

Chief Wiley Enjun's front door. The chief opened the front door with a look of stunned amazement.

"Hey, are you Mel Gibson?" he asked.

"No, Chief, I'm Joe Kent," I replied.

"Well, you could be a dead ringer for him," he said.

"Hey, Chief, could you please be careful with your choice of words? At my age, there are several words that are just a bit scary to me—words like, dead, doctor, cardiac, funeral, hearse, and grave."

The chief said okay and invited me in for a cup of coffee, a cold Shiner Bock, Maeker's sausage, and some freshly baked pecan pie.

The chief then proceeded to explain the legend of the tom-tom. It seems that in the lore and history of the Wannadaince Indian Tribe, there was a young Indian brave named Tomto. Tomto and another Indian brave named Blubber were out hunting for buffalo one day in 17,060 B.C. Well, yeah, the chief said that Blubber was a very unusual Indian name, but one particular Indian squaw had already given birth to nine Indian braves and was hoping that the tenth time would be the charm and she would have a baby Indian girl. When the doctor announced, "It's a boy!" she broke down and started weeping. Actually, she was blubbering, and they all decided that the baby boy would be called Blubber.

It was very difficult to be living in 17,060 B.C. because not only were there none of the modern conveniences that we all know of today, but folks continually had to count both backward and forward. Tomto was born in 17,080 B.C. and was enjoying his twentieth year on Earth, and his friend Blubber was born in 17079 B.C. and was already legally voting and drinking. The first month of the year was December and the first day of the year was December 31. Just six days after the first day of the year, the Indians celebrated Christmas Day and then the next day was Christmas Eve, followed several weeks later by Thanksgiving. The

Talkin' Texan

Indians greatly looked backward to Halloween because not only did they have great fun trick-or-treating, but also autumn would soon be over and they could start enjoying the summer.

Anyway, Tomto and Blubber had been out hunting several days from April 10 until April 6 in the spring of 17,060 B.C. and wanted to take a nice juicy buffalo back to camp for their upcoming winter provisions. The braves were very fortunate to fell a good-size buffalo with their spears, bow and arrows, and their ever-handy battleaxe. The boys cleaned, skinned, and gutted the buffalo and were heading back to camp to get some of the rest of the tribe to help them carry the buffalo meat back to camp.

While they were walking back to camp, suddenly they were confronted by an angry, coiled diamondback rattlesnake ready to strike. The braves were startled but kept their wits about them as Blubber immediately distracted the snake by running circles around it while Tomto used his lightening quick reflexes and grabbed the snake by the tail and slung it into a nearby hollow log. Tomto took a piece of the damp buffalo hide and covered the top of the hollow log and wrapped it tightly to keep the snake from escaping. The boys then merrily went on their way back to camp and told the others of their exploits.

The braves enjoyed the winter and holiday season with their friends and family and looked forward and backward to seeing what had become of the snake that summer after the fall. In the summer of 17,059 B.C., the braves returned to the hollow log to see what had happened to the snake. Tomto slapped the top of the buffalo-skin hollow log several times to see if he could awaken the snake. "Hey," he announced to Blubber, "this sounds pretty good." Blubber agreed and Tomto began pounding on the hollow log with not only his hands but all sorts of things. Within a few short hours, Tomto became very proficient at getting some really great drum beats from the hollow log.

The braves initially called this new discovery the Tomto Tomto, because Tomto was the one to sling the snake into the hollow log and cover it with the buffalo skin and was really great at playing this new musical instrument, but later they just decided to call it the tom-tom. Tomto could make some great sounds come out of his tom-tom, and Blubber suggested he add some words to all these new sounds. Some folks may wonder why this wasn't the birth of the blues, with Indian braves named Tomto and Blubber. The blues would come many thousands of years later with the invention of the saxophone and country-western music happened with the invention of the guitar. Tomto and Blubber are credited with having the first "Rain Dance," the first "Hunting Dance," and the first "Harvest Dance"—and, of course, the first dance.

I thanked the chief for this legend of the tom-tom and for being such a gracious host and headed back on home to San Antone. The chief insisted that I take some extra Maeker's sausage, fresh-baked bread, and the rest of the pecan pie for my long journey back home. The food was delicious and my journey was very full and satisfying.

Texan - English
Za-pot-uh—Zapata
Zapata is probably one of the best-kept secrets for the quality of life and an easy-going style of living in the whole state. If this book is not a success, it will most probably remain that way. Zapata is located on Highway 87 about a hundred miles south of Laredo, or around 150 miles southwest of Corpus Christi. This quiet little border town has a population of less than 8,000 friendly folks, and some of the most authentic Mexican food in the state.

    Nothing against the popular fast-food Mexican restaurants that dominate Texas and the rest of the nation, but have you ever noticed any Mexicans frequenting these establishments? Um, shouldn't that tell you something? Quoting Professor Bob Domonkos, "That stuff is cholesterol-laden gruel" and any relation to that stuff and true Mexican food is pure coincidence. I suppose someone could call a pile of manure a rose bush, but it would still be a pile of manure to me. Visit some of the Mexican restaurants in Zapata and enjoy some authentic Mexican food. Viva Zapata!

    The town of Zapata had about sixteen different names before they finally named the town after Antonio Zapata in the early 1900s. Mister Zapata gave his life and his fortune in an unsuccessful attempt for freedom. There is a very fine movie about his life and times that you might be able to find at your favorite video store. It is quite appropriate that such a nice town is named after this great gentleman and patriot.

    Spaniards discovered this area of the country in the early 1500s. They also discovered the Apache Indians and immediately proclaimed this land unfit for habitat. So, naturally, everyone wanted to move here because they thought the Spaniards had discovered gold or the fountain of youth. The Apache Indians had lived in this part of America for over 11,000 years and upon discovering this, the Spaniards claimed the land for Spain. The Apaches called themselves "Inde," which means "the people." The

Spaniards called themselves "Rulesta Elegante," which means the elegant ruling people. The Spaniards called the Inde people Apache, which means fierce fighters, and the Inde called the Spaniards something that I am not allowed to print, which (loosely translated) means bad smelling, land-grabbing bonzos.

The Spaniards had brought horses to the new world, and the Apache were able to obtain quite a few by some shrewd horse-trading. The Apache men and women shortly became some of the best horse riders in the world. Naturally, the Spaniards wanted these horses back because they thought the Apache had traded for trick ponies. This is when the Spanish and Indian War started. The Apache were superior warriors and were experiencing many easy victories. The Spanish decided that since they couldn't win, they might as well make peace.

Drawing on their past experiences with another Indian tribe in Nacogdoches, the Spaniards offered the Apache reservations for an area up in Oklahoma. The Apache had heard what had happened in Nacogdoches and refused the offer. The Spaniards then tried a new tactic and asked the Indians, "Hey, how about if we build you a really nice Spanish mission?" This sounded so nice and romantic to the Indians, they accepted. After moving into the newly completed Spanish missions, the Indians quickly became very disgruntled and left the new mission. The Indians complained that while the Spanish missions looked pretty good, there was no green grass, flowing rivers, game, or even a decent fishing hole around the mission. There was nothing around but peyote cactus, rattlesnakes, and scorpions. The Indians became very wary of Spaniards bearing gifts. The Spaniards decided to go farther out west in this new world in search of a more gullible tribe and eventually ended up in California.

Later, an Indian tribe of buffalo hunters started moving into parts of Texas, primarily because these same Spaniards told them about lots of gold and the fountain of youth being in this part of

America. It seems that no mater what the nationality, folks always want lots of money and eternal youth. Anyway, this new group of Indians also called themselves "the people." Well, apparently Texas wasn't big enough for the both of them to be called "the people" so this was the start of the Indian Wars. The Apache called this new group of Indians the Comanche, which means "those who always want to fight."

It was most difficult in those days for any Comanche men or women to get a blind date with a member of a different Indian tribe. The Comanche really did fight like cats and dogs. Even today it is very difficult to get a positive reaction to the question, "Hey, do I have a great Comanche for you?"

The Comanche's favorite sport was something they called Indian wrestling, and the sport is still carried on today. Nowadays, it's promoted by the WBA and just called wrestling. There are no longer any Comanche involved in wrestling, and there is a lot more of just talking trash than the Indians would have allowed.

These Indian Wars lasted quite a long time and the Apache would eventually lose these wars. The Apache were primarily farmers and were well known for their ability to grow very large crops. They raised maize, squash, pumpkins, and watermelons. They were famous for their delicious graham-cracker-crust pumpkin pies with whipped cream topping. I don't know how they made the graham crackers; they probably got them from the Spaniards or something. They would get the cream from buffalo milk. The Apache men were responsible for milking the buffalo, which was a very difficult and dangerous task. This is one of the reasons that most of the men were called braves. The Apache women did most of the cooking and therefore most of the whipping, although I've heard there are a few Indian chefs around nowadays. I've tried a few of these Indian restaurants, and the food is not at all like I've imagined. I knew that Indians liked salsa and spicy foods, but I didn't realize they used so much curry. I'm kinda glad I wasn't born Indian and that I have a German heritage, because I really do love bratwurst.

What the Comanche really wanted from the Apache were their famous recipes for pumpkin pie and great cookies. The Apache were fairly easy to raid, because they pretty much had to stay on the farm during harvest season. The Apache had never seen Broadway, because it was way back east, so it was pretty easy to keep them here, whereas the Comanche were buffalo hunters and followed the migrating buffalo herds wherever they went.

The Comanche would send several members of their tribe to spy on the Apache to see if they could find out how to obtain this recipe. Later on in history, these spies would be called Indian scouts, because the Comanche didn't like the term spy. The Comanche eventually defeated the Apache, and the Apache ended up with reservations in parts of Oklahoma. Rumor has it that the Apache discovered oil on this land and became very rich.

The Comanche really didn't care too much about the Apache's successful oil discoveries, because they weren't much into being covered in oily grime. They preferred pumpkin pie and cookie crumbs. The Comanche were thrilled that the spoils of war had brought them the Apache recipes for pumpkin pie and the most fabulous cookies.

Several future events in history would bring the Comanche vast sums of wealth. They sold their pumpkin pie recipe with royalties to the famous Nieman-Marcus store located in Dallas. The next time you happen to be in their cafe enjoying some of this delicious pumpkin pie, go ahead and ask them about this recipe.

The other thing that really helped the Comanche was joining the cavalry and becoming Indian scouts. These scouts became very famous for their tracking ability and being able to sniff out the locations of pumpkin pie and cookies. Usually, the movies will never show the uncanny ability these scouts possessed, but movies have always been a bit lax in portraying recent history.

Talkin' Texan

In the early 1900s, a lady formed an organization called the Girl Scouts, and she was looking for a way of funding their future growth. She was very fortunate indeed that the Comanche decided to bake these delicious cookies for her endeavors. Today, these cookies have become world famous and are enjoyed by millions of folks everywhere. After purchasing some of these cookies, if you were to ask a Girl Scout or her mom if the Comanche baked them, they will deny it. It's probably best not to ask; after all, it *is* a secret recipe.

Outdex

If you know of anything that is missing and should have been included in this book, please forward your suggestions to the attention of the "Outdex."

The following are just a few of the things that I did want to leave out:

- Any mention of the word *homework*, because I do not wish to scare any of my younger readers.
- Any reference to *required reading*—please see above.
- Any reference to the relationship of Texas barflies and the proper use of flypaper.
- Any mention of the great Apache warrior Geronimo and how he kept a U.S. cavalry unit of over five thousand men frustrated for over three years with an eighteen-member Indian band. There are a few Texan towns named after this great Indian chief. The first that comes to mind is Bandera.
- Any reference to "over the hill"—although I have personally been to the mountaintop and can still see it in the distance whenever I look over my left shoulder
- Any mention of women's lib, men's lib, old folks' lib, teenagers' lib, or children's lib.
- Any mention of things being "politically correct"—although "politics do make strange bedfellows" and even stranger laws and decisions.
- Any mention of carpetbaggers, brown baggers, grocery baggers, or sandbaggers. Some are reviled, some are thrifty, some are helpful, some are sneaky, and I usually get them all mixed up.
- Four-letter words—my publisher insisted that I have no four-letter words in this G-rated book. Well, I do have some four-letter words in this book because it's very

difficult to do any type of speaking or writing without using any four-letter words at all. Some writers may be able to write without using any four-letter words, but I found it quite impossible. The sentences just didn't make much sense or could be greatly misunderstood without them. For an example:

"Please don't execute any more prisoners," would say:

"Please execute any prisoners."

Backword

Since all of the really classy books have a foreword and, as you will have noticed, I've included a foreword in this book, I figured that a really, really classy book should have a backword.

For those of you who are computer savvy and familiar with Internet websites, this is where you would be able to click on the "back" button and return to the first page. You don't have to "click" on any back button—just flip the book over and you can start all over again. There's no telling what you may have forgotten:

Did you remember to return your motel key?
Are all your children accounted for?
Did you remember your luggage?
Did you leave any personal items in the bathroom?
Did you remember to pay for this book?

The nice thing about this book is, although it might burn, it will never crash unless somehow it has distracted you while driving.

"If you drink, don't drive."
"If you drive, don't drink."
"When you read, don't drive."
"When you drive, don't read."

I truly hope that I have not offended any of the fine people of my native Texas by having put this book in print. It was with great joy and delight that I put my memories and thoughts of my home state to pen and paper.

The people of Texas have always been the kindest, friendliest, and most helpful of any in this great nation. I'm quite content to have been born and raised in a state with such a great heritage. I do hope that the generosity and openness of Texans will remain unchanged in the years that shall come.

Hopefully, the native Texan language will also endure and remain with all of its pleasantries so that it can be enjoyed by the many millions of visitors to this state each year.

Epilogue

I've probably forgotten more about Texas than most individuals will ever know or care to know. However, if there is anything that you know of that is truly unique or unusual about my home state of Texas, please do not hesitate to contact me through my publisher's marketing department at www.booklocker.com. If I can still remember how to make a web page, you might try www.talkintexan.com. You might also be able to e-mail me through the website if I remembered how to add an e-mail hyperlink.

    I love traveling in Texas, because it's the friendliest state in America, so if you don't happen to see me at any of the bookstores, you'll probably find me in one of the many gift stores throughout the state. This paperback will also be available in all of the local convenience stores, major gasoline stations, and truck stops throughout the state. You'll probably find me hanging out near one of the spinning bookracks, munching some pecan pie, and drinking a Big Red. Some people have Coke bottle shapes, others are shaped like the letter "T," and most of us are fruit shaped, like bananas, apples, oranges, and pears. I'll be the tall fellow with a shape that betrays my love for bratwurst, Shiner Bock beer, pizza, chili dogs, Texas chili, anything fried, cookies, cakes, and especially, Texas pecan pie. I'll be wearing a cap that says Arthur, even though my name is Joe. Please be sure and say howdy.

    My hope is that you will have found this little book as much fun to read as I had in putting my thoughts, memories, and words to paper. My original editor at the Republic of Texas Press is a sweetheart of a lady, filled with an enormous amount of wit and wisdom. She thought this book was a novel idea, and I hope you will feel the same. Perhaps you and I will be able to meet in the near future, share a cup of coffee and some pecan pie, and talk some Texan.

Gift Books keep on Giving

Books do not need assembly; there are no missing pieces and, best of all, they do not require batteries to operate. Gift Books also provide others with the vast amount of knowledge and intelligence you wish to share with them.

We do hope you have enjoyed Talkin' Texan and will want to purchase additional books for your friends, co-workers, in-laws, children, grand children, cousins, nieces, nephews, or some lonesome Texan far, far away from their beloved State of Texas.

Books make excellent gifts for all occasions, especially: Birthdays, Anniversaries, Weddings, Graduations, July 4th, Barmitzvahs, Valentine's Day, Saint Patrick's Day, Easter, Mother's Day, Father's Day, Grandparent's Day, Thanksgiving, and Christmas.

You may purchase any additional books you may need thru: www.booklocker.com, www.amazon.com, www.bn.com, or the authors website, www.talkintexan.com, or simply walk into your favorite local bookstore and request Talkin' Texan by name and ISBN #

Giddy Yup,

Joe